Anonymous

Rand, McNally and Co.'s Illustrated Guide to the Hudson River and Catskill Mountains

Anonymous

Rand, McNally and Co.'s Illustrated Guide to the Hudson River and Catskill Mountains

ISBN/EAN: 9783337377311

Printed in Europe, USA, Canada, Australia, Japan

Cover: Foto ©Lupo / pixelio.de

More available books at **www.hansebooks.com**

ILLUSTRATED GUIDE

TO THE

HUDSON RIVER

AND

CATSKILL MOUNTAINS

By ERNEST INGERSOLL

Seventh Edition.

CHICAGO AND NEW YORK
RAND, McNALLY & COMPANY, PUBLISHERS
1899.

CONTENTS.

	PAGE.
INTRODUCTION	11–24
Character of the Hudson	11
Early History	16
Hudson River Steamboats and Railways	23
NEW YORK TO TARRYTOWN	25–57
The New York City and New Jersey Shores	25
The Burr-Hamilton Duel	26
Revolutionary Forts	30
The Palisades	35, 46
The City of Yonkers	39
Dobb's Ferry and Irvington	44
The Croton Aqueducts	48
The Story of Sunnyside	49
From Irvington to Tarrytown	51
Sleepy Hollow, Past and Present	53
TARRYTOWN TO WEST POINT	58–105
The Tappan Sea	58
Nyack	59
Sing Sing	60
The Story of Arnold's Treason	65
The Battle of Stony Point	68
Peekskill	73
The Passage of the Hudson Highlands	76
The Fall of the Highland Forts	81
The Tour of West Point	88
WEST POINT TO NEWBURGH	106–136
Cro' Nest and Storm King	108
The Culprit Fay	109
Cornwall and Its Attractions	112
N. P. Willis' "Idlewild"	113
The City of Newburgh	116
Washington's Headquarters	121
The Fishkill Shore	125
NEWBURGH TO POUGHKEEPSIE	128–136
Ice and the Ice Harvest	129
Poughkeepsie and Education	133

Stanwix Hall

ALBANY, N. Y.

American and European Plans

THE MOST COMFORTABLE AND PERFECTLY EQUIPPED HOTEL IN THE CAPITAL CITY. IS CONDUCTED LIBERALLY, WITH THE DESIRE TO PLEASE THE MOST EXACTING. HAS AN ABSOLUTELY PURE FILTRATION OF ENTIRE WATER SUPPLY. HAS, BY FAR, THE MOST CONVENIENT LOCATION TO STORES, DEPOTS, BOATS, AND PLACES OF INTEREST.

Free Omnibus and Carriages To and from all Boats

PATRONS ARE ASSURED

Pleasant Rooms, Excellent Cuisine, and Careful Attention.

Our Rates for Each Person are:

FOR ROOM ONLY,
$1.00 and upward per day, according to location, etc.
FOR ROOM AND BOARD,
$3.00 and upward per day, according to location, etc.
FOR ROOMS WITH PARLOR OR BATH
An extra charge will be made.

RESTAURANT AT POPULAR PRICES.

Special Rates will be made for large parties.
For rooms and information, address,

E. E. McCANDLISS.

CONTENTS.

	PAGE.
POUGHKEEPSIE TO KINGSTON	137–154
First View of the Catskills	138
The City of Kingston	142
Cement and Cement Making. Bluestone, etc.	143
Historical Sketch of Kingston	147
The Senate House	150
The Burning of Kingston by the British	151
THE TOUR OF THE CATSKILLS	155–176
Two Principal Entrances	156
The Journey from Kingston	157
At the Gateway of the Catskills	158
Loftiest of the Catskills	161
Stony Clove, Hunter, and Tannersville	163
Parks and Cottagers	165
From Phœnicia to Stamford	168
KINGSTON TO CATSKILL AND TO THE MOUNTAIN RESORTS	177–199
Rhinebeck	177
Saugerties	179
The Story of Clermont	181
Catskill Village	184
Catskill Mountain Railroad and Otis Elevator	186
A Group of Famous Mountain Hotels	187
Kaaterskill Clove and Rip Van Winkle	190
Catskill to Hudson	193
The City of Hudson's Curious History	194
THE CAPITAL CITY	200–216
Historical Sketch of Albany	200
The Tour of Albany	204
The State Capitol Described	205
THE UPPER HUDSON COUNTRY	217–226
The Rollicking Youth of the Hudson	217
Albany a Central Point of Departure for the Tourist	219
Tours North of Albany	220
Saratoga and the Southern Adirondacks	221–222
The Historical Region of Lake George	223
Northern Entrances to the Adirondacks	224
Along Lake Champlain	224
Scenery in the Mountains	224
From Plattsburgh to Saranac Lake	226
ALPHABETICAL LIST OF HOTELS IN THE HUDSON VALLEY AND CATSKILLS	227–232
INDEX	237–249

HOTEL EMPIRE

BOULEVARD AND 63d STREET, NEW YORK CITY.

Patronized by travelers and tourists of the best class from all parts of the world.

A MODERN FIRE-PROOF HOTEL OF THE FIRST CLASS, CONDUCTED ON THE AMERICAN AND EUROPEAN PLANS FOR THE ACCOMMODATION OF THOSE WHO WANT THE BEST AT REASONABLE COST.

FAMOUS for the PERFECTION of its CUISINE and SERVICE.

Its Beautiful and Homelike Appointments and Splendid Location. *Within 12 minutes of all the principal theatres and great department stores.*

Electric cars running to all parts of the city pass its doors. 6th and 9th Avenue Railroad stations one minute's walk from the hotel.

RATES MODERATE.

Music by the Empire Orchestra every Evening.

Send address for our book, "The Empire, Illustrated."

W. JOHNSON QUINN, Proprietor.

ILLUSTRATIONS.

Towing on the Hudson	Frontispiece	
The Palisades	Facing page	28
Tomb of Gen. U. S. Grant	"	30
Sugar Loaf	"	44
Breakneck Mountain	"	60
Slide Mountain and Shandaken Valley	"	76
Cranston's	"	84
View up Hudson from Hotel, West Point	"	100
View North from Upper Road, West Point	"	108
Newburgh	"	116
Washington's Headquarters at Newburgh	"	124
The Poughkeepsie Bridge	"	132
Kaaterskill Falls	"	140
Haines' Falls	"	156
Schoharie Mansion	"	166
Furlough Lodge. Geo. Gould's Summer House	"	172
Fleischman's Settlement, Delaware County	"	180
Otis Elevating Railroad, Catskill Mountains	"	188
The Chasm, Catskill Creek	"	204

THE TEN EYCK

POSITIVELY FIREPROOF.

AMERICAN AND EUROPEAN PLANS.

Most attractive hotel in New York State, opened in May.

H. J. ROCKWELL & SON.

HOTEL KENMORE.

American Plan.
Moderate Rates.
Under the same management.

The Evolution of Dodd's Sister

Rich Cloth Binding, Price 75 cents

> The book is sure to be widely read.
> —*Boston Daily Globe.*
>
> The story is striking, both in subject matter and treatment.—*Philadelphia Call.*

A Tragedy of the Every-Day Life of a Girl

BY

CHARLOTTE W. EASTMAN

Rand, McNally & Co., Publishers, Chicago and New York.

NEW AND RECENT PUBLICATIONS.

ENOCH THE PHILISTINE
A Traditional Romance by LeRoy Hooker.
Striking Egyptian Cover Design. 12mo, cloth, $1.25.

BONNIE MACKIRBY
By Laura Dayton Fessenden, author of "A Colonial Dame." 16mo, cloth, 75 cents. The story of an international marriage.

ROMOLA
By George Eliot. A carefully revised edition with 56 full page illustrations in monogravure. Large type, new plates, two volumes, exquisitely bound in cloth, 8vo, boxed, $3.00.

A DAUGHTER OF CUBA
By Helen M. Bowen. 12mo, cloth, $1.00.

MY INVISIBLE PARTNER
By Thomas S. Denison. 12mo, cloth, $1.00.

PHOEBE TILSON
By Mrs. Frank Pope Humphrey. 12mo, cloth, $1.00.

MARGARET WYNNE
By Adeline Sergeant. 12mo, cloth, $1.00.

ALONG THE BOSPHORUS
A HISTORIC REMINISCENCE OF FOREIGN TRAVELS BY RICH IN ALL THAT MAKES PLEASANT READING
Susan E. Wallace (Mrs. Lew Wallace), author of "Land of the Pueblos," etc. Illustrated. 12mo, cloth, $1.50.

THE FIFTH OF NOVEMBER
By F. Kimball Scribner and Charles S. Bentley. 12mo, cloth, $1.00.

WOMAN AND THE SHADOW
By Arabella Kenealy. 12mo, cloth, $1.00.

ARMAGEDDON
By Stanley Waterloo, author of "Story of Ab," etc. A prophetic romance. 12mo, cloth, $1.00.

A MAID OF THE FRONTIER
By Henry Spofford Canfield. 16mo, cloth, 75 cents.

AT THE BLUE BELL INN
By J. S. Fletcher, author of "When Charles I. Was King" "In the Days of Drake," etc. In exquisite old style English. 16mo, cloth, 75 cents.

ALL ABOUT THE BABY
With appendix scientifically treating on the Limitation of Offspring and Either Sex at Will. By Robert N. Tooker, M. D., author of "Children's Diseases," etc. Illustrated. 8vo, cloth, $1.50.

A CRUISE UNDER THE CRESCENT
By Charles Warren Stoddard.
Profusely illustrated by Denslow. 12mo, cloth, $1.50.

Send for complete catalogue and full lists of our Three Famous Libraries of Beautiful 12mos.
THE AMERICAN LIBRARY, THE TWENTIETH CENTURY 12MOS, THE ALPHA LIBRARY.

Rand McNally & Co.,
CHICAGO. NEW YORK.

LIST OF MAPS.

Section 1.
NEW YORK TO TARRYTOWN.
28 miles from New York City.
Facing page 27.

Section 2.
TARRYTOWN TO NEWBURGH.
27 to 61 miles from New York City.
Facing page 59.

Section 3.
NEWBURGH TO KINGSTON.
60 to 91 miles from New York City.
Facing page 129.

Section 4.
KINGSTON TO COXSACKIE.
90 to 122 miles from New York City.
Facing page 177.

Section 5.
COXSACKIE TO ALBANY.
120 to 147 miles from New York City.
Facing page 195.

PLAN OF WEST POINT.
Facing page 88.

MAP OF CATSKILL MOUNTAINS.
Facing page 168.

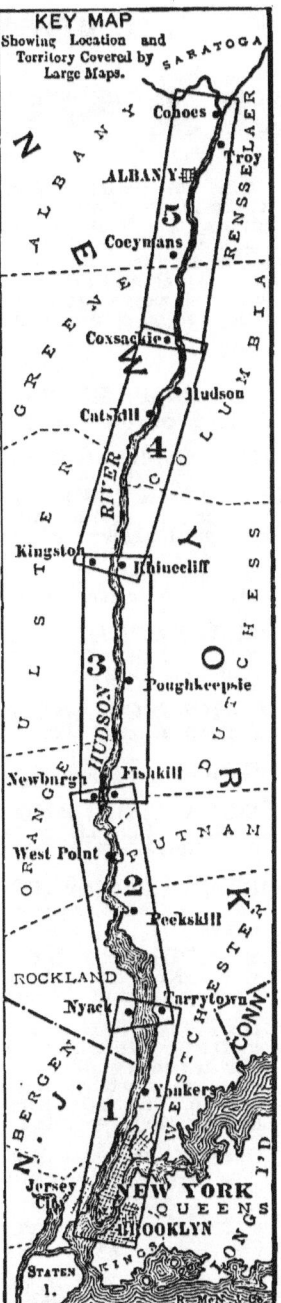

Rand, McNally & Co.'s
SERIES OF
HANDY GUIDES

This new series of American Guide Books gives, in volumes of "handy" size, the information generally desired by travelers seeking pleasure, health, or business. The books are uniform in size and general arrangement. Places or objects of particular importance or interest are noted in black-faced type, and those of less importance in italics. Care has been taken to present everything in the most candid and helpful light, saying little or nothing about that which is deemed worth little attention. Numerous illustrations from photographs, and colored maps supplement the text.

PRICE OF EACH GUIDE.

In Paper Binding, - - - - 25 Cents.
In Flexible Cloth Binding, Rounded Corners, 50 Cents.

The following are now ready and will be revised annually:

NEW YORK CITY, including Brooklyn, Staten Island, and other suburbs. 210 pages; 44 illustrations. Maps of New York City, 28 x 17; Central Park, 10 x 28, and New York and New Jersey Suburbs, 28 x 26.

BOSTON AND ENVIRONS. 154 pages; 24 illustrations. Maps of Boston, 28 x 21; Environs of Boston, 11 x 13½, and Business Portion of Boston, 9½ x 9.

PHILADELPHIA AND ENVIRONS, including Atlantic City and Cape May. 126 pages; 32 illustrations. Maps of Philadelphia, 28 x 22, and One Hundred Miles Around Philadelphia, 28 x 21.

WASHINGTON AND THE DISTRICT OF COLUMBIA. 161 pages; 40 illustrations. Map of Washington, 21 x 28.

CHICAGO. 215 pages; 46 illustrations. Map of Chicago, 31 x 33.

HUDSON RIVER AND CATSKILL MOUNTAINS. 249 pages; 18 illustrations. Five large scale sectional maps showing both sides of the river from New York to Troy.

SOUTHEASTERN STATES. Includes Florida, Georgia, the Carolinas, and the Gulf Coast; 246 pages; illustrations. Map of Southeastern States, 24 x 28.

NEW ENGLAND STATES. 260 pages; nnmerous illustrations. Maps of Maine, New Hampshire, Vermont, Massachusetts, Rhode Island, and Connecticut, printed in colors, each 11 x 14 in size.

COUNTRY AROUND NEW YORK. 180 pages. Describing resorts and routes in Westchester County on Staten Island and Long Island, and in Northeastern and Seaside New Jersey. Forty half-tone illustrations. Twelve route maps in black and white and map of region around New York, north to Hastings-on-the-Hudson; east to Garden City, Long Island; south to South Amboy, N. J.; west to Lake Hopatcong.

Our publications are for sale by booksellers and newsdealers generally, or will be sent postpaid to any address on receipt of price.

RAND, McNALLY & CO., Publishers,

142 Fifth Ave., N. W. Cor. 19th St., NEW YORK.
166-168 Adams Street, CHICAGO, ILL.

INTRODUCTION.

The Hudson River gathers its waters from the central heights of the Adirondacks, and these unite into a stream which at Fort Edward, 180 miles from its mouth, becomes well defined. The river is narrow, tortuous, and rock-obstructed, however, as far as Troy, thirty miles below and 150 from New York, where it reaches the level ground at the foot of the mountains, and begins the stately career of usefulness and beauty which has given it a world-wide renown.

"Rivers are as various in their forms as forest trees. The Mississippi is like an oak with enormous branches. What a branch is the Red River, the Arkansas, the Ohio, the Missouri! The Hudson is like the pine or poplar—mainly trunk. From New York to Albany there is only an inconsiderable limb or two, and but few gnarls and excrescences. Cut off the Rondout, the Esopus, the Catskill, and two or three similar tributaries on the east side, and only some twigs remain. There are some crooked places, it is true, but on the whole the Hudson presents a fine symmetrical shaft that would be hard to match in any river of the world." So wrote John Burroughs (*Scribner's Monthly*, August, 1880), after living many years upon its bank; and he adds:

"Of the Hudson it may be said that it is a very large river for its size; that is, for the quantity of water it discharges into the sea. Its water-shed is comparatively small—less, I think, than that of the Connecticut. It is a huge trough with a very slight incline, through which the current moves very slowly, and which would fill from the sea were its supplies from the mountains cut off. Its fall from Albany to the bay is only about five feet. Any object upon it, drifting with the current, progresses southward no more than eight miles in twenty-four hours. The ebb tide will carry it about twelve miles, and the flood set it back from seven to nine. A drop of water at Albany, therefore, will be nearly three weeks in reaching New York, though it will get pretty well pickled some days earlier.

"Some rivers by their volume and impetuosity penetrate the sea, but here the sea is the aggressor, and sometimes meets the mountain water nearly half-way. . . .

"It is this character of the Hudson, this encroachment of the sea upon it, that led Prof. Newberry to speak of it as a drowned river. We have heard of drowned lands, but here is a river overflowed and submerged in the same manner. It is quite certain, however, that this has not always been the character of the Hudson. Its great trough bears evidence of having been worn to its present dimensions by much swifter and stronger currents than those that course through it now. Hence, Prof. Newberry has recently advanced the bold and striking theory that in pre-glacial times this part of the continent was several hundred feet higher than at present, and that the Hudson was then a very large and rapid stream, and drew its main supplies from the basin of the Great Lakes through an ancient river-bed that followed pretty nearly the line of the present Mohawk; in other words, that the waters of the St. Lawrence once found an outlet through this channel, debouching into the ocean from a broad, littoral plain, at a point eighty miles southeast of New York, where the sea now rolls 500 feet deep. According to the soundings of the coast survey, this ancient bed of the Hudson is distinctly marked upon the ocean floor to the point indicated.

"To the gradual subsidence of this part of the continent, in connection with the great changes wrought by the huge glacier that crept down from the north during what is called the ice period, is owing the character and aspects of the Hudson as we see and know them. The Mohawk Valley was filled up by the drift, the Great Lakes scooped out, and an opening for their pent-up waters found through what is now the St. Lawrence. The trough of the Hudson was also partially filled, and has remained so to the present day. There is, perhaps, no point in the river where the mud and clay are not from two to three times as deep as the water.

"That ancient and grander Hudson lies back of us several hundred thousand years—perhaps more, for a million years are but as one tick of the time-piece of the Lord; yet even *it* was a juvenile compared with some of the rocks and mountains the Hudson of to-day mirrors. The Highlands date from the earliest geological age—the primary; the river—the old river—from the latest, the tertiary; and what that difference means in terrestrial years hath not entered into the mind of man to conceive. Yet how the venerable mountains open their ranks for the stripling to pass through! Of course, the river did not force its way through this barrier, but has doubtless found an opening there of which it has availed itself, and which it has enlarged."

The Hudson is now navigable to Troy for large steamers and shipping; but this, of course, is due to the artificial deepening of the channel, which naturally is unnavigable for ships of even moderate size north of the city of Hudson. Opposite the city of New York, the whole river is from fifty to seventy-five feet deep, and a good depth is maintained as far as Hastings by the scouring force of the tides along the comparatively narrow channel at the foot of the Palisades. Above that point, however, a far less depth of channel actually exists wherever the river is broad, and extensive shallows stretch between it and the shore, so that long wharves, or else dredged approaches to the landing stages, are almost everywhere necessary. The Federal Government has spent large amounts of money in making and maintaining the ship-channel through the grassy shallows north of Catskill, and such harbors as those at Rondout and Saugerties. Moreover, it appears sadly true that the channel of the lower river is constantly growing shallower—dangerously so in the Tappan Sea; and this is due, it is said, to the reckless scattering there of vast quantities of refuse from barges and canalboats as well as of ashes from many steamboats. The principal offenders are the men who carry bricks, and who dump overboard, wherever convenient, on their return trip, the broken bricks and dust rejected from the cargoes they carry to New York. "As there are forty to eighty canalboats in each tow, and from six to ten tows pass up the Hudson every twenty-four hours, it is easy to realize what a vast quantity of these broken bricks must be thrown into the Hudson each year to the detriment of the channel. And not only are the bricks an evil in themselves, but they arrest mud and the natural silt which would otherwise be carried out to sea." These facts are mentioned here in the hope of calling public attention to the evil. A Federal commission has been appointed to examine into the question of deepening and preserving the river channel, but thus far it has done little or nothing.

The river is closed by ice in winter throughout nearly its whole extent. North of the Highlands the closure is usually permanent during January and February, at least, and sometimes longer. Navigation ceases about the end of November, but the winter is by no means a period of idleness upon the Hudson. In its uppermost reaches, the lumbermen are busy, and the owners of water-power. Between Albany and the Highlands there is the vast ice industry (see Chap. IV), and the sports of racing, skating, and ice-boating on the ice; the steam ferryboats continue to run, keeping their paths open.

Below the Highlands the ice is a less certain quantity, not growing solidly from shore to shore, as a rule, and rarely available for cutting and saving, but drifting about in more or less compact floes, that lodge here and there for limited periods, and below Dobbs Ferry the river is entirely open more winters than it is closed. The ice-carriers travel all the year round between the city and Rockland Lake, and lightering and other business on the river near the city proceeds all winter with only rare and brief interruptions. This condition varies with seasons and periods, however; and not only the lower river, but the whole harbor, has been frozen solid for weeks together, as happened during the Revolutionary War.

The river breaks up in March, usually. Burroughs tells us, though in some seasons not till April.

"It is no sudden and tumultuous breaking of the fetters, as in more rapid and fluctuating streams, but a slow and deliberate movement of the whole body of the ice, like an enormous raft quietly untied. You are looking out upon the usually rigid and motionless surface, when presently you are conscious that some point, perhaps a cedar bough used by the ice men, or the large black square of open water which they recently uncovered, has changed its place; you take steadier aim with your eye, and with a thrill of pleasure discover that the great ice-fields are slowly drifting southward. . . .

"After the ice is once in motion, a few hours suffice to break it up pretty thoroughly. Then what a wild, chaotic scene the river presents—in one part of the day the great masses hurrying down stream, crowding and jostling each other, and struggling for the right of way; in the other, all running up stream again, as if sure of escape in that direction. Thus they race up and down, the sport of the ebb and flow, but the flow wins each time by some distance. Large fields from above, where the men were at work but a day or two since, come down; there is their pond yet clearly defined and full of marked ice; yonder is a section of their canal partly filled with the square blocks on their way to the elevators; a piece of a race-course, or a part of a road where teams crossed, comes drifting by. The people up above have written their winter pleasure and occupations upon this page, and we read the signs as the tide bears it slowly past. Some calm, bright days the scattered and diminished masses flash by, like white clouds across an April sky.

"Ducks now begin to appear upon the river, and the sportsman, with his white canvas cap and cape, crouched in his low white skiff, simulates as far as possible a shapeless mass of snow-ice, and thus seeks to drift upon them. . . .

"When the chill of the ice is out of the river, and of the snow and frost out of the air, the fishermen along shore are on the lookout for the first arrival of shad. A few days of warm south wind, the latter part of April, will soon blow them up; it is true, also, that a cold north wind will as quickly blow them back. Preparations have been making for them all winter. In many a farm house or other humble dwelling along the river, the ancient occupation of knitting of fish-nets has been plied through the long winter evenings, perhaps every grown member of the household, the mother and her daughters, as well as the father and his sons, lending a hand.

"The ordinary gill or drift net used for shad-fishing in the Hudson is from a half to three-quarters of a mile long, and thirty feet wide, containing about fifty or sixty pounds of fine linen twine, and it is a labor of many months to knit one. Formerly the fish were taken mainly by immense seines, hauled by a large number of men; but now all the deeper part of the river is fished with the long, delicate gill-nets, that drift to and fro with the tide, and are managed by two men in a boat. The net is of fine linen thread, and is practically invisible to the shad in the obscure river current; it hangs suspended perpendicularly in the water, kept in position by buoys at the top and by weights at the bottom; the buoys are attached by cords twelve or fifteen feet long, which allow the nets to sink out of the reach of the keels of passing vessels. The net is thrown out on the ebb tide, stretching nearly across the river, and drifts down and then back on the flood, the fish being snared behind the gills in their efforts to pass through the meshes. . . .

"The shad campaign is one that requires pluck and endurance; no regular sleep, no regular meals, wet and cold, heat and wind and tempest, and no great gains at last. But the sturgeon fishers, who come later, and are seen the whole summer through, have an indolent, lazy time of it. They fish around the 'slack-water,' catching the last of the ebb and the first of the flow, and hence drift but little either way. To a casual observer they appear as if anchored and asleep. But they wake up when they have a 'strike,' which may be every day, or not once a week. The fisherman keeps his eye on his line of buoys, and when two or more of them are hauled under, he knows his game has run foul of the net, and he hastens to the point. The sturgeon is a pig, without a pig's obstinacy. He spends much of the time rooting and feeding in the mud at the bottom, and encounters the net, which is also a gill-net, coarse and strong, when he goes abroad. He strikes and is presently hopelessly entangled, when he comes to the top, and is pulled into the boat, like a great sleepy sucker."

The Discovery of the Hudson is popularly attributed to that old sea-dog, *Henry Hudson*, whose name it bears. He was not its discoverer, but he became its exponent and exploiter; and is entitled to all the distinction the attachment of his name to this most important and beautiful river is able to confer upon him.

As early as 1524, the Florentine navigator, *Verrazano*, an officer of the French king, Francis I., while coasting the shore of the lately discovered continent, entered the present bay of New York, and ascended it for some distance. How far is not known; but he must have gone at least to the Palisades, for he described the stream as "The River of the Steep Hills." This was the first sight of it by a European of which we have any certain record; and on a map issued in 1629, compiled partly from Verrazano's charts, the name "San Germano" is written at the mouth of the Hudson.

In 1525, the next year after Verrazano's visit, came *Gomez*, a Portuguese, sailing under the Spanish flag along the American continent, in search of that great desideratum of all the early voyagers, a short-cut to the East Indies. He knew nothing about Verrazano, but this opening in the coast attracted his attention, and he entered it—probably on St. Anthony's Day (January 17th), for he gave the river, which he explored for some distance, the name "Rio San Antonio." In Ribero's chart, which was partly drawn from an outline map by Gomez, the country from Maryland to Rhode Island is named the "Land of Estevan Gomez"; and it has even been suggested that the Spaniards who put the whole river under holy St. Anthony's care were the first to notice that grand old cliff in the Highlands which quizzingly symbolizes the saint's nose. "It is true that Dutch Anthonys innumerable have claimed the honor, but until they settle the disputes among themselves, who shall say that Gomez never saw San Antonio's Nose?"

The Dutch, who were the most energetic and intelligent sea rovers and traders of that time, were quick to profit by these and other discoveries. The archives of The Netherlands show that Dutch captains explored all this part of the American coast in 1598, and that they frequented the territory, though without making any fixed settlements, except a shelter in the winter; "for which purpose they erected on the North (Hudson) and

South (Delaware) rivers there, two little forts against the incursions of the Indians" (*N. Y. Col. Doc., Vol. I, p.* 149). This is not at all unlikely, considering the fact that prior to 1598 three Dutch voyages had been made to within 9° of the pole.

Thus Henry Hudson had several predecessors and his mission was not to discover but to examine the river, of which he knew as much as the rest of the world of geographers and naval officers, and more than most of them, for he had had translated for his own use the ancient sailing directions of the Icelanders who were accustomed to visit the northern part of the western continent; and Capt. John Smith had supplied him with notes derived from the voyages of himself, Gosnold, and other "adventurers into Virginia."

Twice this man had tried to reach China by way of the arctic seas north of Europe, and each time had failed to penetrate the ice-fields beyond North Cape. A third time he tried it, sailing from Amsterdam under the Dutch flag, and in the "yacht" Half Moon (*Haalve Maan*), on March 25, 1609. Again meeting a solid barrier of ice, however, he turned his prow westward and held that course until the cliffs of Greenland arose over the tip of his bowsprit. Then he coasted southward, and in September (1609) entered what is now New York Bay, and sailed up our great river, landing now and then, until he reached the head of ship navigation somewhere near the present city of Hudson. Then he sent a boat-load of his men still farther, and they examined the river to beyond the mouth of the Mohawk, and came to the conclusion that this was not a channel through to the East Indies. The mind likes to dwell upon this voyage, whose incidents would be retold here were space available.

"I think," exclaims N. P. Willis, "of all excitements in the world, that of the first discovery and exploration of a noble river must be the most eager and enjoyable. Fancy 'the bold Englishman,' as the Dutch called Hendrich Hudson, steering his little yacht, the Haalve Maan, for the first time through the Highlands. Imagine his anxiety for the channel, forgotten as he gazed up at the towering rocks, and round the green shores, and onward, past point and opening bend, miles away into the heart of the country; yet with no lessening of the glorious stream beneath him, and no decrease of promise in the bold and luxuriant shores! Picture him lying at anchor below Newburgh, with the dark pass of the 'Wey-Gat' frowning behind him, the lofty and blue Catskills beyond, and the hillsides around covered with the red lords of the soil, exhibiting only less wonder than friendliness. And how beautifully was the assurance of welcome expressed, when the 'very kind old man' brought a bunch of arrows, and broke them before the stranger, to induce him to partake fearlessly of his hospitality!"

On the 4th of October, the Half Moon came out of the "great mouth of the great river," and "steered off into the main sea," on a direct course toward Holland, where its commander made haste to report the goodly land and opportunity for trade which he had found and aptly appraised. Commerce at once followed in his track. The Half Moon never returned, but was wrecked at the Island of Mauritius; and a few years later Hudson himself —of whom we know almost nothing outside of the eventful years between 1607 and 1611—was set adrift in an open boat by a mutinous crew, and left to perish in the arctic expanse of Hudson Bay.

An interesting article by Miss Susan Fenimore Cooper, in Vol. IV of the *Magazine of American History*, upon the names which the Hudson has borne, sketches the early history of the river thus:

"When Hudson returned to Amsterdam with the report of his voyage, he spoke of the fine river he had explored as the 'Manhattes,' from the name of the people who dwelt at its mouth. . . . In 1610, a Dutch ship, freighted with goods to suit the savages, anchored in the bay, at the mouth of the 'river of the Manhattes,' and from that date a succession of the small, uncouth, but serviceable craft in favor among the early explorers and commercial adventurers of the period, showed themselves in the waters of the 'Great River of the Manhattans'; the Little Fox, the Nightingale, the Little Crane, the Tiger, the Fortune, passed the Narrows. In 1613, Adrian Block and his comrades wintered in the country, building themselves rude huts, probably of bark, for shelter. It was in consequence of the discoveries made by Block and his companions, in 1614, that the new country first received a civilized name in the charter granted the 'New Netherland Company' in 1616, and at the same period the 'Manhattans River,' having been fully explored, received the legal name of 'De Riviere van den Vorst Mauritius.' That great military genius, Prince Moritz, was then stadtholder, and the idol of his countrymen, his whole life having been a series of battles, sieges, and victories. He was in the full vigor of life and talent when Hudson, with the 'Haalve Maan,' entered the grand stream.

The English, only a few years earlier, had given the name of King James I. to a fine stream in Virginia. It was very natural that the New Netherlands Company should give the name of their stadtholder, Prince Maurice of Orange, to the river whose banks they were about to colonize. The same stream, however, was often spoken of as the 'Groote Riviere,' the 'Noordt Riviere,' the 'River of the Manhattans,' and the 'Rio de Montagne.' The name of Hudson was never, at any time, connected with its waters by the Dutch. In 1624 De Laet wrote his *New World; or, Description of the West Indies*, and at that date he distinctly says that 'the Great North River of the New Netherlands' was by some called the Manhattes River, from the people who dwelt near its mouth; by others, also, Rio de Montagne, or River of the Mountain; by some, also, Nassau, but by our own countrymen it was generally called the 'Great River.'

"By this time the river had been thoroughly explored as far as the mouth of the Mohawk. A regular traffic with the different tribes on its banks had begun; Mohegan and Mohawk, Tappaen and Munsee, brought their peltries to the pale-faces. The rude trading boats, passing to and fro, had already noted and named the different reaches, or *raches*, in the stream, its islands, and some of the hills on its banks, from Manhattas to Beverwyck."

Only one remark needs to be added, a word of explanation of the term *North River*, which is still used commonly in New York City. The "North River" (*Noordt Riviere*) was originally and naturally so called by the Dutch colonists to distinguish it from the "South" (*Zuydt Riviere*), which was the Delaware, and not at all with reference to the "East River," which was on the eastern side of the island. At present the term *North River* is coming to be restricted to the harbor part of it between New York and Jersey City; but half a century ago it was still the designation most commonly applied to the whole stream. The English, indeed, had always spoken of it as Hudson's River, but the Dutch never did so; and the use of the name *Hudson River* by the railway company along its eastern bank has probably done more than any other agency to displace the old term and fasten Hudson's name in popular speech.

From the time of the beginning of English rule in New York until the revolt of the colonists against the Crown, the history of the Hudson is simply that of the development of local trade and sea-going commerce in the eastern colonies. At the beginning of the Revolution, New York was already among the foremost seaports, and the Hudson Valley was the most populous and important highway to the interior, north of the Delaware, and had an especial strategic value from the fact that it furnished a direct water route between the southern seacoast and the English strongholds in Canada. Its possession was therefore of vital importance to the American patriots, since, if they lost it, New England would be separated by the enemy from the southern colonies. During the whole war, therefore, a struggle for the possession of the Hudson went on, and many of the most thrilling and consequential operations of both armies were conducted in this valley, beginning with the capture of Forts Ticonderoga and Crown Point, May 10, 1775, held by the British as the key to the gateway of Canada. Many of these are particularly spoken of in the following pages in connection with the places where they occurred; and here it is intended only to give an outline connecting them chronologically.

After the evacuation of Boston (March 17, 1776), Washington gathered the main body of the army at New York, which was threatened by the British forces, and assembled it upon fortified hills, now included in the city of Brooklyn. After these were captured by the British (August 27, 1776), the American army escaped to fortified camps at White Plains, in Westchester County, where, on July 9, 1776, a provincial assembly had proclaimed New York's adhesion to the Declaration of Independence. Driven from there after the battle of White Plains (October 28, 1776), and the fall of Fort Washington and the neighboring redoubts (November 16, 1776), the remnant of the army was withdrawn to New Jersey, and a line of defense was made east of the Hackensack, leaving the British in possession of the western shore from the Palisades down to Jersey City. Then followed the retreat southward of the American army, and the campaign in the Delaware Valley, marked by the battles of Trenton and Princeton, and succeeded by the terrible winter at Valley Forge (1777–78).

Meanwhile, at the end of 1775, a fruitless expedition invaded Canada, but was repulsed, and, in July, 1777, Burgoyne attempted to descend by the Hudson River route from Canada, and forced his way as far as Saratoga. Sir Henry Clinton prepared to meet him by sending an army northward, which captured the forts guarding the Highlands, enabling a squadron of British war vessels to ascend the river, plundering the villages along the shores, and finally destroying Kingston, where, in the preceding April, the first State Legislature had assembled and adopted the constitution. Nevertheless, Clinton failed to succor Burgoyne, who surrendered his army to Gates at Saratoga on October 17, 1777.

Thus far the operations had been principally in New Jersey and Pennsylvania, but the concentration of the British forces in New York, early in 1778, caused Washington to take the army northward, where the battle of Monmouth was fought on June 29, 1778. The winter was passed in the vicinity of Morristown. In the following summer, in 1779, Stony Point was captured by the Americans, and Washington regained complete possession of the Highlands and the river, which were then scientifically fortified.

From this time on, the Highlands of the Hudson were constantly garrisoned, and, after September, 1778, the main army was quartered in the neighborhood of Newburgh, except when it moved to Virginia for the Yorktown campaign, which resulted in the capture of Cornwallis; after which the army returned to the Highlands to be disbanded, at the close of the war, in 1783.

The principal incident of this period, which saw no local battles after the recovery of Stony Point, was the treason of Arnold, and the arrest and execution of André, in September, 1780.

After the close of the war, business revived more quickly and vigorously, perhaps, along the Hudson Valley than anywhere else. Each of the existing large towns—Newburgh, Poughkeepsie, Rondout, Albany—considered itself a seaport, and strove to bring to itself not only the country trade but foreign commerce. Hudson was called into existence, with a rush, by a company of speculative whaling masters and marine merchants. Turnpikes were built inland from each town. Whaling and fishing craft were built and manned and sent out from the up-river towns. Albany and Troy secured improvements of the upper channel to give them an equal chance. Lines of fast and regular passenger sloops, as well as freight vessels, were organized, and the river towns throve and made good headway, even against New York. But prosperity in this line was brief. In 1807 the first steamboats were introduced, and they ran for years on the Hudson before they were established elsewhere. The tendency of the new conveyance—by cheapening and quickening the carriage of both goods and passengers—to minister to the supremacy of the great town nearest the mouth of the river, was at once foreseen; and when the Erie Canal and the Delaware & Hudson Canal were opened, between 1830 and 1840, and tugs were ready to haul the canalboats and barges straight on to New York, the end of the up-river towns as seaports and rivals of New York City was at hand. It was fully accomplished a few years later by the building of the railway.

Meanwhile, however, the country along both sides of the river had developed, and the townsmen, adapting themselves to new conditions, had built up local trade and manufactures, which have rendered them newly prosperous, and are year by year adding to their numbers and possessions.

These things are highly interesting to the historian, the philosopher, and the man-of-affairs, whose desire for information of this kind has not been neglected in the following pages; but to the ordinary tourist the river remains chiefly interesting for the beauty of its scenery, for the romantic associations that cluster about its past and its present, and for the magnificent homes along its banks, and the conspicuous people who dwell in them.

"I thank God," exclaims Washington Irving, "I was born on the banks of the Hudson . . . and I fancy I can trace much of what is good and pleasant in my own heterogeneous compound to my early companionship with this glorious river. In the warmth of my youthful enthusiasm, I used to clothe it with moral attributes, and almost to give it a soul. I admired its frank, bold, honest character; its noble sincerity and perfect truth. Here was no specious, smiling surface, covering the dangerous sand-bar or perfidious rock; but a stream deep as it was broad, and bearing with honorable faith the bark that trusted to its waves. I gloried in its simple, quiet, majestic, epic flow; ever straight forward. Once, indeed, it turns aside for a moment, forced from its course by opposing mountains, but it struggles bravely through them, and immediately resumes its straightforward march. * Behold, thought I, an emblem of a good man's course through life; ever simple, open, and direct; or if, overpowered by adverse circumstances, he deviate into error, it is but momentary; he soon recovers his onward and honorable career, and continues it to the end of his pilgrimage. . . .

"The Hudson is, in a manner, my first and last love; and after all my wanderings and seeming infidelities, I return to it with a heart-felt preference over all the other rivers in the world. I seem to catch new life as I bathe in its ample billows and inhale the pure breezes of its hills. It is true, the romance of youth is past, that once spread illusions over every scene. I can no longer picture an Arcadia in every green valley; nor a fairy land among the distant mountains; nor a peerless beauty in every villa gleaming among the trees; but though the illusions of youth have faded from the landscape, the recollections of departed years and departed pleasures shed over it the mellow charm of evening sunshine."

HUDSON RIVER STEAMBOATS AND RAILWAYS.

Steamboats—All the lines of steamboats plying upon the Hudson River between New York and up-river landings have their wharves in New York upon the western, or North River, side of the city. They are as follows:

Albany Day Line Steamers leave New York every morning in summer (except Sunday) from Desbrosses Street at 8.40, and W. 22d Street at 9.00 a. m., for Albany and principal intermediate points, arriving at Albany at 6.10 p. m. Fare, $2.00; excursion, $3.50.

People's Line Steamers leave New York every day (except Sunday), from Pier 32, N. R., foot of Canal Street, at 6.00 p. m., for Albany, arriving there at 6.00 a. m. next day. Fare, $1.50.

Citizens' Line Steamers leave New York every day (except Saturday), from Pier 46, foot of W. 10th Street, at 6.00 p. m., for Troy, arriving there at 6.00 a. m. next day. The Sunday steamer touches at Albany. Fare, $1.50; excursion, $2.50.

Mary Powell Steamboat Co.—Steamer "Mary Powell" leaves New York every day (except Saturday), from Desbrosses Street Pier at 3.15 p. m., and W. 22d Street Pier at 3.30 p. m. (from May 15th to October 15th), for Rondout, Kingston, and intermediate points. Saturdays at 1.45 p. m. from Desbrosses Street Pier, and from W. 22d Street Pier at 2.00 p. m.

Catskill Evening Line Steamers leave New York every day (except Sunday), from Pier 43, foot of Christopher Street, at 6.00 p. m., for Catskill, Hudson, and Coxsackie, connecting at Hudson with the *Boston & Albany Railroad*. During July and August extra boat on Saturdays at 1.30 p. m. Fare, $1.00; excursion, $1.70. The new boat "Onteora" began running with the season of 1898.

Saugerties Evening Line leaves from foot of Christopher Street, North River, every week-day at 6.00 p. m. for Hyde Park, Rhinebeck, Barrytown, Ulster Landing, Tivoli, and Saugerties. Fare, $1.00; excursion, $1.50. During July and August Saturday boat leaves at 1.00 p. m.

Kingston Line Steamers leave New York every day from Pier 46, foot of W. 10th Street, at 4.00 p. m., Saturdays at 1.00 p. m., for Rondout and Catskill Mountains. Fare, $1.00; excursion, $1.50.

Newburgh Line.—Steamers leave New York every day from Pier 24, N. R., foot of Franklin Street, at 5.00 p. m., Sundays 9.00 a. m., for Newburgh and intermediate points. Fare, 50 cents; excursion, $1.00.

Poughkeepsie Line.—Steamers leave Pier 24, N. R., foot of Franklin Street, daily (except Sundays) at 6.00 p. m. for Poughkeepsie. Fare, 75 cents; excursion, $1.25.

Railways.—Six railways extend into the Hudson Valley from New York, as follows:

New York Central & Hudson River Railroad.—Station, Grand Central Depot, Fourth Avenue and 42d Street. This road passes up the valley of the Harlem to the mouth of the Spuyten Duyvil, and then closely skirts the eastern margin of the river all the way to Albany and Troy. Its service is frequent and rapid, and a seat on the river side of one of its trains affords the passenger an admirable view of nearly all the scenery. The *New York and Putnam Division* runs northward from 155th Street as far as Sing Sing, touching Yonkers and other smaller towns.

West Shore Railroad.—This railroad has its terminus in Weehawken, N. J., which is reached from New York by ferries from the foot of Franklin and W. 42d streets. It passes through and along the rear of the Palisades to Haverstraw, and thence along the edge of the river through the Highlands, as far as a few miles above Poughkeepsie, when it turns inland. The *Ontario & Western Railway* uses its tracks as far as Cornwall.

Erie Railroad.—This, the first company to reach the lower Hudson, runs by branches from Jersey City to Piermont, Cornwall, and Newburgh. It is reached from New York by ferries from the foot of Chambers and W. 23d streets. Ferry from Newburgh to Fishkill.

The *Northern Railroad of New Jersey* runs from the *Erie* station in Jersey City along the rear of the Palisades, through a historic and beautiful country to Nyack. Ferry to Tarrytown.

HUDSON RIVER GUIDE-BOOK.

NEW YORK TO TARRYTOWN.

Let us begin our Descriptive Tour of the River at the New York wharf of some up-river steamer, say an Albany or Troy day-line boat, and stand as observers upon its deck while the voyage proceeds. Thus both shores of the noble water-way will be under our eyes at once, and we can proceed comprehensively.

Immediately *opposite* us, as the steamer leaves her wharf, stretching downward along the western shore of the harbor, are the wharves, warehouses, sugar-refineries, and railway stations of **Jersey City.** Of the last, the most prominent is the huge arched station and train-house of the *Pennsylvania Railroad*, the great central line East and South. Just above it the tall Lorillard tobacco-works are seen; and a mile farther the elevators, stations, and ferry-landings of the *Erie Railway* (New York, Lake Erie & Western), the terminus of the main line not only, but of the branch to Newburgh and Piermont, and of the *New Jersey Northern Railroad* to Nyack. Still farther on is the river-side terminus of the Delaware, Lackawanna & Western Railroad.

The expanded channel here is crowded with ocean steamships and the white hulls of the boats that run up the river to ports on Long Island Sound and to the ocean beaches. A score of ferry-boats at once are crossing from shore to shore, and three times as many more may be counted in their slips. Great steamers, European "liners," coasters to the Gulf of Mexico, the West Indies, and South America; men-of-war, at anchor; numberless tugs, racing about alone, proudly towing some noble ship to sea, or laboriously dragging a long line of picturesque barges; and innumerable sailing-craft, large and small, foreign and domestic, dignified and ridiculous—all these meet and pass and cross one another's bows with little hindrance, for there is room enough for each.

The **New York shore** shows simply a straight array of wharves and warehouses, crowded with ocean steamships, the names of whose lines may be read in large letters, but these thin out above 23d Street, where most of the Hudson River boats stop (actually at the foot of W. 22d Street) for up-town passengers. The city's available water-front on North River is said to be no less than thirteen miles in extent, but only the lower part of this is devoted to commerce as yet, fortunately for the sight-seeing traveler.

Meanwhile a bushy headland has attracted attention on the New Jersey shore, where **Hoboken** has succeeded Jersey City, north of an invisible boundary line, just above the Erie terminus, and about at the place where the half-dug tunnel underlies the river. This is *Stevens' Point*, opposite 14th Street, New York, the site of "Stevens' Castle," the homestead of the late Commodore Stevens, who formerly owned a large tract of land near it, and founded the Stevens' Institute of Technology, whose buildings now occupy the Point. The man and the place became famous during the Civil War in connection with the huge floating fortress called the Stevens' Battery, which was constructed there, at the commodore's expense, for the defense of the harbor, but was never used.

The lowlands north of this Point are called *The Elysian Fields* —a resort for Sunday afternoon strolling, of which our grandfathers and grandmothers in their young days were very fond, but which has now lost its beauty and good repute together.

Close behind it is seen the rocky front of *Bergen Hill*, a long ridge of trap rock which forms the backbone of the peninsula between the valleys of the Hudson and those of the Hackensack River and Newark Bay, which are two miles west, and parallel with our river. This ridge steadily increases in height and boldness forward; and is occupied north of Hoboken by Hudson City, covering West Hoboken and Union Hill in one municipality. Nearer the water, and next north of the Elysian Fields, comes **Weehawken** a name, like "Hoboken," which is a corruption of an Indian term learned by the earliest colonists. None of these towns, upon close acquaintance, gain much over the unprepossessing appearance they have from the water, and they are inhabited mainly by foreigners, principally Germans.

THE BURR-HAMILTON DUEL.

The Weehawken shore has a melancholy interest as the scene of that sad duel between Hamilton and Burr which ended the

careers of two exceedingly talented men. It took place upon a grassy plateau at the foot of the cliff just south of the present West Shore Railroad ferry-houses, in the early morning of July 11, 1804.

Alexander Hamilton was one of the most cultivated, most talented, honorable, and patriotic men of his time. He had been of distinguished service during the years of the Revolution, and to his genius the financial recovery of the United States at the close of that war was mainly due. Among the men whose public course he combatted was the Vice-President, Aaron Burr, a man of brilliant talents, but of erratic and vindictive character. Burr seized upon the pretext of some idle gossip to make a quarrel with Hamilton, and sent a challenge of such a nature as, according to the social rule of the time, Hamilton felt bound to accept, though well aware that he had been innocent of any real offense. They met at Weehawken, and Hamilton was mortally wounded at the first fire, he making no attempt to reply with his own pistol. His death, the next day, was mourned as a public calamity, and Burr was treated with almost universal execration until he sank into a bitter and miserable obscurity.

On the hill-top above the place where this duel was fought lay the large estate and stone house of the King family. The mansion still stands, but it and the grounds (to which Col. King carried the bowlder against which Hamilton fell, and inscribed it with the initials A. H.) are now occupied by an immense summer garden and amusement place named *El Dorado*, where outdoor spectacular exhibitions were given, with music, and refreshments, and decorous merry-making of all sorts in the open air, until the enterprise became unprofitable.

"What a change is here!" exclaims a recent newspaper observer. "The quintessence of paradox is reached when in this old King house which, after the battle of Brandywine, was the headquarters of Gen. Lafayette, are now quartered 150 chorus girls, who nightly flit across the El Dorado stage. In the great high-studded rooms with fluted cornices, where Lafayette and his staff lived, are now placed little cot beds, five or six in a room; and round the old table which has many a time shaken with the pounding of fists as General and afterward President Washington was toasted in sound old Madeira, now sit a dozen or more Spanish coryphees, who chatter Spanish and eat roast chicken and drink fresh milk every morning.

"It is the same red sun that sinks down behind the blue hills of New Jersey now that sank down a hundred years ago, but what a different scene it said good-evening to then. There was no teeming city across the river, no huge white steamers making up and down, no El Dorado, with its dancing lights and moving crowds, no yellow-haired coryphees. All was different, except the old square stone house. Doubtless before the door stood a gentleman in a cocked hat and buckled shoes and plum-colored small-clothes, and by his side, mayhap, was a lady in a fine hat, wi h waving ostrich feathers, and a King Charles Spaniel chased across the lawn where now chases the white and woolly trick poodle."

The *lofty iron structure in front of the El Dorado grounds* is a structure containing elevators, and supporting a railroad no longer in service. The large wharves and ferry-landings just above it belong to the terminal station of the *New York, West Shore & Buffalo Railroad*, familiarly called "West Shore," which passes through Bergen Ridge by a tunnel immediately in the rear of the station. Its ferryboats run thence to Franklin Street, downtown, and to the foot of W. 42d Street, nearly opposite. Trains of the New York, Ontario & Western Railroad also use this station and the tracks of the West Shore Railroad as far as Cornwall.

Above this point the shore becomes a series of bold rocks, crowned by the straggling houses and breweries of Union Hill and Guttenberg, with the Moorish towers of the distant monastery and church of the Passionist fathers as the only building worth mention. The cliffs gradually increase in height and abruptness, become more wooded, and are sparsely inhabited. They may be reached by an electric railroad from the ferry, connecting northward to Fort Lee and Englewood.

Meanwhile, *on the right* the densely populous, busy part of the metropolis is rapidly gliding astern, and the best residential part, which succeeds it on this northerly high ground along the river, is now hidden by the verdant margin of

Riverside Park and Drive.—This beautiful littoral park, says Ingersoll's *Week in New York*,* lies along the high verge of the Hudson between 71st and 127th streets, and is reached by the Boulevard horse-cars, or, at the upper end, by the cable-cars along 125th Street to Fort Lee Ferry. It was the subject of an appreciative and artistically illustrated article by Wm. A Stiles, editor of the popular horticultural journal, *Garden and Forest*, in

---

* *A Week in New York*, By ERNEST INGERSOLL. Rand, McNally & Co. Annual revision, 1892, p. 116.

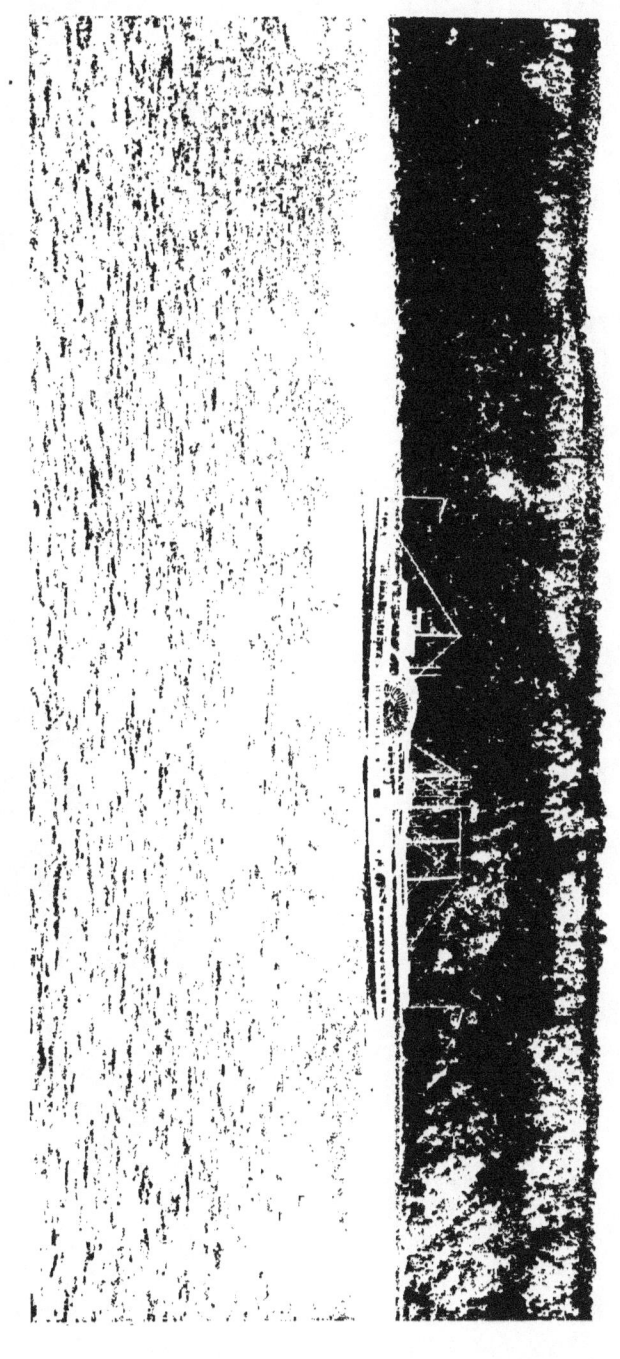

The Century for October, 1885, from which the following remarks are condensed:

From 72d Street to the hollow known in the old maps as "Marritje Davids' Fly" (valley), at what is now 127th Street, the river banks are bold, rising steeply at one point to the height of 150 feet. "Down at the river level lies Twelfth Avenue, while upon the high ground, 800 feet inland, and parallel with the pier line, Eleventh Avenue cuts its way square across the long series of side streets. . . . Between these two avenues, now approaching one and now the other, winds Riverside Drive, following mainly the brow of the bluff, but rising and falling in easy grades, curving about the bolder projections, and everywhere adapting its course so graciously to the contour of the land that it does not look to have been laboriously laid out."

From this drive the views of the river and the wood-crowned heights above are most characteristic. The eye has free range to the north or south along the bright waterway, and covers prospects of great extent and the most varied interest. The crowning view of the whole series is that from Claremont Heights looking up the river. This is at the northern end of the park, where the grounds reach their greatest elevation. Here, overlooking a commanding prospect, and surrounded by quiet lawns, which keep at a reverential distance the "equipage and bravery of fashion," has been placed the **Tomb of Gen. U. S. Grant,** the first soldier of the restored Union, where his body was laid finally to rest amid impressive ceremonies on April 27, 1897.

This temple-like tomb stands 100 feet above the river, and is itself 150 feet high. It is built of flawless white granite from Maine, and is adorned with varied sculptures. The designer was J. H. Duncan; it was erected between 1891 and 1897; and the cost, defrayed by over 5,000 subscribers, was about $600,000. An imposing flight of steps is intended to lead up to it from a riverside landing. Behind this conspicuous and noble memorial are seen the ornate white St. Luke's Hospital, the beginnings of the Episcopal Cathedral, and the new buildings of Columbia University, of which the central one is the domed library. These stand on Morningside Heights, half a mile east of the river.

This part of New York, just north of *Claremont Heights,* used to be *Manhattanville,* and the name is still heard in the neighborhood. The great buildings embowered in trees, upon the distant eminence, are those of the Convent of the Sacred Heart and attached institutions. A half-mile farther, where the white monuments of Trinity Cemetery (the burial-ground of Trinity Church) gleam among the foliage, the naturalist Audubon lived for many years, and there he is buried. The fine residences just north of the cemetery are built upon the grounds once surrounding his mansion, and form an undivided cluster called *Audubon Park*. This neighborhood was formerly the village of *Carmansville*, and it contains several benevolent institutions, among which the city's Asylum for the Deaf and Dumb is conspicuous by reason of its dome. It can accommodate 450 pupils, and dates from 1817, when only one other institution of its kind existed in the country—that at Hartford, Conn.

Then comes the elevation **Washington Heights**, of Revolutionary memories and modern social pre-eminence, with *Jeffrey's Hook* thrown out at its base. This and the Highlands northward are now threaded by streets, and dotted on the water-front with costly estates and great houses which enjoy an almost rural seclusion. The foliage of the trees that beautify the shore hides these houses almost completely; but it may be mentioned that among them are the former country-seats of James Gordon Bennett and A. T. Stewart.

The next hill northward is now included under the district name *Inwood*, but earlier it was called Cock Hill. It forms the extreme northern end of Manhattan Island. The little point and landing at its base is *Tubby Hook*, named from an ancient ferryman, Tibers. Between this hill and Washington Heights is a deep vale through which the United States Government is now digging a canal by which barges of slight draft may pass from the Hudson to the Harlem and East rivers. Just behind it is the historic King's Bridge, and beyond, across the Spuyten Duyvil, are the war-scarred heights of Tippet's Hill.

Historical.—All this is ground of deep interest to Americans, for it is identified with the early struggles of the Revolutionary War, in the dark days of '76. The defeat of the Patriot army, in the battle of Long Island, made it evident that New York, too, must be abandoned to the foe. The sick and wounded were hurried to New Jersey; the military stores and baggage were conveyed up the Hudson to a fortified post at Dobbs Ferry, and Washington moved his headquarters to King's Bridge, where the old post-road and present Broadway crosses the Harlem. Thus driven from the city, the American army set to work to establish itself on these rocky heights, between the Hudson and the Spuyten Duyvil (see map), and upon this, the highest point, a

TOMB OF GEN. U. S. GRANT.

fortification was constructed named *Fort Washington*. It was a strong earthwork, in the form of a pentagon, occupying, with its ravelins, the lofty hill between 181st and 186th streets. Just to the northward, on the same rocky heights, was the redoubt called *Fort Tryon;* to the eastward was *Fort George*, looking down upon the Harlem River, while immediately below, a water-battery was erected upon Jeffrey's Hook. Cock Hill (now Inwood), Tippet's Hill, and the vicinity of King's Bridge were also fortified. Though these works were slight, their positions were naturally of great defense. Meanwhile, both armies maintained strongly protected fronts, stretching across the whole breadth of Manhattan Island, and separated by the transverse valley north of Central Park. Skirmishes were of almost daily occurrence, and most frequently at the cost of the patriots, who, in addition to their wonted wretched condition, were dispirited to the last degree. Desertions from the camp were so numerous as to materially reduce its strength, and to disquiet even the bravest and most sanguine of the leaders themselves. Boats and ships-of-war were daily bearing the British flag triumphantly up the East River, and even up the Hudson, despite the obstructions upon which so much reliance had been placed. The *chevaux de frise*, formed by old sloops sunk in the river, and the wonderful submarine batteries, were but straws in the way of the British vessels; and the guns of Fort Washington and its twin fortresses Lee and Constitution, across on the Palisade shore, were quite as contemptuously disregarded.

Washington, at this time, desired, as did most of his officers, to evacuate Fort Washington, but was overruled by his respect for the wishes of Congress, which insisted that the post should be held. After the battle of White Plains (October 28, 1776), the whole army devoted itself to strengthening Fort Washington, and negligently allowed Lord Howe to get a supply of flatboats through the Spuyten Duyvil to King's Bridge, enabling him to ferry his troops over, and thus invest the works on every side. The following day (November 15th), the fort was summoned to surrender, but refused. The next morning, Magaw, who was in command, proceeded to dispose of his forces, amounting in all to nearly 3,000 men, the greater part of whom were stationed outside of the fort, for want of room within. The south side of the fort was menaced by Lord Percy with 1,600 men, and to oppose him, Col. Lambert Cadwallader was dispatched with a Pennsylvania force of only half that number. Col. Rawlings of Maryland, with a company of riflemen, was placed by a small battery northward (Fort Tryon), to oppose Knyphausen, who, with his Hessians, was posted with cannon near King's Bridge. Col. Baxter of Pennsylvania held Fort George, to oppose an attack by Mathew from the Harlem side. The fourth proposed attack of the enemy was under Col. Sterling, who, as a feint, was to drop down the Harlem River on flatboats to the left of the fort.

The enemy's several assaults were made simultaneously, beginning about noon of the 16th, by booming cannon and volleys of musketry. Knyphausen's division, commanded by himself and by Col. Rahl, conquered all the opposing obstructions of woods and rocks, and, despite the bold defense of Rawlings, soon drove him and his force back to the fort. The Americans under Baxter were no less steady in their resistance, but with no better fortune. Baxter himself was killed, and his men driven back into the fort. Cadwallader, in the meanwhile, was making a brave defense to the southward against the enemy under Lord Percy; but he, too, was at length compelled to retreat under the additional pressure of an attack by Gen. Mathew—who had previously driven in Baxter's division—and of the threatened approach, on the rear, of Col. Sterling. Thus were the assailants victorious at all points, though only after the most obstinate resistance everywhere, and with a terrible loss in killed and wounded.

Washington and several of his officers were eager spectators of the disastrous struggle, from the opposite shore of the Hudson. When he saw the flag, which heralded the second summons to surrender, carried into the ill-fated fortress, he hastily wrote a note to Magaw, promising to bring off his garrison if he could sustain himself until evening. This message was daringly delivered by Capt. Gooch of Boston, who passed and repassed safely across the river and amidst the balls and bayonets of the British. The embassy was, however, too late. Magaw and his garrison were wholly in the power of their opponents, and nothing remained but to surrender themselves prisoners-of-war, with no other terms than the retention of their swords by the officers, and of their baggage by the men. "It was," said Lee, at the time, "a cursed affair."

Thus ended the military history of Fort Washington, although it was repaired, and as Fort Knyphausen, was long afterward garrisoned by the enemy.

The **New Jersey bank** here is equally interesting historically, and closely connected with the foregoing incidents.

A wagon road runs along the base of the crags, and people live there in rustic fashion. Some factories—especially the great oil-works at **Shadyside** (anciently Bull's Ferry)—exist lower down, but above Guttenberg nothing of the sort mars the bank. Many of the residents are fishermen who set shad-nets in the spring. *Undercliff* is the new landing for the Fort Lee Ferry and electric railroad, which runs to Fort Lee Village, Leonia, and Englewood. Wagon-roads climb inland, here and there, offering enjoyable rambles; and the landings at Shadyside, Edgewater, and Pleasant Valley are accessible several times a day, from Canal and W. 22d streets, New York, by the steamer *Pleasant Valley* (fare, 10 cents). This rocky wall is still Bergen Ridge; but two miles above Weehawken, and opposite Washington Heights, Bergen Ridge trends inland behind a new and much higher wall of trap-rocks, which thereafter front the river for many miles—the Palisades of the Hudson. In the ravine-like space between the two ridges, which enables a wagon road to reach the plateau upon the summit, a village has long existed called **Fort Lee** after the fortification built upon the heights above it in 1776.

For many years **Fort Lee** has been an excursion point and picnic-ground, and gradually it became the resort of a rough element, who would land there by the barge load and hold no sy revels. A few years ago, an attempt was made to redeem the place, and prepare it for a pleasure resort acceptable to a good class of customers. A great hotel has been built, and abundant means of refreshment and amusement are provided, while the scale of prices is moderate, and during the summer steamboats make frequent trips back and forth, from Canal, 13th, and 31th streets, New York, while the ferry at W. 129th Street (reached by the 125th Street cable cars) runs all the year round; but fashion has never smiled upon the place, though the view from its Palisades is worth a much longer journey.

Historical.—The Revolutionary record of this western shore is intimately connected with that of Washington Heights.

The promontory in which the Palisades begin was fortified, early in 1776, by two strong redoubts, of which the principal and uppermost one was named Fort Lee, after the eccentric Charles Lee, and was commanded by Greene, while the other was called Fort Constitution. After the fall of Fort Washington there remained no longer any hope of obstructing the passage of the Hudson at this point, and preparations were at once begun to abandon these Jersey forts also; but before it could be effected, Lord Cornwallis, crossing the river with a British detachment of 6,000 men, endeavored to surround and capture this garrison also. His attempt was a failure. The American troops got safely away to the Hackensack, but were obliged to relinquish to the British all their artillery, except two twelve-pounders, and a great quantity of provisions and military stores. Washington's army, depleted by these losses, discouraged, melting away under expiring terms of service and desertion, totally unprepared to face the inclemency of the weather, or to build fortified winter quarters, was obliged to abandon even this poor line of defense and hasten southward to the Delaware River.

After that the New Jersey shore was nominally in the possession of the British, but was not regularly garrisoned, and became the scene of an incessant guerrilla warfare. Just north of the present Guttenberg, where the woods begin at Shadyside, there was in those times the landing of Bull's Ferry to New York, where a farmer's road came down through a ravine. Between this road and the river a high and narrow ridge of rocks formed a headland, known since 1779 as *Block-house Point*, in memory of a fierce and fruitless encounter which occurred there, and which was the occasion of a celebrated poem.

The winter of 1779–80 was a season of almost unexampled severity. Sleighs crossed the Hudson for weeks without interruption, and artillery was brought from Staten Island on the ice. Fuel became so scarce in New York that $20 a cord was paid for wood, and the British authorities were forced to break up old ships to supply their troops with something to keep the fires going. Anticipating an equal scarcity the following winter, a great number of British sympathizers spent the next summer on these heights, west of the Hudson, in cutting down the forests covering Bergen Ridge, and turning the logs into cordwood. But the American army along the Hackensack constantly sent out foraging parties, so that the Tory wood-cutters found their occupation precarious in point of profit and dangerous to life and limb. Moreover, most of these men had fled from inland places to the protection of the Royal army, including many who were guilty of robbery and other crimes, committed, in that lawless interval, upon friend and foe alike. Hence the whole crowd were known as "refugees," and were so execrated by both sides that not only had they good cause to dread the American troopers, but were left by the British commander to build block-houses and defend themselves as best they might. Several such minor forts were constructed by wood-contractors along the hill-top, but the most important one stood on this point above Bull's Ferry. It was a large block-house of logs, inaccessible on two sides, and defended by breastworks and an *abatis* upon its vulnerable northern front, where the point of land was continuous with the plateau.

In the summer of 1780, Washington was encamped near Suffern's, N. Y. His men were badly provisioned, and he knew that there had been collected on Bergen Neck, for the use of the British and the Tories, a large number of horses, cattle, swine, and other desirable live stock, protected by these Refugees. He, therefore, ordered Gen. Anthony Wayne to take several regiments of Maryland and Pennsylvania troops, including cavalry, destroy it, and secure as many cattle and other provisions as possible.

Wayne marched quietly to Liberty Pole (now Englewood),

where he divided his command. A part went straight to the river above Englewood Landing, and hid themselves in the woods, while Wayne led the remainder down the back roads to the top of the ridge near Fort Lee, where he turned southward and was soon discovered by the wood-cutters, who fled to their block-house and prepared to resist the onslaught.

While Wayne, with the infantry and artillery, moved steadily against it, the cavalry under Maj. Moylan, mounting an extra man behind each dragoon, swept on to the pastures of Weehawken and Hoboken, gathered up every four-footed beast they could find, and drove them with the utmost haste toward Washington's camps; a raid long remembered there.

Meanwhile, Wayne had made a most spirited attack, but the defense was obstinate, and his little six-pounders were too light to demolish the fortifications. Moreover, when success seemed near, word came that the English were crossing in force and were likely to intercept and capture the whole expedition. A retreat was therefore ordered, and the command hurried away, having suffered a loss of sixty-four men in killed and wounded. Wayne and Washington were both deeply disappointed; and their disgust was not lightened by learning that the reported reinforcements was a false alarm, and that, moreover, if tradition may be believed, the enemy was almost out of ammunition and must have succumbed in a few moments. The door of this blockhouse may now be seen in the museum of Washington's headquarters at Newburgh.

This skirmish was a source of so great satisfaction to the British, that the King himself sent his personal congratulations to the Refugees, who did really make a most gallant defense; and it inspired Maj. André, then on the staff of Sir Henry Clinton, in New York, to write his satirical verses, "The Cow Chase." They make a long rollicking ballad, especially interesting from the coincidence connected with the last verse, which runs thus:

> And now I've closed my epic strain,
>   I tremble as I show it,
> Lest this same warrio-drover Wayne
>   Should ever catch the poet.

On the day this was printed, in *Rivington's Gazette*, Maj. André was captured as a spy; and the commander of the division of the American army to which his captors belonged, and where he was tried and executed, was Gen. Anthony Wayne!

Palisades of the Hudson is the term long since applied to that escarpment of roughly columnar basaltic trap which gushed out of a crack in the earth's crust in early Triassic time, and now, with its foot-slope of fallen fragments, forms the western wall of the river for twenty miles to the Tappan Sea. The face is nearly straight, almost uniform in height, rising from an altitude of 350 feet, half a mile above Fort Lee, to 550 feet near its northern extremity.

The front is everywhere precipitous, and the bare rock is exposed in that vertical formation characteristic of basalt, from which has come the name; a natural suggestion to the early comers here, who were so familiar with stockades made of logs set on end. Breaks sufficient to enable wagon roads to descend to the river occur in only three places, and scarcely more opportunities exist for the hardiest foot-climber to descend; it is in fact a narrow ridge, flat-topped, tree-grown, and falling suddenly away on the inner side into a deep valley dividing it from Bergen Ridge.

This long escarpment, so gray and undiversified, half bare of trees, and showing only here and there a little house, or, worse, a great scar where men are tearing down the rocks to cut into paving-blocks or crush as road-metal, is more forbidding than beautiful as seen from a steamer's deck or from the opposite bank, with the broad river to dwarf its height; but when one skirts its base in a canoe, especially at morning or on a somewhat cloudy day, the grandeur of height and warmth of color are perceived, and better justify the encomiums of early writers.

A road runs along the top, and it is possible to stroll upon the very edge from Fort Lee some two miles, as far as the end of Englewood Avenue, opposite Spuyten Duyvil, and there to enjoy one of the most striking scenes America has to show; a privilege, however, that too few avail themselves of. "The opposite low, verdant shore, for a long distance to the north, affords a varied and charming picture; while below, the eye reaches to the far-off metropolis and its crowded bay. The palisade wall, apparently so uniform, is broken into pinnacles and deep clefts, and all the scene, from a close survey, is full of picturesque variety."

One would suppose that this lofty, breezy ridge so near the city, and affording views so extended and superb, would have long ago been fully occupied by country-houses and summer pleasure-places, but such are few and inconspicuous. Formerly a famous hotel—the Palisade Mountain House—stood upon the cliff opposite Riverdale, but it was burned in 1884.

The **Eastern side** of the river now presents a vivid contrast to the solitary and inaccessible Palisades. It is low, verdant, and thickly inhabited. Having passed the heights of Fort Washington and Inwood, the **valley of the Spuyten Duyvil** (Dutch *'Spyt den duivel*) opens to view, but the stream itself is hidden by the railroad drawbridge underneath which the tide flows in and out between the Hudson and the Harlem. This marks the northern end of Manhattan Island, and affords an opportunity for the main tracks of the New York Central & Hudson River Railroad to reach the bank of the Hudson from its city station in the Grand Central Depot, on 42d Street. The railway station against the rocks, just north of the valley, is *Spuyten Duyvil*, where the 30th Street branch, which follows the lower river's edge, joins the main line. At the end of the vista up the valley is seen the neighborhood of King's Bridge, which was the scene of several hard skirmishes in the early part of the Revolution, and later was held as the northern outpost of the British army in New York.

Irving's facetious explanation of the curious name of this stream or tideway has long been laughed over by the readers of "Diedrich Knickerbocker's" *History of New York;* but it may not be generally known that the tale which follows is only an enlargement of a real and fatal exhibition of foolhardiness on the part of a young Dutchman; long before Stuyvesant's time, however. The story will bear repeating, as Diedrich tells it, and is as follows:

Anthony Van Corlear, the trumpeter of Governor Stuyvesant, was sent post-haste, upon the appearance of the ships of the English Duke of York in the harbor, to warn the farmers up the river and summon them to the defense of New Amsterdam. He had reached this stream, where there was then no bridge. "The wind was high, the elements in an uproar, and no Charon could be found to ferry the adventurous sounder of brass across the water. For a short time he vapored like an intelligent ghost upon the brink, and then, bethinking himself of the urgency of his errand (to arouse the people to arms), he took a hearty embrace of his stone bottle, swore most valorously that he would swim across in spite of the devil (*en spyt den duyvel*), and daringly plunged into the stream. Luckless Anthony! Scarcely had he buffeted half-way over, when he was observed to struggle violently, as if battling with the spirit of the waters. Instinctively he put his trumpet to his mouth, and, giving a vehement blast, sank forever to the bottom! The clangor of his trumpet rang far and wide through the country, alarming the neighbors round, who hurried in amazement to the spot. Here an old Dutch burgher, famed for his veracity, and who had been a witness of the fact, related to them the melancholy affair, with the fearful addition (to which I am slow in giving belief) that he saw the duyvil, in the shape of a huge moss-bunker, seize the sturdy Anthony by the leg, and drag him beneath the waves. Certain it is, the place has been called Spuyten Duyvil ever since."

The high point of land between the Spuyten Duyvil and Hudson, now covered with residences, the Mohicans called *Nipnichsen*, and the Dutch *Constable's Point*, after its owner. At the time of the Revolution, when owned by the Tippet family, it was repeatedly fortified and known as Tippet's Hill, but no incident of much public moment happened there. This little cross-valley seems to have been thickly inhabited by Indians. It was here that Henry Hudson had that fight with the "Manhattoes," or Island Indians, who wished to board his little vessel, and got shot for their pains. One great attraction, no doubt, was the abundance of fish—a recommendation that still holds good. Great hauls of shad are made every spring off the mouth of the Spuyten Duyvil, and the angling for striped bass and the like, along its rocky course, furnishes amusement to many a leisurely citizen.

The city of New York long ago overflowed Manhattan Island, and its limits extend northward on this side to Yonkers, three miles above the Spuyten Duyvil. This lofty and beautiful shore, however, still keeps its early village names, *Riverdale* and *Mount St. Vincent*, and is dotted with the country-like estates of wealthy citizens, such families as that of the late Wm. E. Dodge, the philanthropic merchant; the Appletons, of the famous publishing house; Robert Colgate, ex-Postmaster-General James, and others. These are in *Riverdale*, whose railway station is next above Spuyten Duyvil, at the water's edge. A mile farther up is seen the station for *Mount St. Vincent*, a locality taking its name from the great convent on the hill-top, where were formerly the castle-like residence and estate, "Font Hill," of the actor, Edwin Forrest.

"**Mount St. Vincent**," remarks the editor of *Picturesque America*, "is an extensive Roman Catholic convent-school for girls, which is famous for the excellence of its educational system; but, unfortunately, the huge building erected here can not be said to form an attractive feature of the river scenery. It is out of harmony with the landscape, and . . . utterly dwarfs Font Hill, which, before the erection of the vast unhandsome mass behind it, was a striking and interesting feature of the river shore. Now, if one can manage to shut out from his vision the mammoth pile behind it, he can get a partial idea of its claims to the picturesque. It must be admitted, however, that a castle on the banks of the Hudson is a piece of sheer affectation. The pile looks very small from the river, and must necessarily disappoint those who associate size and grandeur with the idea of a castle, although one frequently finds abroad castles with no better pretension in the way of extent, however superior may be their claims on the ground of antiquity."

The convent is more than a school, however, for it is the headquarters in America of the great order of Sisters of Charity, numbering over 1,500 under its immediate jurisdiction, and forming a general home hospital and retreat.

After the heights of Mount St. Vincent have been passed, the land sinks somewhat, and busy civilization reappears. The new station *Ludlow*, at this point, recalls the old-time rural property here of the Ludlow family. Then succeeds

The City of Yonkers.—The water front, where the railway, and steamers, and street-cars meet at the central wharf, is solid with warehouses, for here are many important manufacturing establishments—mower and reaper works, gutta-percha and rubber, silk, carpet, and hat factories, machine and elevator works, and the shops of the Eagle Pencil Company. Above these, embowered in trees, rise the shops and houses of 35,000 inhabitants. Yonkers is connected with New York not only by the Hudson River Railroad, but also by the New York & Putnam Railroad, and is a calling place for all lines of steamers. It has a score of churches and a long list of religious, benevolent, and fraternal societies; a high school and seven grammar schools, but no public library; paid police and fire departments, with police and fire-alarm telegraphs, connected with New York's system; four banks and a safe-deposit company; electric street-cars, which run to the suburbs north, east, and south, and pass Getty Square, the City Hall, and the most central hotels. The leading social clubs are the *Yonkers*, whose house is 1017 Broadway, and the *City*, on Getty Square—an open space in the center of the city where several streets converge. There is an athletic club (63 Main Street), with good grounds; but the facilities for aquatic sports have given these pre-eminence there, and along the shore, at the northern suburb *Glenwood*, a station on the Hudson River Railroad, are the houses of the Corinthian and Yonkers Yacht clubs, the Yonkers Boat Club, and the Yonkers Canoe Club. The Bicycle and Photographic clubs should also be mentioned. It is thus apparent that athletic and outdoor sports receive an unusual amount of attention at the hands of its citizens. The National Guard is represented by the Fourth Separate Company, whose armory is on Waverly Street.

The town, as a whole, has no great pretensions to beauty— though Warburton Avenue, and some other streets in the northern part, fronting the river, are rapidly acquiring it—and contains little of interest to the stranger. Two objects, however, are worthy of attention, the more so as they successfully recall the early history of the locality. These are the *City Hall*, called "Manor Hall" because the building was the home of the Lord of the Manor of Phillipsburgh in colonial times; and *St. John's Protestant Episcopal Church*, a beautiful house of worship, with an interesting story. The best hotel is *Arlington Inn*, on South Broadway.

Henry Hudson, and the Dutch traders after him, found here a Mohican village, named Nappechemak, at the mouth of a rapid little stream, now spelled Nepperhan. Settlements were made by the Dutch West-India Company in this township as long ago as 1639; at least, lands were purchased of the native Indian Sachems at that early period, and soon thereafter occupied. These, after a time, passed into the hands of a burgher of Manhattan, Adriaen Van der Donck, who acquired a far wider area than the present city covers, and was, by royal patent, created a Patroon, whose estate was called Colondonck. It has been supposed that "Yonkers" is a corruption of his patronymic, but a better explanation is, that when a village began to grow up at this landing it was called the *Jonk Heer's* (i. e., young lord's), in compliment to the Patroon; whence Jonker's, and gradually (the *j* being like the English *y*) the modern spelling. At that time this village was called Upper Yonkers, and the region now covered by Van Cortlandt Park, in New York City, was Lower Yonkers. The latter was conveyed to the Van Cortlandts, who intermarried with the Van der Doncks; and the upper half was later sold to Frederick Phillipse, the first.

The Phillipse or Phillips family, which owned extensive lands northward, and whose favorite residence theretofore had been at "Castle Phillipse," yet standing by the old mill in Sleepy Hollow, at once took possession, and obtained from the English King a patent creating the property into the Manor of Phillipsburgh. Phillipse had anticipated this dignity, not perfected until 1693, by erecting, in 1682, the front part of the present City Hall as his manor-house; and it was completed by the addition of the back part in 1745. This old house is still elegant, and in its time must have been a very notable place. Having put his house in order, the now reigning lord of the manor, a second Frederick Phillipse, bethought him of more heavenly things, and erected a stone church, as he was bound to do by reason of owning the living. It was, of course, of the Established Church of England, was called *St. John's,* and was completed in 1752; but services had been held in the parish ever since 1694.

At this time one of his daughters, *Mary,* born in the manor-house, July 3, 1730, was growing up to be the belle of all the country-side. A few years later (1756) George Washington, then a colonel wearing the laurels which he alone, almost, had brought from the disastrous Braddock campaign, was visiting in New York at the house of Beverly Robinson, a man of wealth and cultivation, who afterward became prominent as a leader of Tories, and especially in connection with the Arnold and André affair. Robinson's wife was the eldest daughter of Phillipse, and there Washington met and fell in love with her younger sister, the beautiful Mary Phillipse. The affection was not declared, however, and the young Virginian went back to his plantations, confiding his secret to a friend who wrote him frequently of the social doings of the young lady and her friends. Finally, Washington was informed that a suitor had appeared in the person of Col. Roger Morris, who had been an associate on Braddock's staff, and was advised to make haste to come to New York and contest his claim He did not do so—why, no one knows—and the belle became the wife of his rival; but there is no foundation for the tradition that Washington had offered himself and had been refused.

Yonkers grew apace, and the Nepperhan, which had been trained to work a saw-mill, and hence had come to be called Saw Mill Creek even in Van der Donck's time—soon turned the wheels of several mills, and to-day is hidden between factories. When men were taking sides at the approach of the Revolution, the Frederick Phillipse of that day—third lord of the manor—endeavored to remain neutral; but, although Washington stayed more than once under his roof, he fell under suspicion of a leaning toward royalty, and his property was confiscated by act of Legislature in 1779, and was sold by the Commissioners of Forfeiture in 1785—the year of his death in England. Complications followed, which were cleared up by a sale of the whole thing to John Jacob Astor, from whom the Government had to re-buy it, at a very long advance, in order to confirm the tenants and holders of parts in their titles. The manor-house was occupied as a private residence by various families until 1868, when it was purchased by the Village of Yonkers, and finally became the City Hall in 1872. It was the scene of a notable historical celebration in 1882; and in front of it now stands a lofty and admirable Soldiers' Monument to citizens who fell in the Civil War.

The *Revolutionary history of Yonkers* was full of lively incidents, though no battle of moment occurred near it, except the memorable engagement in the harbor in 1777, between the British frigates *Rose* and *Phenix*, at anchor, and the oared gunboats of the patriots, which were rowed out of the mouth of the Nepperhan, having in tow a large tender, filled with combustibles, intended to be placed alongside of the frigates as a fire-ship. The sailors, however, kept it off by means of spars, and a heavy fire of grape and canister compelled the gunboats and their brave crews to seek shelter near shore. The attempt was witnessed by Generals Heath, Clinton, and others, and came very near succeeding.

During the whole war—after the American army, in 1776, had retreated from its hills, following the disastrous campaign about White Plains—Yonkers was the center of the uncovered "neutral" tract between the British posts at King's Bridge and those of the American army above. This unlucky tract was the foraging ground of both parties, and the rendezvous of the opposing bands of reprobates known as the Skinners and the Cow Boys—the former claiming to act in the service of the Americans, and the latter under the British banner. As far as the quiet folks of the devoted neighborhood were concerned, there was not much choice between the rival bands, since they both served themselves, no matter whether at the cost of friend or of foe. What with the escapades of these fellows, and with the marches and counter-marches above and below them, and with now and then a serious skirmish, the "neutral ground" was a busy region at the time, and abounds in such reminiscences of adventure as J. Fenimore Cooper has utilized in his story *The Spy*.

St. John's Church persisted, and for many years was an interesting relic of colonial architecture; but in 1870 it was replaced by the present spacious, costly, and very beautiful Gothic building on Getty Square, which contains a carved font of Italian marble and workmanship, a beautiful pulpit of brass, and several memorial windows of high artistic excellence.

This structure largely exceeds in size the earlier church; but the south wall includes, near the base, a large part of the wall of the original church, and the low, arched, old-fashioned door, which has thus been preserved as a fitting relic of the early condition. Attached are a series of picturesque parish buildings connecting the noble church with the rectory; and in the wall which incloses the church yard is arranged a public drinking-fountain, having an artistic bronze tablet where the invitation to drink is coupled with the appropriate citation, John iv; 13, 14: *Whosoever drinketh of this water shall thirst again; but whosoever drinketh of the water that I shall give him shall never thirst, but the water that I shall give him shall be in him a well of water springing up into everlasting life.*

The best part of Yonkers is northward of the business center, especially along Warburton Avenue, a street which lies parallel with the river and part way up the hillside, where the tall brownstone steeple of the Baptist Church is conspicuous from the water. Above this street are Palisade Avenue and (North) Broadway, while Alta and Park Hill avenues (see p. 24) are other very handsome streets, bordered with beautiful residences. An interesting walk is to climb the hill, from the trolley-car line to Broadway, and go out along it for a mile or more. This is the old turnpike, and really a continuation of Broadway in the city of New York, so that it comes rightly by this name, which, in fact, is applied to it in all the river towns, at least as far as Sing Sing. The road is macadamized, laid with water, and lighted by gas far north of the city, and bordered by elegant properties, of which the residence of C. H. Lillienthal, indicated from the river by a brown-stone battlemented tower, is a good example. A far more famous homestead, however, is that somewhat above, to be recognized from the river by a lofty gray tower, surmounted by an ornamental iron railing; for this is the country-house of the late Governor and Presidential candidate, Samuel J. Tilden, who became known throughout the Union as the Sage of "Greystone." The large grounds are especially noteworthy for the magnificent trees that grow in forest-like profusion along the avenues of approach and on the river slopes.

Next above Yonkers comes *Hastings*. The village itself, where there are a railway station and small steamboat landing, and the works of an asphalt pavement concern, is of small account; but the high shore is closely set with homes of wealthy men, of which Dr. Huyler's, just above the landing, is most conspicuous by reason of its clock-tower and windmill. Just below this is the yellow boat-house of the Tower Ridge Athletic Club, whose grounds for tennis, etc., are elaborately laid out on the hill above.

The village is much the same as when T. Addison Richards sketched here, thirty years ago, and wrote out his impressions for *The Knickerbocker* (magazine), thus:

"The hamlet—for, the more stately villa-edifices apart, such it is—lies snugly nestled in the depths of a beautiful glen, or spreads quietly away upon its verdant acclivities and lofty terraces, looking into the shades of old woods, and listening to the murmurs of running brooks below, and gazing far up and down the broad river above. In the olden time, that is to say in the days of our revolution, the region around was the domain of the worthy farmer, Peter Post, whose patriotism on one occasion subjected him to an experience which he remembered, no doubt, with less pleasure than we do now. At the period referred to he assisted the patriots, under Col. Sheldon, to surprise a party of marauding Hessians, beguiling them into the belief that the Americans, whom they were pursuing, had moved on in a certain direction, while they were snugly ambushed conveniently in the rear.

"'The Hessians, deceived by his answer,' says the story, according to Bolton, in his *History of the County of Westchester*, 'were proceeding at full gallop through the lane, when a shrill whistle rang through the air, instantly followed by the impetuous charge of Sheldon's horse. Panic-stricken, the enemy fled in every direction, but the fresh horses of the Americans carried their gallant riders wherever a wandering ray disclosed the steel cap of the brilliant accouterments of a Hessian. A bridle-path leading from the place of ambush to the river was strewed with the dead and dying, while those who sought safety in the water were captured, cut to pieces, and drowned. The conflict, so short and bloody, was decisive. One solitary horseman was seen galloping off in the direction of Yonkers, and he alone, wounded and unarmed, reached the camp of Col. Emmerick in safety. Here he related the particulars of the march, the sudden onset and retreat. Astonished and maddened with rage, Emmerick started his whole command in pursuit. Poor Post was stripped for his fidelity, and after having a sufficient number of blows inflicted upon his person, left for dead.'"

Earlier than this, however, Hastings had acquired notoriety from the fact that there Cornwallis embarked his army for the subjugation of Fort Lee, following the capture of Fort Washington.

A charming walk or bicycle-run of 1½ miles may be taken from Hastings northward to Dobbs Ferry, along the old post-road, which is shaded all the way, mainly by ancient locust trees; and no walls or high hedges prevent a view of the orderly and tasteful grounds that continuously border the avenue.

Dobbs Ferry is an exceedingly pretty village, whose homely

SUGAR LOAF.

name is the bequest of the ancient family of Dobbs ("Dobb—his ferry," says Mr. Sparrowgrass), who whilome farmed and ferried the contiguous land and water. As early as 1698 there lived here or hereabouts a Jan Dobs and his wife, who were members of the now venerable old church in Sleepy Hollow. The village covers hill and dell, rising charmingly from the river shore to the crests of lofty ridges, and is planted thick with sumptuous homes. There is one summer hotel, the "Glen Tower," whose yellow front and fine grounds overlook the river below the station, and a boarding-house or two; but none of the villages in this part of the country are "resorts," being composed almost wholly of those who own and occupy their premises the most of, if not all, the year. Just above the village is "Nuits," the residence of F. Cottinet, a beautiful Italian structure of imported Caen stone. Adjoining it, northward, stands "Nevis," the estate of the late Col. James Hamilton, son and biographer of Alexander Hamilton, and next beyond, the home of George L. Schuyler.

Dobbs Ferry was an important post in the Revolution, and the rendezvous of each army alternately. It was here that the British troops mustered after the battle of White Plains, and before marching to the assault upon Fort Washington. In January, 1777, Lincoln and his detachment of the patriot army encamped here a while. Later (1781), Washington established the American army headquarters at the Livingston manor-house, somewhat inland from the village, and the mansion was subsequently identified with many political events. There, in 1783, George Clinton and Sir Guy Carleton, the British commander, met to confer on the subject of the evacuation of the city of New York by the British forces. Although known as the Livingston manor-house, this house did not come into the possession of the Livingston family until after the Revolution. It was originally built by a Dutch farmer, who leased it from the lord of the Phillipse manor; the Phillipse estate being sequestered by the Government at the close of the war, this farm was purchased by Peter Van Brugh Livingston, with 500 acres, and it became henceforth known as the "Livingston Manor." The fortifications were mainly by the present railway station—one of the best examples of those *bijous* of architecture in rose granite, red sandstone, and hardwoods with which the New York Central Company is ornamenting the river route from one end to the other—and were intended for the protection of the rowboat ferry to Paramus, now Sneden's Landing, directly opposite, and a mile or two above the northern boundary of New Jersey. These batteries were a sore vexation to the British ships, which were wont to cruise up the river, and attempt to ravage the shores. In July, 1781, some British frigates that had passed up the river a few days before, took advantage of wind and tide to return to New York, thus exposing themselves to a severe cannonading from these batteries. They returned the fire, but without effect; and Thatcher relates that on board one of them, the *Savage*, a box of powder took fire, whereupon twenty men leaped into the river, only one of whom, an American prisoner, reached the shore. This vessel was nearly sunk by the well-directed balls. The first treasonable interview between Arnold and André was to have been held here, but by some mischance did not take place. A monumental tablet marks this house.

The Palisades, to glance again at the western shore, here attain their highest point, which is found in *Indian Head* (550 feet) directly opposite Hastings. Somewhat below there the precipitous wall is broken by a ravine, in the mouth of which have been built several summer hotels and dancing pavilions, resorted to by cheap steamboat excursion and picnic parties, more noisy than nice in their methods of amusement. A ferry connects the place with Yonkers. This ravine is called *Alpine Gorge*, and a road zigzags up to the top of the ridge and over to the village of Closter, N. J. It was formerly known as *Closter Landing*, and here Lord Grey disembarked his dragoons on that evening in October, 1778, when he galloped over to the Hackensack Valley, and surprised and massacred Col. Baylor's company of patriots, despite their surrender and calls for mercy— an act which British as well as American historians have execrated as a disgrace, not only to Englishmen, but to all humanity.

This part of the river used to be called the *Great Chip Rock Reach*, a term which extends to the end of the Palisades, where New Jersey is left and New York State (Rockland County) begins on that side of the river. Here, opposite Dobbs Ferry, is seen a deep glen, up which goes the old highway to Tappan, and so southward into New Jersey. This was known as Paramus when, in 1776, Cornwallis landed here and marched his men up the old road, but now it is *Sneden's Landing*. The Sneedens (or Snydens) were a family of Tories, early advertised as enemies by the local authorities. The shore gradually bends backward, and we see before us the broadening space of the **Tappan Sea**—the name given to the lake-like expanse of the river from the Palisades north to Croton Point. A mile above is *Piermont*, whence a wharf a mile or more long, bearing derricks and coal-pockets, juts out to deep water. It was built many years ago by the Erie Railway Company to facilitate the river shipment of their freights, when it was expected to be the chief, if not their only, river terminus. Now it is devoted almost entirely to the transfer of coal from cars to barges. The coal business of the Erie Railway is very large, giving nearly as much revenue as their passenger traffic; and all of it destined for New York comes this way, while that for New England is transferred at Newburgh.

"Few portions of the Hudson," as Richards has remarked, "are so rich in natural beauties as the vicinage of Piermont, where the mighty mirror of the Tappan Sea reflects the purple shades and the golden sunshine of grand mountain acclivities and of most picturesque headlands. Back of the village, on the west, the land steps in noble terraces from the waterside to the lofty crests of Tower Hill. To the southward, the Palisades rise in majesty; and above, the bay is shut in by the superb cliffs of the promontory, known as Point-no-Point, or more familiarly as the Hook Mountain."

This *Tower Hill*, by-the-by, is one well worth the attention of climbers. It can be reached by way of Nyack, or more easily by the Northern Railroad of New Jersey, and will well repay a walk to its summit, where there is an observatory. From this platform the hills and valleys of Westchester County, the Sound, and Long Island and the Atlantic Ocean can be seen; to the south, the heights of Hoboken bound the horizon; to the west, the Orange Mountains—some peaks of which are more than forty miles away—the Ramapo Gap, and the site of Tuxedo Park; and, finally, to the north a vast sea of mountain tops, comprising some of the Catskill and Berkshire ranges, stretches darkly and grandly to the distant horizon. It is a view that always pleases and almost invariably calls forth superlative exclamations of delight.

For many years one of the cottages on the Piermont slope was that of *Lewis Gaylord Clark*, the friend of Irving, his associate in the publication of *Salmagundi*, and long-time editor of *The Knickerbocker*. Sparkill, a favorite summer residence with city people, and historic old *Tappan*, where André was hung, and where so many other things of life and death happened during the War for Independence, are only just back of the shore hills.

From Dobbs Ferry to *Irvington*, to return to the *eastern shore* of the Tappan Sea, is about 1½ miles, and may be covered by a delightful walk along the old *Croton Aqueduct*. Walk from the railway station along the main street of Dobbs Ferry as far as its turn to the right, when the stile and path down to the top of the aqueduct will be seen. This path leads straight across the fields, giving occasional glimpses of the river and of the finest houses, in a much better way, and at far less expense of time and labor, than by following the roundabout course of Broadway. Mrs. Henry Draper, widow of the eminent scientific author, lives near where the aqueduct is first encountered; and farther on Gen. Samuel Thomas; while the comfortable and spacious country-house of the late Cyrus W. Field is seen upon the higher ground to the right, above Broadway. As Irvington is approached, the houses along a deep glen form the *Abbottsford* neighborhood, and are owned by such prominent persons as David Dows and Joseph Stiner (the house with a large dome) and others.

THE CROTON AQUEDUCTS.

The aqueduct alluded to above is that "old" one which has conducted water from the Croton River to New York for half a century. It was finished in 1842, is of brick, and is placed on or near the surface, occasionally tunneling under high ground, and again spanning some ravine upon arches, as particularly across Kill Brook in Sing Sing, where the structure is most picturesque —a single stone arch seventy feet high, and having a span of eighty-eight feet. In general, it follows the old post-road, and is traceable by its white stone ventilating towers nearly all the way from the mouth of the Croton to the beautiful High Bridge by which it is carried across the Harlem River. It conducts nearly 100,000,000 gallons a day, but long ago proved inadequate, and after much preliminary work the construction of a second conduit from the Croton Valley to the city was begun in January, 1884, and was completed in 1890.

The New Aqueduct consists of a brick tunnel, laid in an almost perfectly straight line from Croton Lake to the Harlem near High Bridge, through the solid rock, and at an average depth of 500 feet below the surface. This tunnel is thirty miles long and fourteen feet in diameter, and delivers over 300,000,000 of gallons each twenty-four hours. At times as many as 10,000 men were employed upon it, and the total cost was $25,000,000. Nothing to equal it in magnitude of engineering is known in any other part of the world.

The Croton flows from the Highlands southward to its debouchment into the Hudson at Sing Sing. It drains a basin, popularly called the Croton water-shed, having an area of 338 square miles, above the present Croton dam. This region is a hilly country full of ponds and brooks, the surface of which is gravel overlying a hard and impervious gneissic rock. Much of it is covered with second-growth woods, and the cleared portion is devoted mainly to dairying. The rapidity of the main river and many of its tributaries has, however, invited the utilization of the water-power and many mills and factories have sprung up, while the population of the valley has greatly increased, and hotels and boarding-houses are enlarged and added to annually. Most of these, deliberately or accidentally, drain their refuse into the Croton, and thence into the city's drinking supply. Thus far the oxygenating power of the sunshine and running water have sufficed to overcome these befoulments and keep the water wholesome, if not as pure as when sent down from the hills and filtered through the gravel-beds; but the time will soon be at hand when it will be vitally important to check this menace to the health of the metropolis by reserving a broad park-like margin along the principal streams, and around the many artificial reservoirs which store the winter's rains against summer's drouth, from human occupation; or perhaps, finally, by evicting the whole population of the water-shed Those interested in the details of construction and management of this wonderful aqueduct and system of water-supply will find a valuable illustrated article upon it in *The Century* (magazine), Vol. XVII, December, 1889, p. 205.

Irvington, the river-landing and railroad station next north of Hastings, at the foot of the Tappan Sea, is a village of comparatively recent growth, inhabited, in great part, by the families of gentlemen whose place of business is in New York. "The river is here about three miles wide, and the sloping hills that look over this tranquil bay are literally covered with beautiful villas and charming grounds. At no point on the Hudson are there more evidences of wealth and refinement, and this locality around Irvington is noted as one of the most aristocratic suburbs of the great metropolis. Many of these palatial structures are furnished with the choicest that art and wealth can produce, and are the abodes of luxury, culture, and the most exquisite taste."

THE STORY OF SUNNYSIDE.

This village is named in honor of Washington Irving, whose fancy and pen have informed the whole district with immortal interest. As usual, it is delightful to walk, or wheel, or drive along the ancient highway through and northward of Irvington; but the object of special interest, **Irving's home at "Sunnyside,"** can not be seen from that road, since it stands close to the river bank, three-fourths of a mile distant. It is only half a mile north of the railway station, however, and is excellently seen from the windows of the railway cars, or with less distinctness from a steamer's deck. It is a many-gabled, vine-clad cottage, covered with stucco and shadowed by grand trees. When Irving bought the place, in 1835, the locality was vaguely known as Dearman's, for it was not until 1854 that a sufficient settlement accumulated to be set off from Tarrytown and called Irving. This farm contained, at that time, ten acres, and there stood upon it a small stone house called "Wolfert's Roost" (*roost*, rest), from a former owner, Wolfert Acker, who had been one of the Committee of Public Safety in '76, and had come here to set up his Rest and take his ease. Later, eight more acres were added to "Sunnyside," as the author styled his new property. The main facts in its history have been pleasantly told by Mr. Clarence Cook, in an article in *The Century* for May, 1887, reminiscent of his schoolboy life in Tarrytown, when he enjoyed Irving's friendship. He tells us that Irving at once called in the services of a sympathetic artist, George Harvey, who, while he enlarged and modernized the house, kept all the "old-times" air and picturesqueness which had struck the author's fancy—the "little old-fashioned stone mansion, all made up of gable-ends, and as full of angles and corners as an old cocked hat," as the owner himself has described it. Over the entrance to the porch may still be read the inscription *George Harvey, Boumr.*, the last word an abbreviation for "Boumeister," which Mr. Irving had raked up as Dutch for architect. The beautiful growth of English ivy that clothes the front of the cottage has all grown from a slip brought from Melrose Abbey by a friend, Mrs. Renwick. This lady was a Miss Jeffrey, of Lochmaben, Dumfriesshire, Scotland, and was the heroine of Burns' *Blue-eyed Lassie* and of another song. Such is Mr. Cook's assertion, contradicting the popular statement that the ivy grew from slips given to Irving by Sir Walter Scott at Abbotsford.

The interior of Mr. Irving's house, according to Mr. Cook, hardly corresponded with the promise made by the outside. "As I remember," he says, "it was plainly but comfortably furnished; and, compared with almost any house lived in by a person of Irving's position, to-day would certainly be said to have a bare look. . . . There was nothing in Irving's surroundings, or in his way of life, to suggest the literary man. His house might have been that of any gentleman bachelor, with a happy turn for indolence, with no expensive tastes, but with an inborn relish for the simple pleasures of country life."

This historic house has recently been rebuilt and greatly enlarged.

The old highway from Irvington to Tarrytown is especially beautiful and is bordered by noble properties, mainly between it and the water. As seen from the river, the residences about Tarrytown rise tier upon tier. That on the hill, with the pointed tower, is "Cunningham Castle." Near it are the still stately ruins of the burned home of the painter, *Albert Bierstadt;* and a long list of names of men prominent in the world of business would be found on the door-plates of the mansions ensconced among those umbrageous trees. Most conspicuous among them, as is appropriate, is the tall square marble tower of the late *Jay Gould's house,* "Lyndehurst," which rises like a bright monument above the green bank of foliage. It is interesting not only as the former residence of the most powerful, and, since the death of Commodore Vanderbilt, the most picturesque business man of the country, but from the fact that it was originally "Paulding Manor," the country-house of William Paulding, a nephew of the hero of the André capture, and cousin of Admiral Paulding, U. S. N. He was a prominent merchant of the early decades of this country, and was Mayor of New York at the time of Lafayette's visit in 1824; and his house represents the best type of Tudor architecture. It is best seen from a northerly direction.

The windows of all these mansions look out upon the **Tappan Sea** (or *Zee*), so named because the Tappan Indians were found along its western shore by the Dutchmen. Many a story might be told of its waters and circling shores, one of which Irving has left us in his *Chronicle of Wolfert's Roost*, relating to the Revolutionary period, when every farmer had to be upon his guard against the bandits that infested this debatable land between the lines of the opposing armies. The story may not be veritable history, but it is a picture of those times, nevertheless:

"While this marauding system prevailed on shore, the Great Tappan Sea, which washes this belligerent region, was domineered over by British frigates and other vessels of war, anchored here and there to keep an eye upon the river, and maintain a communication between the various military posts. Stout galleys, also, armed with eighteen-pounders, and navigated with sails and oars, cruised about like hawks, ready to pounce upon their prey.

"All these were eyed with bitter hostility by the Dutch yeomanry along shore, who were indignant at seeing their great Mediterranean plowed by hostile prows; and would occasionally throw up a mud breastwork on a point or promontory, mount an old iron field-piece, and fire away at the enemy, though the greatest harm was apt to happen to themselves from the bursting of their ordnance; nay, there was scarce a Dutchman along the river that would hesitate to fire with his long duck gun at any British cruiser that came within reach, as he had been accustomed to fire at water-fowl.

"About this time, the Roost [i. e., Sunnyside] experienced a vast accession of warlike importance in being made one of the stations of the water-guard. This was a kind of aquatic corps of observation, composed of long, sharp, canoe-shaped boats, technically called whale-boats, that lay lightly on the water, and could be rowed with great rapidity. They were manned by resolute fellows, skilled at pulling an oar or handling a musket. These lurked about in nooks and bays, and behind those long promontories which run out into the Tappan Sea, keeping a lookout, to give notice of the approach or movements of hostile ships. They roved about in pairs; sometimes at night, with muffled oars, gliding like specters about frigates and guard-ships riding at anchor, cutting off any boats that made for shore, and keeping the enemy in constant uneasiness. These musquito-cruisers generally kept aloof by day, so that their harboring places might not be discovered, but would pull quietly along, under shadow of the shore, at night, to take up their quarters at the Roost. Hither, at such time, would also repair the hard-riding lads of the hills, to hold secret councils of war with the "ocean chivalry"; and in these nocturnal meetings were concerted many of those daring forays, by land and water, that resounded throughout the border."

With such a history, is it surprising to learn that Irving should hear such traditions as the following:

"Before closing this historic document, I can not but advert to certain notions and traditions concerning the venerable pile in question. Old-time edifices are apt to gather odd fancies and superstitions about them, as they do moss and weather-stains; and this is in a neighborhood a little given to old-fashioned notions, and who look upon the Roost as somewhat of a fated mansion. A lonely, rambling, down-hill lane leads to it, overhung with trees, with a wild brook dashing along, and crossing and recrossing it. This lane I found some of the good people of the neighborhood shy of treading at night; why, I could not for a long time ascertain, until I learned that one or two of the rovers of the Tappan Sea, shot by the stout Jacob during the war, had been buried hereabout, in unconsecrated ground.

"Another local superstition is of a less gloomy kind, and one which I confess I am somewhat disposed to cherish. The Tappan Sea, in front of the Roost, is about three miles wide, bordered by a lofty line of waving and rocky hills. Often, in the still twilight of a summer evening, when the sea is like glass, with the opposite hills throwing their purple shadows half across it, a low sound is heard, as of the steady, vigorous pull of oars, far out in the middle of the stream, though not a boat is to be descried. This I should have been apt to ascribe to some boat rowed along under the shadows of the western shore, for sounds are conveyed to a great distance by water, at such quiet hours; and I can distinctly hear the baying of the watch-dogs at night from the farms on the sides of the opposite mountains. The ancient traditionists of the neighborhood, however, religiously ascribed these sounds to a judgment upon one Rumbout Van Dam, of Spiting Devil, who danced and drank late one Saturday night, at a Dutch quilting frolic, at Kakiat, and set off alone for home in his boat, on the verge of Sunday morning, swearing he would not land till he reached Spiting Devil, if it took him a month of Sundays. He was never seen afterward, but is often heard plying his oars across the Tappan Sea, a Flying Dutchman on a small scale, suited to the size of his cruising-ground; being doomed to ply between Kakiat and Spiting Devil till the day of judgment, but never to reach the land."

Tarrytown, whose port, railway station, and business streets are seen immediately above Irvington, which, indeed, it formerly included, is a beautiful and long-established village with considerable trade and manufacturing, as well as a large population of families whose business is in New York. The name is said to be from the Dutch *Terwen Dorp*, or Wheat Town, in reference to the leading product of the district; this the English half-translated into Terwen Town, and then corrupted into Tarrytown. It abounds in irregular, beautifully shaded avenues, lined by costly and elegant houses, crowding all citizens of small means into the low-lying streets along the water-front. The ornamental arrangement of the grounds about the new station here will attract attention, as well as the great fountain, given as a present to the public by the Rev. and Mrs. E. C. Bull.

SLEEPY HOLLOW, PAST AND PRESENT.

Those who delight to seek out places of historical and poetic association will not fail to stroll about Tarrytown, and will wander out to **Sleepy Hollow** in search of the scene of the romance of Ichabod Crane and Katrina Van Tassel, and of that frightful apparition, The Headless Horseman; and will not fail to visit the *grave of Washington Irving*.

Sleepy Hollow is the narrow valley of Pocantico Creek, which flows into the Hudson half a mile north of the railway station, where the jutting out of Kingsland's Point—marked by a light-house—forms a small bay. The name is regarded as a half-contemptuous translation of the Dutch words *slaperig haven;* and Irving himself tells us why.

"Not far from Tarrytown," he writes, "there is a little valley, or rather a lap of land, among high hills, which is one of the quietest places in the whole world. A small brook glides through it, with just murmur enough to lull one to repose, and the occasional whistle of a quail, or tapping of a woodpecker, is almost the only sound that ever breaks in upon the uniform tranquillity."

"Sleepy Hollow," in the phrase of Clarence Cook, whose article was referred to a few paragraphs back, "is still very much the same lazy country road it was in the old days when we school-boys wandered along it in the summer afternoons, picking blackberries from the wayside vines." Following the turnpike road [Broadway] down the hill we come to Beekman's mill-pond, and crossing the pretty stream, the Pocantico, on the bridge over which Ichabod galloped, pursued in his mad flight by the headless horseman, we reach the old Dutch church, surrounded by the graves of many generations—those of the earlier settlers clustering thickly about the church itself, while the newer graves people the rising ground toward the north.

"It is in this newer portion of the cemetery that Washington Irving lies. His grave is in the middle of a large plot purchased by him in 1853, six years before his death. The stone that marks his grave is a plain slab of white marble, on which are engraved his name and date alone, without any memorial inscription. The path that leads to the entrance gate of the plot is so worn by the feet of visitors that a stranger hardly needs to ask his way to the church.

"It would not have been easy to find a place more in harmony with the associations that gather about Irving's name as a writer, than the spot in which he is buried. Even to-day, with all the changes that have been brought about by the growth of the neighboring settlement, the spirit of peace and quiet that used to brood over the region hovers there undisturbed. Irving's own words in the *Legend of Sleepy Hollow*, describing the grave-yard, the old church, and the stream that plays about its feet, reflect with the faithfulness of a mirror the scene as we behold it to-day.

"Here is the church, a small building with rough sides of the country stone, surmounted by a picturesque roof, and with an open bell-turret, over which still veers the vane pierced with the initials of the Frederick Felypsen * who built the church and endowed it in 1699. In our rambles about the grave-yard we used to find the bricks of light-colored clay, brought from Holland, and of which, so tradition said, the church had originally been built, or which had, at any rate, been largely used in its construction."

Above Irving's grave, and those of his many relatives, the land swells into a knoll surmounted by the *memorials of the Delavan family*. These consist of a tall shaft of granite, observable from far out on the river, and supporting a grand figure; and of six marble statues, one representing Jesus, and the others symbolical figures of Immortality, Faith, etc., disposed about the pedestal of the column among the graves. This eminence, called Battle Hill, overlooks the highway, the Pocantico Vale, and the sweetest part of the Tarrytown slope. In 1779 it was crowned by a fortification of the Patriot army, but received no assault. Remains of the earthworks may yet be traced; and their site is still further marked by a small cannon, mounted upon a granite carriage, and having near it a pyramid of projectiles. This gun bears an inscription informing readers that it is the rifled steel cannon which caused Napoleon III. to make its inventor a member of the Legion of Honor; but why this red-painted modern weapon and its vulgar personal advertisement should be accepted as an historical monument anywhere, and, above all, in this City of Peace, is a curiosity of inconsistency remaining unexplained.

The present bridge is, of course, a very modern affair, replacing that one which Irving knew, and which itself had no memories of the old colonial times of which the great romancer wrote. But the tranquil and weedy pond below it is the same as that of the days when the burghers brought their grist a horseback to be ground at Wheat Town; and the identical old mill is still stand-

---

* Frederick Philipse the first, whose first manor-house, or "castle," still stands a little way down the stream by the old mill.

ing under the trees at the foot of the pond, by its moss-grown dam. Near it is the old Philipse manor-house, or Castle Philipse, whence the family moved to Yonkers when their newer manor-house was built there. It is stanch as ever, but is sadly belittled by the sumptuous homes of modern days, and can scarcely be seen for the foliage. This house, the mill, and the dam are all well seen from the railway while the train is crossing the mouth of the Pocantico, north of the station.

The shortest road to Sleepy Hollow from the station is along the street that leads up the railway track, and gradually bends to the right. It is a walk of twenty to thirty minutes, through an unpleasant part of town. Much more interesting is the longer way up the hill to Broadway, then northward to where, at a brick church, a wide road descends toward the left; this must be followed around the cove to the bridge and pond, beside which are the old church and the cemetery. Two hours will amply suffice to walk around this way and back to the station, and to see all that the casual tourist will feel an interest in; but the distance is too great for feeble pedestrians. Carriages are always waiting at Tarrytown station, however.

The Monument to André's Capture.—About half-way to Sleepy Hollow, on Broadway, stands a monument commemorating one of the most interesting episodes of the War for Independence—the capture of André, the story of which is told in the next section. It was originally a simple, small obelisk, erected in 1853 by the people of Westchester County, upon a pedestal bearing the following inscription, with some additional sentiments of appreciation:

On this Spot,
The 25th Day of September, 1780, the Spy,
MAJOR JOHN ANDRÉ,
Adjutant General of the British Army, Was Captured by
John Paulding, David Williams, and Isaac Van Wart,
All Natives of this County.

To this was added, upon the centennial anniversary of the incident, in 1880, a bronze statue of a minute-man, specifically representing John Paulding, which is poised effectively upon the top of the obelisk, and a bronze panel, by Theodore Bauer, depicting the capture of André in a very spirited way. These were the gift of a citizen, John Anderson; and it is unfortunate that this fine little monument does not stand where it can be seen to better advantage. The little stream below it is now called André's Brook; and near the monument there formerly stood a great whitewood, long known as the André tree.

Other stirring adventures occurred at Tarrytown in those days. Lying between the two armies, it was alternately occupied and abandoned by each, and always exposed to the marauders that infested the whole region. Here were landed, in 1777, Vaughan's troops to co-operate in the attack on Fort Montgomery; and at another time, a vigorous cannonade was poured from its intrenchments upon an English flotilla. One of the liveliest local stories is that of the successful surprise, by a body of American militia, of a large corps of British refugees, gathered at the tavern of Elizabeth Van Tassel. The enemy were amusing their evening hours with cards, when Major Hunt and his volunteers rushed into the apartment, the Major exclaiming, as he brandished over the table the huge stick with which he was armed:

"Gentlemen, clubs are trumps!"

The luckless card-players were avenged by other and counter incidents in the strife, as in the capture, by Colonel Emmerick, of the Continental Guard, which was quartered in Requa's house, when four of the patriots were killed and the remaining dozen were taken prisoners; and again, in the spring of 1782, when a party of refugees, commanded by Lieutenant Akerly, captured three American militia-men, named Yerks, Van Wart, and Strong, the last of whom was hanged on the spot.

A steam-ferry connects Tarrytown with Nyack; and the *Crystenah* and other boats ply regularly between Tarrytown and New York, and also to and from certain up-river landings.

TARRYTOWN TO WEST POINT.

The Eastern shore of Tappan Sea, north of Tarrytown, is studded with the country-seats of prominent persons. At the mouth of the Pocantico, occupying *Kingsland's Point* (behind the light-house) and the neighboring river lands, are the long-occupied houses of the Kingsland family, one of whom was a noted mayor of New York. Higher up the hill, not far from Sleepy Hollow, lies the old estate of Gen. James Watson Webb, one of whose sons is now conspicuous as the acting third vice-president of the New York Central Railroad. One of his neighbors is Mrs. Anson G. Phelps, and another is William Rockefeller, president of the Standard Oil Company, who occupies the ancient chateau "Rockwood," in which the Aspinwalls and other noted families have dwelt in past years. A little farther north, near Scarborough station and landing, the Scarboroughs, Remsens, etc., reside in the summer, and here is the Shepard Memorial Church.

The Western shore of the Tappan Sea is nearer to those who travel upon steamers, and must not be overlooked in our description. The Palisades, which the Mohicans said were erected by the Great Spirit to protect his favorite abodes from unhallowed eyes of mortals—is this a bit of sun-myth, referring to the declining king-of-day?—have given place to a graceful blending of valley and hill, stretching northward to a bold promontory which, in some states of the weather, becomes sublime in its aspect. The scenery of the Tappan Sea and its boldly sculptured shores varies widely, with the state of the atmosphere, from the most tame and prosaic condition to an appearance of bold grandeur or idyllic beauty. "The voyager," remarks the landscape artist Richards, "might very reasonably think himself in fairy-land, should he chance here on a quiet, sunny summer day, when the clear still waters reflect the whiteness of a hundred lazy sails, and the sunshine of the all-encircling hillsides; or he might forget that he is upon the bosom of a decorous and peaceful

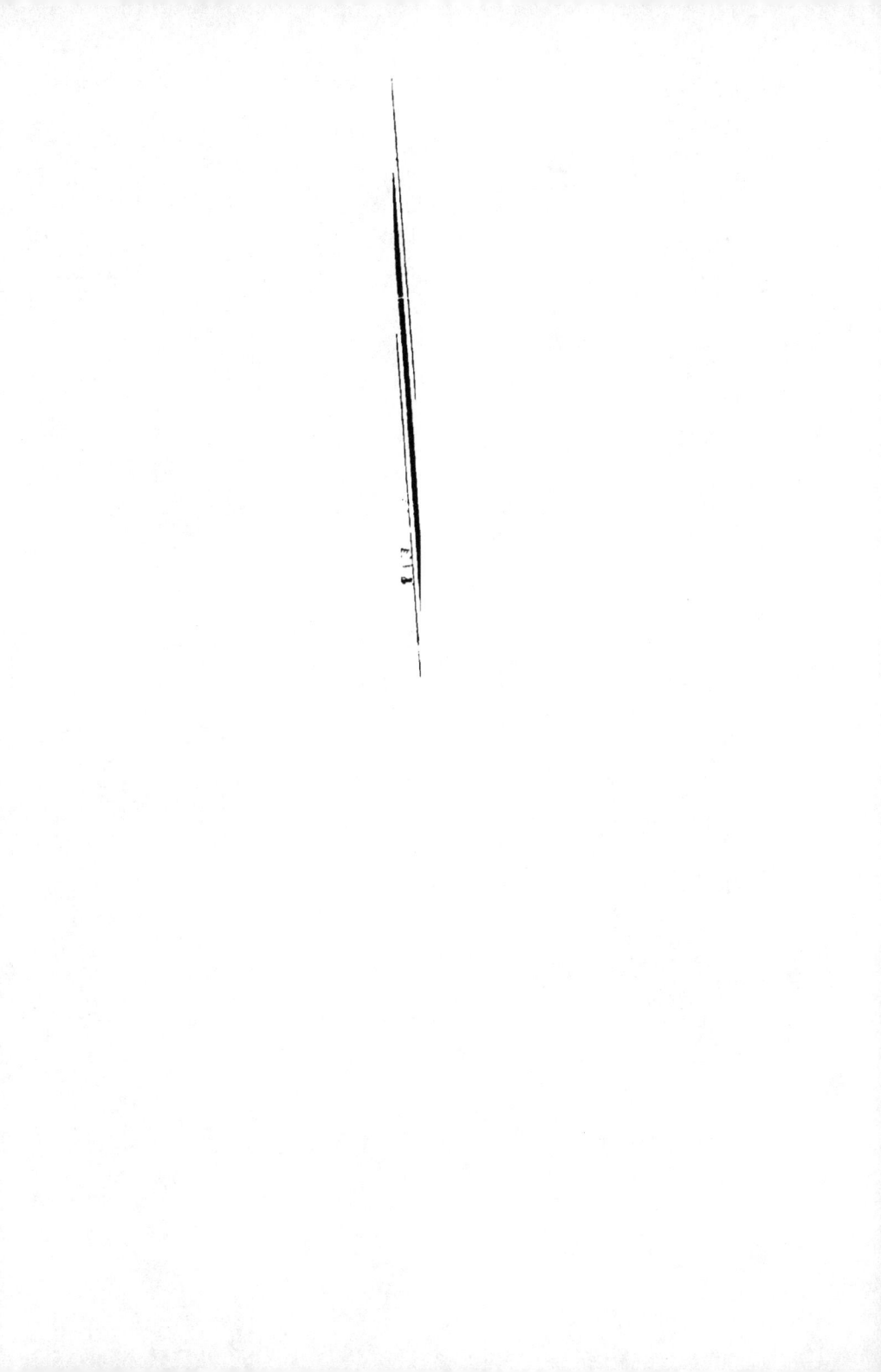

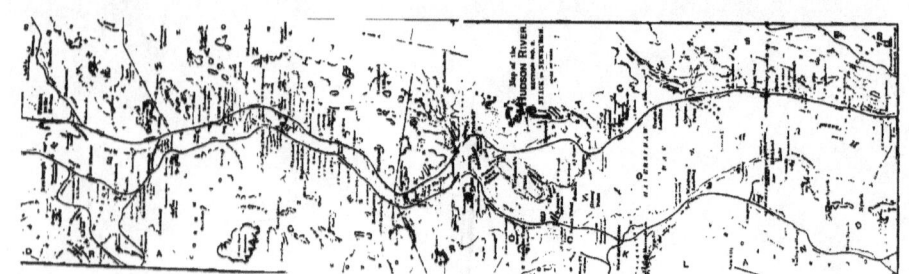

river, should storm and tempest darken the mountains and valleys, and rudely awaken the dreaming floods."

Nyack, just beyond the Piermont jetty, is the only town of importance on the western side of Tappan Sea. It is a pretty and prosperous village at the terminus of the Northern Railroad of New Jersey. Of late years, it has become one of the favorite suburban summer residences, and for some reason has especially attracted many of the South Americans of wealth or prominence who live in New York and Washington.

The village includes, besides Nyack proper, South Nyack, West Nyack, and Upper Nyack. In winter it has some 5,000 inhabitants, and settles down into a steady-going manufacturing town, in which nearly everybody is concerned, directly or indirectly, with making shoes, or else with building yachts and boats. In summer, however, Nyack is increased by three or four thousand summer residents, who fill the hotels and boarding-houses, and find plentiful amusement in rambling and boating over her hills and along her shore. The large building seen in the southern part of the town, near the water, is the "Tappan Zee Hotel," while the still larger "Prospect House" is visible higher up the hill. Both of these are summer houses. A ferry connects Nyack with Tarrytown, the steamboat *Rockland* making hourly trips; and this way runs the tally-ho coach between New York and Tuxedo, twenty-two miles west, stopping for lunch at the capital St. George Restaurant, near the landing.

The Northern Railroad of New Jersey makes its northern terminus at Nyack, a few blocks from the landing, and affords almost hourly communication with the city. This road is leased to the New York, Lake Erie & Western, and is a model of a suburban line.

Its trains leave from the "Erie" station, in Jersey City (23d and Chambers streets, New York, by ferry), and run up along the western base of Bergen Ridge, until this breaks, and allows the road to reach the river-side again at Nyack. It is a charming country—that behind the Palisades. The broad meadows of the Hackensack are first seen, then the narrower valley of its eastern tributary, the Overpeck; and quaint old villages are strung along, with an almost continual line of modern cottages and summer homes. This is a favorite field for New York artists, some of the foremost of whom dwell at Ridgefield Park, Leonia, and

Englewood. It abounds in quaint relics of colonial times, as at Ridgefield, Tenafly, Closter, Tappan; and was the scene, in the earlier years of the Revolution, of some of the most stirring incidents of that war. Altogether, the ride by rail from Jersey City to Nyack is scarcely less interesting than that by river.

Nyack is also touched, at West Nyack, $2\frac{1}{2}$ miles from the river, by the West Shore Railroad, and it has a daily line of steamboats to and from New York.

This part of the Hudson, above Nyack, the pilots term *Tappan Reach*, and it is overshadowed by the extension of the Palisades, locally called *Hook Mountain*, but more anciently known as *Mount Verdrietig Range*. This range is elevated in the middle into the rounded dome of Ball Mountain, and ends northward in the bold promontory which has already excited our admiration. The southern prominence of this headland is Verdrietig Hook; the farther one, where the shore makes a slight bend westward, is Diedrich Hook, or Point-no-Point. These hills are about 700 feet high, rough and uninhabited, but pleasing in outline and color; their extraordinary name, which is spelled in every possible way except the right, is a Dutch adjective meaning doleful, sad. The reference was probably at first to the point or hook (Verdrietig Hoek), where baffling winds often make trouble for the sailorman, and render his passage of the cape "tedious," and afterward the name was extended to the whole range inland.

Sing Sing, perched upon the hills of the eastern shore, is just in advance on the right, as the steamer comes opposite Point-no-Point, with the famous *State Prison* in plain view by the edge of the water.

This odd designation has been accounted for by various facetious expedients. Irving says, truly, that it is a corruption of a Mohican place-word, *O-sin-sing,* referring to the rocky nature of the site ; and then adds in his droll humor :

"Some have rendered it, O-sin-song, or O-sing-song, in token of its being a great market town, where anything may be had for a mere song. Its present melodious alteration to Sing Sing is said to have been in compliment to a Yankee singing-master, who taught the inhabitants the art of singing through the nose."

Others say the name is a variation of that of a Chinese ruler, Tsing Sing, and was brought over by a Dutch sailor who had traded with the Celestial Empire. It comes, however, from the red man's tongue, and means a stony place; and well is the neigh-

BREAKNECK MOUNTAIN.

borhood named, for a more rugged spot of hill and ravine, and a wilder upheaving of rock and bowlder, one could hardly ask for within the streets of an orderly Christian town.

The village of Sing Sing must be kept quite distinct from the prison. It is by no means a sort of penal colony, as the public is too apt to regard it, but "an ancient, prosperous, and picturesque suburb of New York," where some 10,000 excellent people dwell amid surroundings that for health and beauty can hardly be matched in the whole valley. The town lies upon rocky hills and overlooks the most varied, and perhaps the most beautiful, river landscape along the valley. Just north of the town, as the traveler upon the steamer has before now observed ahead of him, the river is invaded by a long projection from the eastern shore, which has quite cut off his view. This is *Croton Point*, and the water between it and the Sing Sing shore is *Croton Bay*, or the estuary of *Croton River*, which the Indians called Kitchawonk.

As one stands upon any of the village streets facing the river, his glance not only takes in a long southward sweep of the opposite shore with its irregular highlands, but embraces, in most pleasing perspective, the several summits north of Verdrietig Hook, which have the sharpness and pose of real mountains, though only five or six hundred feet in height. But the eye, moving on northward, kindles with increasing pleasure as it ranges across the foreground of sail-dotted bay, and beyond the green and diversified interception of Croton Point, to the expanse of Haverstraw Bay northward, where the farther shore rises, far inland, into the blue and irregular mountains of Orange County, over at the head of the Ramapo. One is constantly surprised by glimpses, through the trees and across gardens that fill the foreground with life and color, throwing into artistic remoteness the shining river and cool blue hills, of bits of this scenery which are *picturesque* in the truest sense of the word; and that is a term which can not be applied discriminatingly to much of the Hudson River scenery, even where it is both interesting and full of charm. This rare outlook, the salubrity, the shady and well-kept streets, the excellent water and drainage, and the many educational advantages, have drawn to Sing Sing a large number of wealthy people whose business interests are in New York; and one may see there many costly and beautiful homes, and many fine churches and school buildings. Besides the public schools, this town possesses no less than four military boarding-schools for boys and a seminary for girls, besides two business colleges. In addition to its churches, the Sing Sing Camp Meeting, on the heights a mile north of town, is largely attended in summer by the religious people of the whole region.

In the early part of the last century, capital was largely invested here in *silver and copper mines*, and some of the older families still have in their possession silver spoons and copper utensils which were fashioned from the products of those mines. The copper mines, a little south of the prison, can still be explored by the curious, but the opening to the silver mines, which were on the north bounds of the prison, is now covered by the track of the Hudson River Railroad. Judging from the various and long corridors extending hundreds of feet under the waters of the Hudson, immense sums must have been expended in the development of these mines. Garnets of some size were frequently found in the same locality, and farther north there were traces of gold.

The capital invested in these old mines was truly sunk in the ground; but that which has been put into the many factories at Sing Sing has given a good return. The Arcade File Works here is the oldest in the country, and now employs 150 men; while the factory of the much-advertised Brandreth's Pills has extensive works adjoining the doctor's park-like home grounds along the railway. A shoe factory employing 225 hands, two foundries for plumbers' castings, a manufactory of cotton-gin machinery, and another of cotton-gin saws, are noticeable among the rest. These industries nourish the town industrially and keep it brisk. It has two strong banks, an excellent water and fire-department service, electric and gas lights, and an assessed valuation of nearly $4,000,000. Sing Sing has thirty trains daily to and from New York; the steamer *Sarah A. Jenks* plies daily, going down in the morning and back at night; and a small steamboat makes four round trips a day between Sing Sing and Haverstraw; and the village has electric street-cars.

The State Prison is about one mile south of the station, next the water. Little of it can be seen from a passing steamer, and still less from the railway, which passes underneath it through deep cuttings. The remarkable whiteness of the buildings is due to the fact that they are constructed of dolomite, a coarse marble quarried on the spot, and extensively used as building-stone in this and other river towns. This prison was founded in 1826, when Capt. Elam Lynds took a party of 100 convicts from Auburn Prison to this spot, and set them at work to wall themselves in. By 1829 this had been accomplished, and the main building was ready. It is now nearly 500 feet long, and has 1,200 cells, besides many shops, in which shoes, saddlery, furniture, and other articles were formerly manufactured by convict labor. The confinement of women in this prison was discontinued many years ago. About 1,700 persons now find here the quiet, if not the peace, which complete seclusion from society affords.

Rockland is the name of the little village, immediately opposite Sing Sing, opened to view as the steamer rounds Point-no-Point. It is set in a narrow, shady ravine north of Hook Mountain, and is the port of *Rockland Lake*, a large sheet of water lying a mile or more inland, and about 150 feet above the landing. On this lake is cut a large portion of the ice used by New York City, and 1,000 men are employed in harvesting and shipping the product, which is brought down the ravine by a cable railway, and sent to the city in huge barges. Rockland Lake is also a place of summer resort, and has upon its borders an extensive grove, which is a favorite place for farmers' picnics and excursions from the city.

The ice business of New York may be said to have originated at Rockland Lake, where lived the men who were the founders, many years ago, of the Knickerbocker Ice Company. At first, supposing that ice could not be preserved otherwise, they dug a hole in the ground holding about 125 tons. The ice was taken from this pit, placed in a box holding one ton, mounted upon a truck whose wheels were merely sections of round logs, and hauled aboard a boat which then ran down to New York from Haverstraw one day and returned the next. The delivery in New York was made in springless one-horse carts. How rapidly and far the business has outgrown these rude beginnings we shall see later.

The long, low promontory reaching out from the eastern shore here, and separating Croton Bay from the broad expanse of Haverstraw Bay above, is called **Croton Point**; but the extremity of it, cut off by a cross-stream, is distinguished as *Teller's Point*.

At the head of Croton Bay, where the Post Road crosses it, stands the venerable Van Cortlandt manor-house, built by that fine old patroon in 1683, long before his descendants built the two mansions on the Mosholu, in New York; and it remains one of the best examples extant of early colonial architecture. The Van Cortlandts and Phillipses intermarried at an early date, and became virtual masters of all this land on the west bank of the river, from here to the Harlem. It was off Croton (Teller's) Point that the British war-ship *Vulture*, in which André came to his fatal conference with Arnold, anchored to await his return, and received Arnold instead, after having been driven from the neighborhood of Verplank's Point, to André's ultimate discomfiture.

Beyond these narrows, the shore recedes eastward, and the steamer enters the broad expanse of **Haverstraw Bay**, or *Haverstroo* (oat-straw), as the Dutch wrote it. The eastern shore is a mass of hills, increasing northward to where the Highlands form a rugged wall across the whole northern horizon. Westward, the hills strike inland in the lofty and abrupt Verdrietig ridges, on whose farther (southern) slopes the trout brooks combine in Pond's Patent to form the Hackensack; and in the wide tract of comparative lowlands between this range and the Highlands lies the village of **Haverstraw**, with the historic headland *Stony Point* jutting out beyond it.

The Hudson is here five miles wide—the broadest part of its course—and, as the channel keeps well over in the line of the sweep of the current along the western bank, details on the *eastern shore* are not well seen from a steamboat deck. The railway ride along that shore from Sing Sing to Peekskill is, however, a very pleasant experience, passing the stations *Croton*, *Cruger's* (near where Baron Steuben so diligently drilled the recruits in '76), and *Montrose*, whence is obtained the best southern view of the Highlands of the Hudson. The view from Croton is one of the most attractive landscapes of the whole river. The eye glances backward across the long and graceful outlines of Croton Point to the western mountains, which surprise us by their bold and towering profiles, one behind the other, and blue with distance. Across the shimmering, sail-dotted expanse of the bay are tiers of green hills sweeping from High Tor around almost to the Dunderberg, and blue wisps of smoke prettily indicate the prosaic brick-yards of Haverstraw. This Croton shore is a place famous not only for rod and line angling, but also for its shad fisheries.

The glimpse from a passing steamer or railway train is all that the casual traveler will care to see of Haverstraw, which is a village that has grown up behind some two miles of brick-yards, where hundreds of men are mining and molding and baking the fine clay sediment that settled in the eddies of that nook in the by-gone time when the stream was wider and deeper than now. They even build coffer-dams out into the river to rescue from its bed the valuable brick-clay, and far more than half of all the brick made along the whole course of the river comes from these yards, which reach to Grassy Point, the steamboat landing.

The tall peak of the Verdrietig Range, which overshadows the town, is **High Tor**—a good old Devonshire word. It is 810 feet in altitude, and may be ascended by a good though steep path, beginning half a mile south of the station, where the semaphore-post stands. The view is a very wide and pleasing one, and well repays one for the exertion.

Through the depression at the hither base of High Tor comes the old turnpike from the south, famous in Revolutionary annals, and underneath this gap is the long tunnel of the West Shore Railroad, which emerges upon the high ground overlooking Haverstraw, and keeps along the ridge around the meadows in which the Minnissickuongo loiters before falling into Stony Point Bay. The sudden *view of Haverstraw Bay*, which bursts upon the sight as you leave the tunnel, is one of the noblest pictures in the world. On the western side of the creek is the station *West Haverstraw*, behind which may be seen the eminence of *Treason Hill*, where, in the stone house of Dr. Joshua Hett Smith, Arnold and André perfected their nefarious bargain. The house still stands prominently on the hillside, above the railway track, about a mile north of the Haverstraw Station.

THE STORY OF ARNOLD'S TREASON.

The story of Arnold's treason and André's fate is briefly this: Benedict Arnold was a member of a good family, who distinguished himself early in the war for skill and gallantry, and quickly rose to be a major-general. His financial management, while in command at Philadelphia, led to his being arrested, court-martialed, and sentenced by Congress to be reprimanded by the commander-in-chief. This sentence Washington carried out as considerately as he could. Arnold, nevertheless, was deeply embittered, but dissembled his anger; and, having been conspicuous for valor at Ridgefield and Bemis Heights, where he received grievous wounds, readily obtained, at his own request, when reinstated in the early autumn of 1780, the command of the West Point district, the key to the Hudson. He had previously, however, been in negotiation with Sir Henry Clinton, the British commander at New York, for a desertion to the Crown; and the plan had now so expanded as to include the surrender of this most important group of posts with their garrisons. The time was ripe, as Washington was about to lead a large part of the army out of the way into New England. Whether Arnold initiated this base plot, or whether, while smarting under what he esteemed great wrongs, he had listened to the temptings of the enemy in the person of the noted Tory and officer, Beverly Robinson, is a matter of dispute, but the latter seems more likely. At any rate he was given command of the Highland forts, and took up his residence at "Beverly," the abandoned homestead of Robinson, nearly opposite West Point, where his family joined him. (See page 86.)

Here he began at once to intrigue with Clinton through Robinson, using a Haverstraw Tory, Joshua Hett Smith, as messenger. Finally Clinton sent his sloop of war *Vulture* up the river, bearing as his emissary his adjutant-general, Maj. John André, accompanied by Beverly Robinson as adviser. Arnold was awaiting its coming. André was put ashore in what is now the southern part of Haverstraw village, and there, on the 21st of September, under the shadow of High Tor, the two officers met in a secret discussion of the treachery and its payment. They consulted until daybreak, when Arnold persuaded André to go with him to the house of Dr. Smith (who had previously assisted them), where breakfast was prepared. While at breakfast, cannon were heard booming, and it was learned that Livingston had opened upon the *Vulture* from a battery on Verplank's Point, compelling the ship to drop down to a safer anchorage off Teller's Point. After breakfast André received the plans of the West Point works and armament, numbers of troops, etc., which he wanted, and Arnold rode home.

André passed the day expecting to go aboard the *Vulture* that night, but Smith refused the risk of taking him there, and nothing remained but to attempt a journey overland, with Smith as guide. Arnold had furnished them with suitable passes, under an assumed name, but as André wore the conspicuous uniform of his rank, he borrowed a long overcoat with which to conceal it. They started about sunset, and crossed the King's Ferry between Stony and Verplank points to the east side of the river, but could not get beyond the American lines that night. Early next morning the two proceeded, safely passed the American pickets, and then, almost within sight of the British lines, Smith turned back and André went on alone.

It happened, however, that an irregular outpost of the three militia-men, Paulding, Williams, and Van Wart, was watching the road here near Tarrytown. They stopped André, who, mistaking them for a Tory outpost, instead of showing the pass which would have caused Paulding, their spokesman, to let him go on, avowed himself a British officer who must not be detained. The exhibition of the pass after that imprudence did not satisfy the young patriots. They compelled him to dismount, searched him, and found in his stockings the terrible documents. He offered his captors immense bribes to release him, but they refused, and took him to the nearest American commander, Colonel Jamieson. This officer kept the prisoner, but indiscreetly allowed André to write, under his assumed name, to Arnold. Meanwhile, Washington had not gone to Connecticut as soon as he anticipated, but this very morning was starting and proposed to take breakfast with Arnold and afterward to inspect the new fortifications at West Point—the very day their garrisons were to be scattered so as to appear unable to resist the pretended attack, and the surrender was to be consummated. All were sitting at a late breakfast when the messenger delivered André's note to Arnold. Excusing himself, he hastened to his barge by an obscure lane, now called Arnold's Path, and rowed down to the *Vulture*, which hastened away with him to New York, leaving André to his fate.

An hour or two passed before the evidences of the treachery were presented to Washington. He immediately prepared for an attack, but none was offered, and then organized a court-martial, which, in spite of André's immediate and frank avowal of all the circumstances by which, as the prisoner himself wrote, "was I betrayed into the vile condition of an enemy in disguise within your posts," and of a vigorous defense and many protests; sentenced him to death as a spy; and, furthermore, to be hung, as Nathan Hale had been, years before, in New York. He was thus executed, in full uniform, upon a hilltop near Wayne's headquarters at Tappan, and buried on the spot.* The unhappy fate of this courageous and talented man excited universal sympathy, but the cooler judgment of that time, and history since, have justified his execution. A monument was erected to his memory in Westminster Abbey when, in 1821, his body was taken there for reburial; and in 1878 a memorial was built upon the place of his execution by the late Cyrus W. Field, at the request of Dean Stanley, but the latter was destroyed by bucolic fanaticism. The three militia-men were rewarded by congress-

---

* The coincidence of the poem of the *Cow Chase* has already been mentioned (p. 35); another curious coincidence is that the great whitewood tree in Tarrytown which overspread the spot where André was caught, and which is described by Irving in the *Sketch Book*, was destroyed by lightning on the very day that the news of Arnold's death reached that town!

ional medals and pensions, and now each has his monument at Tarrytown or Peekskill. Arnold received from the English government a part of his promised reward (about $30,000) and a colonel's commission. He was sent to wage war in the Carolinas, and was distinguished by his ferocity against the country people whose farms and villages he ravaged; but, as few English officers would associate with him, he was sent to England, where he lived out his life in disgrace and loneliness. But had he succeeded, in what a different estimation might he have been held, and how divergent might have been the course of history!

Sailing past the low meadows and brick-yards of *Grassy Point*, with a glance at Montrose Point and Oscawanna Island, a picnic resort near the opposite shore, attention is concentrated upon the rocky headland jutting out from the western shore a mile or two in advance, where a light-house crowns an eminence of tragic fame. That is **Stony Point**, the scene of one of the most brilliant exploits in American annals; and the projecting shore opposite it, which forms the northern boundary of Haverstraw Bay, is **Verplank's Point**.

Here, in colonial days, the greatest public ferry on the Hudson, and for that reason called the *King's Ferry*, plied between Stony and Verplank's points as a part of the principally traveled road between New England and the South—for there was no "West" in those days. This ferry was extremely useful in the military movements of the Continental army, and the possession of these two points became vitally important in 1779, when the second series of hostile operations began against the Highlands. Hence the history of Stony and Verplank's points is closely connected, and may appropriately be told here.

THE BATTLE OF STONY POINT.

Stony Point was naturally so-called, "stony" in those days meaning *rocky*, rather than as we now use the word; Verplank's Point had been so termed since it had been bought by Philip Verplank from Stephen Van Cortlandt, the local Patroon, whose only granddaughter and heiress Verplank had married. The river here became narrow, and fortifications would command the ascent of the channel by any ships then owned by either party. Therefore the re-fortification of the Highlands, after the withdrawal of the British in 1777, included these two headlands in its scheme. The season of 1778 was passed in operations elsewhere, but with the advent of the summer of 1779 circumstances began to draw both armies hither, and the Americans at once proceeded to erect defenses upon each headland. Aware of this, Sir Henry Clinton, the British commander at New York, as soon as his Southern expedition returned, led his fleet and a large body of troops northward to put a stop to these preparations. The bulk of his force, under Vaughan, was landed on the eastern shore and ordered to march to the rear of Verplank's Point, where a small but complete and scientific battery and block-house (Fort Lafayette) had already proved useful in defending the ferry from piratical boats. A lesser detachment, with Sir Henry commanding in person, landed at Haverstraw and marched against the block-house which already protected the party of workmen building redoubts upon its summit. Warned of the intended attack, the Americans set fire to the block-house and fled to the hills. Sir Henry took possession, and during the night artillery was landed, and with vast exertion was dragged up and mounted in the empty embrasures; and at daylight a cannonade was opened upon Verplank's Point. The little garrison of Lafayette replied with spirit, but were outmatched, cut off from escape, and forced to surrender. Nobody was killed on either side.

This happened in early June, 1779. The British immediately set themselves to finish and arm the series of redoubts upon Stony Point, until they had constructed "a little Gibraltar," which they boasted was quite impregnable. The only land approach to it was by the causeway road to the ferry across a marsh, which was defended by an abatis and picket stations. The rock gradually increases in height as it recedes from the mainland, nearly to the extreme point of the peninsula, whence, from a height of not less than 50 feet, it suddenly descends, on its northern, eastern, and southern faces, to the river. Verplank's Point also had been greatly strengthened, no less than seven carefully constructed and well-armed redoubts having been built there, holding a heavy garrison.

At this time, warned by these operations that the English were in earnest in their efforts against the passes of the Hudson, Washington had concentrated his army at and above West Point, with headquarters at New Windsor, succeeding with the greatest difficulty in forestalling the enemy, largely on account of the apathy with which Congress and the people together regarded the army at that time. Partly to inspire a greater public interest by some showy movement, Washington now organized a body of picked men, styled the Corps of Light Infantry, and called to their command Gen. Anthony Wayne, then at his home in Pennsylvania, knowing that his dashing character was precisely fitted to the work intended for this quick-moving, hard-hitting body of men. The corps and its impetuous commander, "Mad Anthony," as he was nick-named, were stationed at Fort Montgomery, and ordered to retake Stony Point if it could be done. The full account of the reconnoitering, in which Washington himself took part; of the slow, secret, and exceedingly careful preparation, and finally of the assault, forms one of the most romantic tales in American history; and it is no wonder that many a mythical incident has become entangled into it, even in the writings of Irving, Lossing, and Sparks. These excrescences have been cleared away by the monograph of Dawson, which has been followed in the ensuing sketch.

In the afternoon of July 15th the attacking force gathered as near to Stony Point as was prudent, preserving the utmost secrecy as to their movements. So excessively bad were the narrow mountain roads that it was 8 P. M. before the little army of about 1,000 men reached Springsteel's farm, where it was formed into two solid columns, leaving the cavalry of "Light-Horse Harry" Lee and a body of infantry as supports. Each column was led by a company of picked men, in front of which was a "forlorn hope" of twenty volunteers with axes. When all was ready, orders were given, and for the first time the men understood what was expected of them. Each soldier and officer placed in his hat a piece of white paper to distinguish him from the enemy in the *melée* that was to ensue; and it was ordered that no gun should be fired, but that the assault should be made wholly with the bayonet, and in silence: and the officers were ordered to put to death, instantly, the first man who should attempt to load his musket or break from the ranks. The watchword given was "The fort's our own," and each man was instructed to give it "with a Repeated and Loud voice," "when the Works are forced—and *not before.*"

As midnight drew near, the two columns advanced side by side in perfect stillness. As they approached the marsh, behind the rocky fortress, the right column, with General Wayne at its head, turned toward the right and crossed the marsh, still flooded with some two feet of tide, in order to gain the beach on the south side of the Point, while the other, under Butler and Murfree, crossed the relics of the bridge to an attack of the northern and western front. These movements were quickly discovered by the pickets, and the garrison was aroused and fully ready for defense on all sides by the time Wayne had waded through the marsh and Butler had swerved around to the northern slope; and, notwithstanding the noisy firing which was immediately begun by Murfree's North Carolinians in front as a feint, the assailants on both sides were received with a storm of bullets and grape-shot.

"By moving along the beach, Wayne's column easily turned the abatis, and was at first somewhat sheltered from the artillery, but the redcoats filled every point of rocks on the slope, and poured down a constant and well-directed fire of musketry and bad language. Not a patriot faltered, however, and with funereal silence and steadiness the column pressed upward without firing a musket. Turning the inner abatis, the front ranks were within the enemy's lines, and Wayne stood by, 'spear in hand,' to direct the movement, when a musket-ball struck him on the forehead and, glancing, grazed the skull.

"Stunned by the blow he instantly fell, but as quickly raised himself on one knee and shouted, '*Forward*, my brave fellows; forward!' and turning to Captain Fishbourn and Mr. Archer, his aides, he requested their assistance in moving into the works, where, in case his wound should prove mortal, he desired to die. The troops desired no other incentive, and they dashed forward, bayonet in hand, climbing up the rocks from the beach to avenge the fall of their commander and to sustain the honor of the flag. The advance of the right column, headed by its commander, Lieutenant-Colonel Fleury, led the charge, followed closely by the regiment commanded by Colonel Febiger; and as the former officer sprang up the rampart, and seized the colors of the post and the honors of the day, in broken terms, nearer French than English, he shouted the watchword, '*The fort's our own!*' Almost at the same instant the head of the left column of attack, led by Lieutenant-Colonel Stewart, and driving before it the portions of the garrison which had opposed its progress, also entered the works from the opposite side. Further resistance would have been madness, and the enemy . . . cried lustily for mercy."

No time was lost in turning the guns of the captured fortress against the shipping in the offing, which cut their cables and slipped out of range; and against Verplank's Point, which wisely refrained from wasting ammunition in replying. The attack consumed only about twenty minutes, and by 2 o'clock A. M. the entire garrison had been secured. About twenty were killed and seventy-five wounded on each side (Wayne recovering from his knockdown in a few moments), and twenty-five officers and about

450 privates were captured, besides the wounded, while some sixty escaped. Money rewards and medals were given to Wayne and the leaders in the assault. The ordnance and stores captured were appraised at over $180,000, and paid for by Congress in cash, which was distributed among the troops engaged, and there was universal rejoicing and a revival of courage.

Washington was sensible, however, that in the face of the immediate dispatch of a large force from New York by Clinton, Stony Point could not be held, and he contented himself with destroying the place as well as he could quickly do, and taking away the spoil, which was safely done—with the exception of one large cannon—in spite of the guns of Verplank's Point. The British soon came in force, landed at Haverstraw, resumed possession of and repaired Stony Point, but, failing to beguile "Mr. Washington" into risking a disadvantageous battle, they soon returned to New York, leaving garrisons in these fortresses stronger than ever. The expulsion of the marauding Tryon from Connecticut by Putnam, and the brilliant capture of Paulus Hook (Jersey City) by the Cavalier, Lee, which immediately followed the Stony Point victory, aroused mightily the weakened confidence and zeal of the Continental army, and rekindled the spirit of patriotism throughout the whole weary country. At the end of October, Sir Henry Clinton, alarmed for the safety of New York, withdrew many of his outlying troops, and both Stony and Verplank's points were evacuated by the "redcoats" and again taken possession of by the "rebels," who re-opened the King's Ferry. In 1782, Verplank's Point was made his temporary headquarters by Washington, when he went there with his army to meet the French allies returning from Virginia on their way to embark at Boston for France, and the soldiers spent September and October in rest and merry-making. On the one-hundredth anniversary of the capture of Stony Point, commemorative exercises were held on the spot, and the battle was fought over again; the cadet battalion from West Point participating. The light-house on the Point stands upon the site of the fort's magazine, and there is a railway station near it.

Verplank's Point is now covered with a scant village, farms, and brick-yards. Behind it, on the south side, a great *ice-house* will be noticed at the extremity of what is called Green's Cove.

This is the lowest ice-house on the river, and one of the oldest, and is filled from *Lake Meahagh*, which expands inland behind it.

As the steamer rounds Verplank's Point, or the West Shore's train leaves Tomkins Cove (where now an enormous amount of lime is burned, and broken stone and gravel are sent to the city by the ship-load), and creeps along the base of *The Dunderberg* (the mountain on the left), with *The Spitzenberg* towering inland behind Verplank's, it is entering the **Hudson Highlands.** The Hill Country—Wequehachke of the Mohicans—rises in billows of bush-clothed rock ahead, where the river seems to end in a *cul de sac;* and at the right, a pretty town is half hiding in a ravine, half scrambling up the sides of green bluffs, where several brooks come down into a quiet bay. This is

Peekskill.—Whether or not it be true that Capt. Jans Peek, a Dutch navigator, got stuck in the mud here, soon after the voyage of Henry Hudson, and spent the remainder of his life in contentment by the faithless stream which he had mistaken for the main river, and which came to be called Peek's Kill in consequence, certainly the record of the town goes far back toward the beginning of local history.

In 1664, several Dutchmen bought land here at Sachoes—as the place was called by the local band of Indians (Kitchawonks)—and it was royally confirmed in 1665, as Ryck's Patent. By 1764, several English families had settled near here, and before the end of the century the village was of importance, and had several churches. Peekskill was not itself the scene of any very striking incidents of the Revolutionary War, but it was in the midst of the theater of almost constant campaigns. Fort Independence was just above the village, as its ruins testify. Troops were quartered here from time to time, and Washington often visited the town and Continental Village, a fortified camp a few miles northeast. At one period, Gen. Israel Putnam was in command, and here "Old Put" caught the spy, Palmer, and wrote that famous note to a British officer, who interposed in his behalf: "Edward Palmer, an officer in the enemy's service, was taken as a spy, lurking within our lines. He has been tried as a spy, condemned as a spy, and shall be executed as a spy." Annexing, two hours later, that curt addendum, "P. S. He is hanged." Here too, in the old rural cemetery by the hospital-church (St. Peter's), is buried John Paulding, the captor of André, to whom the city of New York has erected a monumental shaft. He died here in 1818, leaving several sons, one of whom, Admiral Paulding, became distinguished as a naval officer.

Peekskill has grown steadily, and has remained the residence of many families whose branches became rich and famous elsewhere; while it has attracted to it, as a summer home, many prominent New Yorkers. The most widely known of these, no doubt, are the Rev. Henry Ward Beecher, whose farm, in which he took the greatest delight, was two miles east of the landing, and Chauncey M. Depew, president of the New York Central Railroad, whose pillared house is *not* shaded by magnificent chestnuts, as one might expect to see from the great crop of stories which that genial humorist professes to have gathered in his native village. That this should be a favorite place of summer residence is not surprising. The situation, at the southern entrance to the Highlands, is most pleasing and healthful; and the rivers and hills present ever-changing pictures that sometimes attain to grandeur in their effects of sun and shade. The streets wander in all sorts of directions up and down and around the hills, and are densely shaded, while every house has spacious gardens, the smallest of which are thriftily kept. The country roads are excellent, and charming drives may be taken in every direction.

"Gallows Hill, with its folk lore and revolutionary legends; its rudely marked graves, wherein lies the dust of patriot dead; its ruins of the magazines destroyed by Tryon and his Tory crew, the dismantled ovens, and the 'Wayside Inn,' in which André tarried after his arrest, are less than three miles away. In the east room of this old-time hostelry are yet shown the marks of his military boots, made as he restlessly paced up and down its narrow limits. The tomb of Paulding, one of his captors, is just to the eastward, and St. Peter's Church, built in 1767, and in which Washington once worshiped, stands but a few yards away, guarding the dust of Maj.-Gen. Seth Pomeroy, the first commander-in-chief of the patriot army. The Indian spring from which the Mohicans drank, and which ebbs and flows with the tide, is on the north side of Gallows Hill, overlooking the site of Continental Village. Here are found the remains of the revolutionary barracks. West of the Wayside Inn is the Van Cortlandt mansion, built by ex-Lieutenant-Governor Gen. Pierre Van Cortlandt, a distinguished patriot and statesman of colonial and revolutionary days. Six miles to the south is the Van Cortlandt manor-house, built by Stephanus Van Cortlandt in 1683."

The social and educational advantages of the town are noteworthy. Of the schools, the most widely known is the Peekskill Military Academy, founded in 1838, and occupying the large buildings whose telescope-dome is visible from the river. It and the Worrall preparatory military school are under the control of the regents of the State University. A large school for girls is St. Gabriel's, under the care of the Protestant Episcopal Church. The conspicuous brick buildings next the river are the convent, school, and chapel of the Roman Catholic Sisterhood of St. Francis (third order), who conduct, in the "Academy of Our Lady of Angels," a large school for girls. These pious women also have the care of an orphanage containing over 1,000 little waifs of humanity. The public schools also are ample and well managed; one standing on the historic eminence, *Drum Hill*, wherein, it has been written, are stored the drum-beats of the Revolution, to be evoked by him who treads upon its surface. The nucleus of a free library has been established, and all sorts of benevolent, educational, and fraternal societies exist.

Peekskill is strong commercially. The population now approaches 10,000, but the village government is retained. The leading industry is the making of stoves, in which $1,000,000 is invested and 1,000 persons are employed. This dates from 1835, when the present great Union Stove Works were founded, followed since by seven or eight other establishments. The making of brick, fire-brick, and the machinery and apparatus used in brickmaking, form another extensive series of industries. In addition, this thriving village has several machine shops, two paper mills, and a large number of lesser factories of various kinds, including a yacht and boat building yard. The town has public water and a complete sewerage system; is lighted by gas and electricity; maintains uniformed police and fire departments, and free mail delivery. Its public buildings are good, and the new Depew Opera House is of the first class. There are two long-established banks, four weekly newspapers, and an energetic board of trade. Peekskill is the terminal station of the suburban trains of the Hudson River Railroad, which, with other trains, gives it hourly communication with New York (forty three miles); is a calling-place for the steamer *Emmeline*, which runs daily between Haverstraw and Newburgh; and has a daily New York boat of its own in the *Chrystenah*. A ferry crosses the river to Jones' Point (Caldwell Landing).

Peekskill lies mainly upon the southern bank of *Peekskill Bay*, which receives three creeks — the Peek's Kill, or Sachoes, and its two branches, Annsville and Sprout creeks; the Canopus, and a third. The railway crosses the bay through a fleet of anchored pleasure boats, and then curves around the base of a spur of the Highlands called *Manito Mount*. At the head of this little bay, where a level plateau, long known as Roa Hook, stands about eighty feet above the streams on each side, is the

State Camp of Instruction for the National Guard. Here, during the summer, each regiment is brought in turn to encamp and be drilled in the practical work of campaigning. Though the men live in tents in true soldier style, the grounds have been carefully arranged in respect to sewerage and sanitation, the "streets" of tents are lighted by electricity, a large mess-hall forms an eating-house for the officers, a wharf offers a convenient landing-place for steamers, and a model battery affords object lessons in artillery practice. Remembering that almost every point within view was fortified, and every vale a camping-ground, in the war for our independence, no spot more appropriate, as well as delightful, for the purpose could have been chosen. A ferry communicates with Peekskill, and visitors are welcomed at the camp at all suitable hours.

The Passage of the Hudson Highlands now begins. This is regarded as the culmination of the journey in point of scenery, but is perhaps anticipated with too large expectations by most travelers. The railroads on each side skirt the water's edge through the whole length of the gorge; now and then dodging through a tunnel or behind a rocky wall, but, on the whole, giving as good a view as one obtains from the boats; better, in some respects, for the mountains, when looked at from the water's edge, appear taller than from the high decks of a "day-liner." Of the two railroads, that upon the eastern bank offers the more interesting outlook, since it commands a sight of all the old forts, West Point, and the Cro' Nest group of hills; but the view from the western shore is also very interesting. None of these heights much exceeds 1,500 feet, and this is attained only in Storm King, so that it is only by courtesy that they can be called "mountains." All are merely huge hillocks of primitive rocks—a part of the Archæan framework of the continent—covered with brush, from which all the tall timber was long ago taken away, and the newer trees are cut as soon as they become of useful size. Fortunately, however, this brush is close and green, for no fires have swept through it for many years, and, to the casual glance, looks like the original forest. At several points, however, the cliffs have been and continue to be cut away to supply crushed stone, leaving ugly scars, and marring the banks with unsightly buildings. Upon none of these hills are there any signs of agriculture, for there is no cultivable soil, nor many residences, since their ledges are too steep and inaccessible. All civilization, therefore, is near

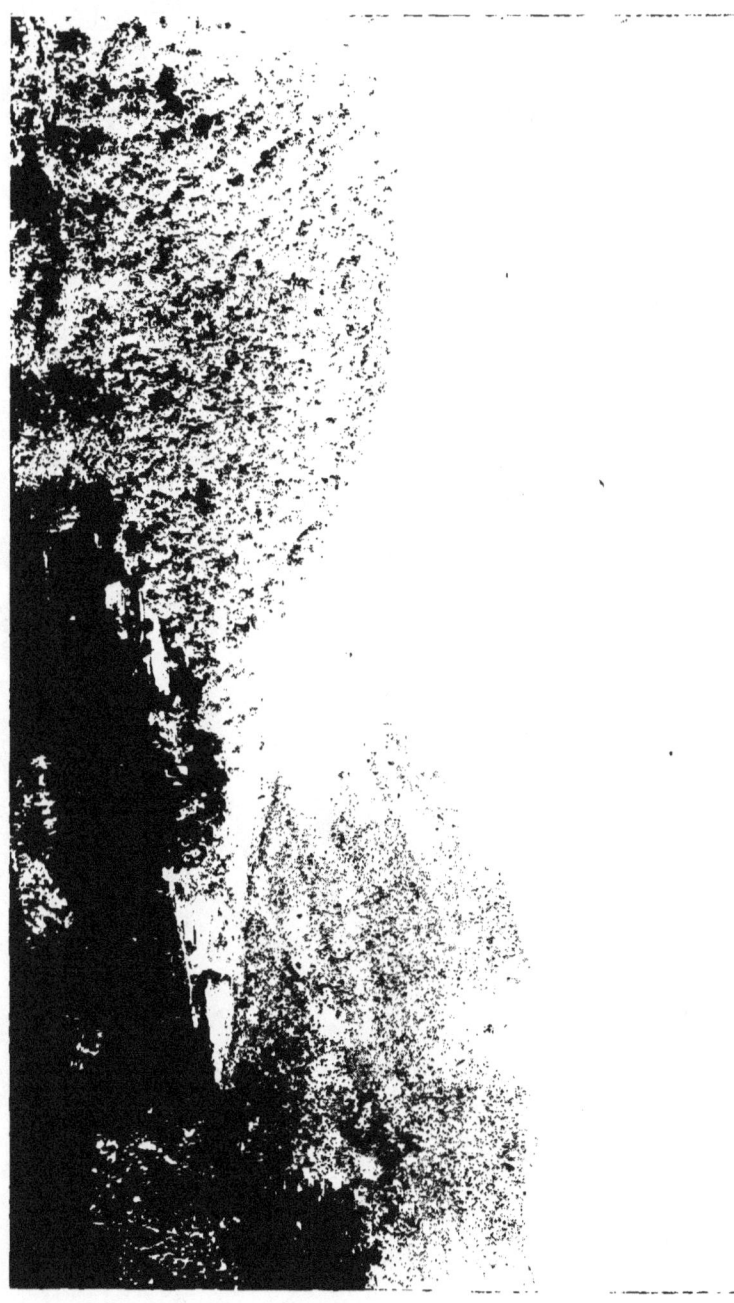
SLIDE MOUNTAIN AND SHANDAKEN VALLEY.

the water's edge, except upon the plateaus about Cranston's and West Point, and about Garrison's opposite, where it is masked by trees, for the most part. In the moonlight, or upon a day when a storm is raging in these narrows, or with the twilight shadows filling the gorge, half hiding and half revealing the jutting rocks and swelling hills, a majestic and picturesque interest of no mean degree belongs to the scene; but in the broad light of a clear summer noon, as most tourists see it, the passage of the Highlands is monotonous, and far from the "grand" or "sublime" spectacle it has often been styled. These Highlands appear to best advantage, undoubtedly, from a distance, as when approaching them from the south, or gazing backward from Newburgh.

"The passage of the Hudson," Willis once remarked, "is doomed to be re-written, and we will not swell its great multitude of describers." Amen! But another remark of Willis is well worth repetition in this connection:

"The qualities of the Hudson," says the genial author of *Rural Letters*, "are those most likely to impress a stranger. It chances felicitously that the traveler's first entrance beyond the seaboard is usually made by the steamer to Albany. The grand and imposing outlines of rock and horizon answer to his anticipations of the magnificence of a new world; and if he finds smaller rivers and softer scenery beyond, it strikes him but as a slighter lineament of a more enlarged design. To the great majority of tastes, this, too, is the scenery to live among. The stronger lines of natural beauty affect most tastes; and there are few who would select country residence by beauty at all, who would not sacrifice something to their preference for the neighborhood of sublime scenery. The quiet, the merely rural—a thread of a rivulet instead of a broad river—a small and secluded valley, rather than a wide extent of view, bounded by bold mountains, is the choice of but few. The Hudson, therefore, stands usually foremost in men's aspirations for escape from the turmoil of cities, but, to my taste, though there are none more desirable to see, there are sweeter rivers to live upon."

But apart from the question of scenery, the passage of the Highlands is full of entertainment to every one interested in colonial history, or in the modern manifestations of summer pleasure-seeking.

Here at the southern entrance, where the foot of the Dunderberg is stretched out against the current, is **Kidd's Point** (with its village and railway station, *Jones' Point*, or *Caldwell Land-*

ing), where the ground has been dug over and over in search of the renowned pirate's buried treasures.

"On the strength of a cannon fished from the water," we are told, "an audacious adventurer proclaimed that Kidd's pirate vessel had foundered in a storm on this spot, with untold treasures on board, and that the vessel had been penetrated with a very long auger, which had brought up pieces of silver in its thread. A stock company was formed; shares were readily sold; and a coffer-dam, with powerful steam-engines, was built over the supposed resting-place of the ship."

The fact that the rocks contain traces of silver, etc., has caused much unprofitable prospecting in this region, occasionally revived.

The Dunderberg (Thunder Mount) itself is a massive hill, 1,100 feet high, along the base of which are small farms upon a terrace that plainly marks an ancient river bank. A ferry runs hourly between this place and Peekskill; and picnic parties often ascend to the summit, where an attractive view rewards them for a not very arduous climb. This summit has been bought by a corporation, which proposes to erect a hotel there, and to make a pleasure-park upon Jones' Point, at the base, connecting the two by a spiral gravity railway about thirteen miles long. It will be interesting to learn, when this is done, whether it dislodges the mischievous and rollicking little goblins who were wont, in the good old times, to make merry upon the mountain, during the storms that the ancient sloop-captains suspected them of contriving out of pure devilry.

"One time," the veritable Diedrich Knickerbocker assures us, "a sloop, in passing by the Dunderberg, was overtaken by a thunder-gust that came scouring round the mountain, and seemed to burst just over the vessel. Though tight and well ballasted, she labored dreadfully, and the water came over the gunwale. All the crew were amazed, when it was discovered that there was a little white sugar-loaf hat on the mast-head, known at once to be the hat of the Head of the Dunderberg. Nobody, however, dared to climb to the mast-head and get rid of this terrible hat. The sloop continued laboring and rocking, as if she would have rolled her mast overboard; and she seemed in continual danger either of upsetting or of running on shore. In this way she drove quite through the Highlands, until she passed Pollopel's Island, where, it is said, the jurisdiction of the Dunderberg potentate ceases. No sooner had she passed this bourn, than the little hat sprung up into the air like a top, whirled up all the clouds into a vortex, and hurried them back to the summit of the

Dunderberg, while the sloop righted herself, and sailed on as quietly as if in a mill-pond. Nothing saved her from utter wreck but the fortunate circumstance of having a horseshoe nailed against the mast—a most wise precaution against evil spirits, since adopted by all the Dutch captains that navigate this haunted river."

Our course turns almost at right angles around the protruding foot of the Dunderberg as we ascend the river, and we find ourselves entering the narrowest and straightest of its reaches, called *The Horse Race*, or, more shortly, *The Race*—a treacherous place for sailing craft. The mountain on the immediate right is *Manito*, and beyond it is seen the profile of *Anthony's Nose*, pierced at the tip by a railway tunnel. On the left, an amphitheater of foot-hills opens backward to the slope of *Bear Mount* (1,350 feet high), north of which are the loftier slopes of *Mount Rascal*, *Black Rock*, and other summits in the rear of Cro' Nest. Between the Dunderberg and Bear Mount, and across the hollow at our left, winds the ancient road that Clinton followed in '77, and along which Wayne's troops crept stealthily on that eventful June evening when they went to attack Stony Point; and *Sinnipink*, one of the many ponds hidden in those hollows (Highland Lake of modern picnickers, careless of the old traditions), has been "Bloody Pond," or "The Hessians' Lake," to the country people ever since the Fort Montgomery fight.

Tradition says that several of the hated mercenaries fell upon its shores, and were thrown into its dark waters; and the older and more experienced among them, who have seen the vainglory of scoffing youth brought to contrition again and again, relate that still upon overcast and gusty nights, such as come among those mountains in midsummer, ghostly apparitions, in helmets and vast riding-boots, may be seen flitting across the dark bosom of the pond; and that there floats to the frightened ear the whispering of commands in a strange tongue, and the rattle of ghostly sabers and harness. This thrilling rehearsal of a sanguinary past is more artistic fiction than most of the tales one hears, but it is fiction nevertheless. Yet the truth is even more horrifying; for into that pond were thrown, after the capture of Fort Montgomery, all the bodies of the American dead, unshrived and forgotten.

Down by the riverside, here, is *Iona Island*—a grape farm and a resort for picnics, which come from the city in barges, or by the railroad that skirts its inland border where it is separated from the mainland by a marshy inlet, called Doodletown Harbor —the seaport of Doodletown, a city of the hills, a mile or two above this peaceful Piræus.

Anthony's Nose, or St. Anthony's Nose, as it used to be written sometimes, is the long ridge sloping down to the river on the right, and causing the bend in the current at the top of the Horse Race. The explanation of this extraordinary name for a very ordinary heap of rocks, some 1,228 feet high, has set everybody guessing. It was just the provocation needed by Irving, who accounts for it by one of his ridiculous Knickerbocker stories. A more serious explanation is that given by Freeman Hunt as told him by Gen. Pierre Van Cortlandt, the owner of the mountain, in 1835, as follows:

"Before the Revolution, a vessel was passing up the river, under the command of a Capt. Anthony Hogans; when immediately opposite this mountain, the mate looked rather quizzically, first at the mountain, and then at the captain's nose. The captain, by the way, had an enormous nose, which was not unfrequently the subject of good-natured remark, and he at once understood the allusion. 'What!' says the captain, 'does that look like my nose? Call it then, if you please, *Anthony's Nose.*'"

Anthony's Nose may be reached, on land, by a road which branches off to the left somewhat over a mile beyond Annsville, on the road from Peekskill to Garrisons. Excavations have been made for the piers of a railway bridge there, but the work long ago ceased.

Montgomery Creek is the modern name of the pretty stream in old times called Poplopen's Kill—after an influential Indian who dwelt in its valley—the mouth of which is in the ravine directly opposite Anthony's Nose. Down this deep and narrow ravine come the waters of a large circle of highland brooks and ponds, tumbling in pretty cascades. On the elevated headlands that confront one another and the river at the mouth of this ravine, there were erected, early in the Revolutionary War, two forts, *Montgomery,* on the northern side, and *Clinton,* a less important outwork, on the southern bluff. Their guns would sweep the river in both directions, and the greatest reliance was placed upon their ability to resist assault, and guard against any further ascent of the Hudson by British ships. How well they answered these expectations, in 1777, may be read in any history. The ensuing notes closely follow the narrative in Lossing's *Life and Times of Philip Schuyler:*

THE FALL OF THE HIGHLAND FORTS.

In September, 1777, Gen. Burgoyne, with an army of British regulars and Hessian and Canadian auxiliaries, was attempting to carry out the instructions of the British ministry, who wished him to open communication along the Hudson between the English forces in Quebec and those in New York, and thereby cut the United States in two. As Mr. Ruttenber remarks, it was Sherman's "march to the sea," without Sherman's success. He had been checked and invested by Schuyler and Gates near Saratoga, and wrote to Sir Henry Clinton in New York that he must be relieved by October 12th if he were to be saved. Clinton, who had been waiting for slow reinforcements from England, made all haste, as soon as these arrived, to go to Burgoyne's relief, and late in September his war ships and flatboats, carrying and conveying from 3,000 to 4,000 men, started up the Hudson.

The American forces of this district, not exceeding 2,000 men, were commanded by Gen. Putnam at Peekskill, while Gen. George Clinton, Governor of the State, was in special charge of Fort Montgomery, with his brother James as commander of Fort Clinton. Putnam sent a statement of the threatening attitude of the enemy to Gov. Clinton, then presiding over the first session of the first State Legislature, at Kingston, and begged reinforcements, but none were to be had.

The defenses of the Hudson were concentrated here where the river was narrow and curved, and the rough hills formed a natural protection to the flanks of the position. Besides these two forts, *Fort Independence* stood on the shoulder of Mount Manito, just above Peekskill; and the navigation of the river was obstructed by a *boom and chain* stretched from Anthony's Nose to the point of rocks just below the present iron railroad bridge at the foot of the crag upon which Fort Clinton stood, and the place is still known as Chain Point. A railway suspension bridge has been planned to span the river precisely at this place, and an excavation for its pier has already been cut on Anthony's Nose, but work has ceased. A part of this **Fort**

Montgomery chain was brought from Lake Champlain, where Schuyler had made it serve a similar purpose in 1775; and there were moored above it some gunboats, intended to prevent an enemy from reaching it in boats to cut a passage through.

The strength of these defenses determined Clinton to avoid a direct attack, and attempt their downfall by stratagem. Landing at Verplank's Point, then unguarded, he impressed the rather heedless Putnam with the belief that the first objects of his attack were Peekskill and Fort Independence. Putnam drew reinforcements from the forts that could ill spare them, and took up a defensive position in the hills; but instead of assailing him, the British commander suddenly recrossed, with 2,000 men, at the King's Ferry, in a dense fog on the morning of October 6th, leaving about 1,000, chiefly loyalists, at Verplank's Point to keep up the aspect of menace toward Peekskill. At the same time, the war vessels were ordered to anchor off Fort Independence, within cannon shot of the Highland forts, and to fire upon them and upon the vessels above the chain.

"Piloted by a Tory, Sir Henry made a forced circuitous march from Stony Point around the southern and western bases of the Dunderberg, through rugged defiles, for several miles, and at 8 o'clock, in the pass between that height and Bear Mount, his force was separated into two parties, in each of which were many Hessian hirelings. One division, composed of 400 loyalists under Col. Beverly Robinson, and 500 British regulars and Hessians, was led by Lieut.-Col. Campbell, and directed to go around Bear Mount, and fall upon Fort Montgomery; while the other division, destined for Fort Clinton, and full 1,200 in number, was led by Gen. Vaughan, accompanied by Sir Henry. Ex-Gov. Tryon was left in the valley with a rear-guard.

"Meanwhile Gov. Clinton, who, on Sunday evening, was informed of the landing of troops at Verplank's Point, and who had brought to Fort Montgomery 400 recruits, had sent out a reconnoitering party at dawn on Monday morning. Three miles south of the fort, this party fell in with the British advance guard, and made a sharp, running fight as it retreated to the breastworks, and reported the approach of the enemy, whose advance was contested all the way from the Dunderberg. Gov. Clinton then sent a messenger to Putnam for aid. The man turned traitor and deserted to the British. Putnam, in the meantime, was astonished at hearing nothing from the enemy, who, he supposed, was about to attack him at Peekskill. He went out to reconnoiter in the afternoon, and did not return until firing was heard in the direction of the forts, and when, at the instance of Col. Humphreys, reinforcements had been sent—though too late—from the camp at Continental Village near Peekskill."

Such is the account which Lossing gives; but the published diary of one of Clinton's officers says that he himself, on the second night before the attack, personally informed Putnam of the position of affairs, and was refused attention; and that he returned, and took part in the whole fight, and was among the prisoners. He declared that he found Putnam at "Beverly," where the "young Ladys and the mother, the night Before the Fort was Taken, Entertained Gen. Putnam with that Pleasing attention that he forgot what he had been informed of the night before, by myself." As the husband and father of these ladies was in the attacking party, it is fair to surmise that they knew what was going on, and were exercising their fascinations for the express purpose of distracting the attention of the American officer from his duties of defense.

While Campbell was making his way around Bear Mount, Vaughan and Sir Henry pressed toward their goal, along a way near the river. At a narrow pass, between Lake Sinnipink and the steep bank of the Hudson, they encountered an abatis, and there they had a severe fight with the Americans. These were pushed back, and, at about 4 o'clock in the afternoon, both posts were invested. At 5, a demand for the surrender of Fort Clinton—which was scarcely more than an outwork—was sent in, and scornfully refused, whereupon a simultaneous assault upon both fortresses was made by the troops, and by the vessels-of-war in the river. Lossing proceeds:

"The garrisons were composed mostly of untrained militia. They behaved nobly, and kept up the defense vigorously, against a greatly superior force of disciplined and veteran soldiers, until twilight, when they were overpowered, and sought safety in a scattered retreat to the neighboring mountains. Many escaped, but a considerable number were slain or made prisoners. The brothers who commanded the forts escaped. The Governor fled across the river in a boat, and at midnight was with Gen. Putnam at Continental Village, concerting measures for stopping the invasion. James, forcing his way to the rear, across the highway bridge, and receiving a bayonet wound in the thigh, safely reached his home at New Windsor. A sloop of ten guns, the frigate *Montgomery*—twenty-four guns—and two row-galleys, stationed near the boom and chain for their protection, slipped their cables and attempted to escape, but there was no wind to fill their sails, and they were burned by the Americans to prevent their falling into the hands of the enemy. The frigate *Congress*—twenty-eight guns—which had already gone up the river, shared the same fate on the flats near Fort Constitution, which was abandoned." [Both frigates were built at or near Poughkeepsie, and never went to sea.] "By the light of the burning vessels, the fugitive garrisons made their way over the rugged mountains, and a large portion of them joined Gen. Clinton at New Windsor the next day. They had left many of their brave companions behind, who, to the number of 250, had been slain or made prisoners. The British, too, had parted with many men and brave officers. Among the latter was Lieut.-Col. Campbell. [Sir Henry himself narrowly escaped a grape-shot.]

"Early in the morning of the 7th of October, the river obstructions between Fort Montgomery and Anthony's Nose, which cost the Americans $250,000, were destroyed, and a light flying squadron, commanded by Sir James Wallace, and bearing a large number of land troops under Gen. Vaughan, sailed up the river on a marauding expedition, with instructions from Sir Henry to scatter desolation in their paths. It was hoped that such an expedition would draw troops from the Northern army [Gates'] for the protection of the country below, and thereby assist Burgoyne."

From all this, however, Burgoyne received no advantage, mainly owing to one of those miscarriages of plans which seem to have been constantly happening in that war, where English spies and couriers were always coming to grief. On the morning of the 9th, when Gen. Clinton was leaving New Windsor with the little force he could hastily gather, in an attempt to keep pace with the British squadron on that side of the river, and resist their landings, while Putnam, who had abandoned Peekskill, endeavored to protect the people of the eastern shore—on this morning, two strangers blundered headlong into the camp from the south, and failed to discover that they were among the soldiers of the American instead of the *English* Clinton—because these were clothed in captured British uniforms not yet dyed—until carried to the governor's quarters. Then one of them hastily swallowed something, whereupon an emetic was administered and a *silver bullet* was thrown up. He swallowed it again, but under a threat of being immediately hanged and opened, was made to take a second emetic with the same result. The bullet, yet preserved in Albany, was an elliptical shell, joined together in the middle, containing nothing more than an announcement of the victory, "and noth-

CRANSTON'S.

ing between us and Gates"; but its failure to reach Burgoyne deprived him of hope, and led to his surrender only a few days later (October 13th). Nevertheless, Clinton's capture of the Highlands was of indirect service to him, for when Gates heard of it, and of the depredations of the men and ships ascending the Hudson, he felt inclined to grant to Burgoyne easier terms than were at first proposed, and hasten southward to drive back the invaders.

Forts Montgomery and Clinton may still be traced, though reduced by a century of weathering, and overgrown with trees and brush. The former is easily accessible by a path which leads up from the railroad track at the little tool house a hundred yards below the station *Fort Montgomery*, which is the station for a farming and summering village, of the same name, on the turnpike. The latter may be reached by an exceedingly pleasant walk of a mile from Fort Montgomery Village.

As the steamer swings around Anthony's Nose, and enters *Crescent Reach*, masses of mountains loom up ahead—the true Highlands. On the left, the heights of **Cranston's**—marked by its two great hotels—and of **West Point**, crowned by the ruins of Fort Putnam, fall steeply down to the river, whose bank there is a line of rugged precipices, beneath which the railroad runs along the beach; and on beyond are seen the summits of **Cro' Nest**. On the right, the conical, detached elevation of **Sugar Loaf** is prominent near at hand, while in the distance are the clustered heights of **Bull Hill** (Mount Taurus), **The Turk's Face** (Breakneck), and **South Beacon Hill**. The land on the right is in Putnam County, which succeeds Westchester County at Anthony's Nose; and that on the left is in Orange County, which begins at Fort Montgomery, where Rockland County terminates, and Monroe County corners between them at the mouth of Montgomery Creek.

Along the elevated highway, on the western side, which, though not far away, is quite out of sight from the river, dwell many persons of note, whose estates come to the brink of the bluff. Near Fort Montgomery lives John S. Gilbert; then the Pells; and a little farther, just opposite Sugar Loaf, J. Pierpont Morgan, the merchant philanthropist. Farther up this beautiful road are the elegant places of Alfred Pell, Charles Tracey, Capt. S. B. Roe, on the Satterlee estate, the "Benny Havens" cottage, and John Bigelow, at "The Squirrels." Here the line of crags is broken by a ravine, where, in times of freshet, a stream leaps over a ledge in the pretty cataract, long ago named *Buttermilk Falls;* and on the plateau at the head of this ravine is the village of *Highland Falls,* which is not only a market town and place of shipment for dairy products and fruit in large quantities, but a resort for summer boarders. At the mouth of the ravine is a steamboat-landing, touched at by several lines of boats, and the railway station *Cranston's*. It is a busy spot in summer. The "Parry House" is a flourishing hotel on the hillside, south of the ravine; while on the northern bluff, overlooking the river, and conspicuous from steamboats or the Hudson River Railroad trains, is "Cranston's Hotel," one of the oldest hotels in the valley. In summer "Cranston's," as the whole locality is familiarly styled, is a very lively, populous, and fashionable place, and a ferry is operated between the landing and Garrison's. The day-line boats, however, stop only at West Point, where stages from Highland Falls meet the boat and trains.

The Eastern Shore, here, is comparatively low, and the Hudson River Railroad had no serious difficulties to encounter. There, too, the ancient highway is near the river, and along it are many fine residences. The first of these, noticeable, is that of F. A. Livingston, on the southern side of a little cove. The upper side of this cove is formed by a small rocky headland, where a small wharf and some stone buildings are visible. This is **Beverly Dock,** where Benedict Arnold embarked in his barge to flee to the *Vulture,* on the morning of André's arrest; and whence Washington and his staff took a boat for West Point a few moments later. And "Beverly," the mansion and farm of Col. Beverly Robinson, was a quarter of a mile back, upon the fertile terrace at the foot of Sugar Loaf. The locality still bears that name, but the house was burned in the spring of 1892. It was a quaint old-time mansion, and visitors used to be shown, in the principal bedchamber, the names of many officers of the Continental army, carved on the mantel-piece by them as from time to time they spent one or more nights there. Just above is the residence of Mrs. Underhill; and near by, at "Glencliffe," in a brick house on this bluff, dwelt Hamilton Fish, Sr.

It now appears that Sugar Loaf is the southernmost of a range of connected hills parallel with the river, and with the greater heights eastward; and the eye will be attracted to a lofty white building perched upon the very summit of the hill, next northward. This is the tomb of the late Wm. H. Osborne, and the prospect from the tower embraces the whole extent of the Highlands. On the northern slope of the same hill, much lower down, is the new house of a son, also made of white limestone quarried on the property. A little way beyond, and not seen from the river, is the spacious estate of Samuel Sloan, president of the Delaware & Lackawanna Railroad Co. The hill behind him is named *Redoubt Mountain*, and is crowned by Mr. Sloan's skeleton tower, which gives a view of great breadth and beauty. Still farther north, on the same high ground, is the old and favorite *Highland Hotel* (stages meet the train at Garrison's station); "Cedar Crest," the residence of J. M. Toucey, general manager of the New York Central Railroad; and the home of the Rev. Walter Thompson, rector of St. Phillips-in-the-Highlands. Nearer the river, and in sight of passengers on steamboats, is a line of costly properties. The first above the estate of the late Secretary of State Hamilton Fish, upon a point directly opposite Cranston's Hotel, is "Arden," the estate of Col. T. B. Arden, above which is that of H. W. Belcher, still the residence of his widow; then comes the home of Hamilton Fish, Jr., marked by its huge red chimneys; then the home of Mrs. Col. S. M. Benjamin. The yellow and white house just above the station is that of W. Livingston; upon the bank of the cove beyond lives John T. Sherman; and beyond that is seen the Gouverneur estate, now occupied by Gen. Louis Fitzgerald.

This collection of costly and splendid country-seats, including many not mentioned, because not conspicuous, constitutes a district termed **Garrison's**. It has a railway station that is important to the general public, mainly the station for the Highland and Croft hotels, and for the *Ferry to West Point* (fare 15 cents). The locality, then known as *Mandivel's*, saw much marching and camping of troops, and contains the remains of batteries, but experienced no fighting.

The traveler has now arrived under the shadow of the bold promontory of primitive rock, flanked by shaggy cliffs, and commanded by wooded heights in the rear, which constitutes **West Point**, and bears upon its plateau the **United States Military Academy**.

THE TOUR OF WEST POINT.

West Point is probably the most interesting stopping-place upon the Hudson for the casual traveler; and every one is strongly advised to arrange his journey so as to spend a few hours there. It is possible to reach or leave the place almost hourly by boat or one or the other of the railways; and a hotel exists, where a longer halt may be made in comfort when the house is not crowded. A favorite plan is to go up from New York on a morning boat, spend three or four hours at the Post, and return by the afternoon boat down. Midday, however, is the least favorable time, as the drills, parade, and other picturesque incidents take place mainly toward sunset. Twenty-four hours can be pleasantly and profitably spent here.

From the steamboat landing roads diverge right and left up the hill; that to the left goes to Cranston's; that to the right to the Military Academy. An omnibus and carriages meet all trains and boats; and if you have baggage and are going to the hotel, it is advisable to ride; otherwise, the distance up the hill is none too great to be walked.*

At the top of the first slope, leave the road, and take the footpath slanting upward toward the right.

The Riding Hall is here seen on the right, at the brink of the bluff—a brick building with an arched roof, completed in 1855, when Gen. (then Colonel) Robert E. Lee was superintendent.† It is floored with tan-bark, and here the cadets are taught horsemanship and cavalry exercises. *This is the most interesting of all the drills.* Outside stairways admit spectators to galleries; but these are small and uncomfortable.

Just beyond it are the *stables*, with quarters for 100 horses. These and all equipments pertaining to this arm of the service are cared for by the detachment of regular cavalry stationed here.

---

* The fixed tariff of charges is as follows: Each passenger to or from wharf or railroad station, 25 cents; each trunk or box, in baggage wagon, 25 cents. Two-horse carriage, first hour, $2; after the first hour, $1.50; late at night, $2 per hour. Those residing or on duty at the Post pay at a reduced rate.

† Nowhere was the defection of Col. Lee to the support of his State, in 1861, more keenly and sadly felt than at West Point, where he had been admired and loved for every soldierly and manly attribute. It is pertinent to note here, that out of 278 cadets in the Academy at the time of the attempted secession of the Southern States, 86 of whom were from that region, only 56 were "discharged, dismissed, or resigned" to go into the Rebellion.

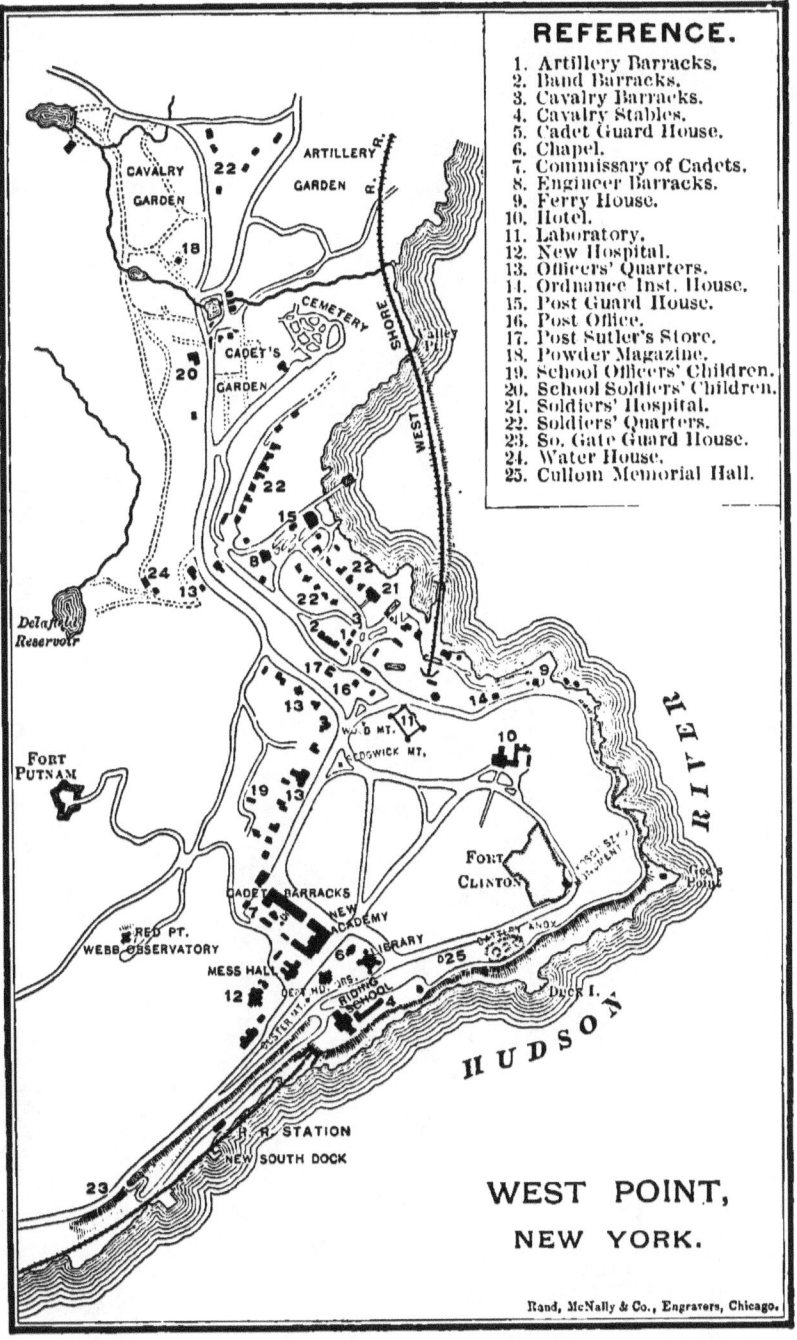

The *path* brings the visitor out upon the **main street** of the Post, which here skirts the edge of the plateau. At his left, facing the river, is *Grant Hall*, or the Mess Hall, as it is more familiarly known.

This building may be visited between meal hours by those who wish to see the collection of fine portraits which adorns its walls. The list is now as follows: 1. Maj.-Gen. John F. Reynolds. 2. Maj.-Gen. John Sedgwick. 3. Col. J. J. Abert. 4. Maj.-Gen. John M. Schofield. 5. Gen. U. S. Grant. 6. Gen. William T. Sherman. 7. Gen. Philip H. Sheridan. 8. Maj.-Gen. E. O. C. Ord. 9. Brig.-Gen. Wesley Merritt. 10. Capt. Bradford R. Alden. 11. Brvt. Maj.-Gen. G. K. Warren. 12. Brvt. Maj.-Gen. Thomas Swords. 13. Maj.-Gen. George Meade. 14. Brvt. Maj.-Gen. R. O. Tyler. 15. Col. J. Gilchrist Benton. 16. Maj.-Gen. J. B. Ricketts. 17. Maj.-Gen. George B. McClellan. 18. Maj.-Gen. C. F. Smith. 19. Brvt. Maj.-Gen. Stewart Van Vleit. 20. Brvt. Brig.-Gen. T. J. Rodman. 21. Maj.-Gen. H. W. Halleck. 22. Brvt. Maj.-Gen. G. W. Cullum. 23. Brig.-Gen. Robert Anderson. 24. Maj.-Gen. H. W. Slocum. 25. Col. J. M. Wilson. 26. Brig.-Gen. Daniel Tyler. 27. Brig.-Gen. Geo. Stoneman.

Beyond Grant Hall is the *Hospital*. Immediately in front of the observer, the new *Academic Building*, which was finished for use in 1895; and at his right is the *Administration Building*, or Post headquarters, on the east side of the street. It is not open to visitors in general, but makes appropriate a few words here as to the organization and status of the school.

The United States Military Academy dates from the close of the Revolution. It was natural that a nation, welded, as the American had been, in the slow fires of a long war, and keeping its military chiefs in the highest civil offices, should think of future wars, and the education of young men to soldierly duties. Washington, Knox, and others urged the organization of a National Academy where regular instruction in the art of war should be given; and in 1794 Congress authorized a corps of artillerists and engineers which should be kept stationed at West Point, and under constant training; and enjoined the attachment to it of thirty-two students, or "cadets." In 1798, this corps was enlarged; special instructors "in the arts and sciences" were appointed, and *cadet* became a definite rank between that of sergeant and ensign (now second lieutenant). The cadets are thus regularly members of the army, and subject to its laws the same as other commissioned officers. Formerly, they were enlisted for five years, but now for eight; and the United States claims their services for four years after graduation, though the Government is not in duty bound to find a commission in the army for every graduate. Step by step, the school was segregated and enlarged, until in

1812 it was opened to 260 students, and assumed somewhat of its present form. The first superintendent was Gen. Jonathan Williams, and one of his professors was F. R. Hassler, who afterward became distinguished in the Coast Survey. Others succeeded him, until 1817, when *Col. Sylvanus Thayer*, now revered as the "Father of the Academy," took command, and brought the school into a far higher condition than it had previously known. It was he who introduced the present uniform, organization, rules of study, reports, etc., substantially in vogue to-day, and to which the Academy owes its discipline and effectiveness. He remained until 1833, when he resigned, and was followed by other officers in more rapid succession, until now the rule obtains that the superintendent and officers detailed to the Post or school shall not, as a rule, serve more than four years. The "professors," however, each of whom has charge of an educational department, are appointed for life, or as long as they continue to give satisfaction; and have the assimilated rank of lieutenant-colonel, or colonel, after a service of ten years, and are subject to retirement. They are thus army officers, in effect, and their assistants are wholly derived from the service. Thus the military idea is diffused throughout the whole course of training, which is mainly scientific and practical; too much so, in the opinion of some modern critics, who insist that the literary side of the education is too little regarded.

West Point, however, is not only a school, but a regular army post—perhaps the oldest in the United States, as such; and the *superintendent* is commander of the whole Post, including the Academy, and having in his staff the usual adjutant, quartermaster, etc., as at any army station. Next in rank to him is the *commandant of cadets*, who is commander of the *Cadet Battalion*.

This battalion is divided into four infantry companies, each commanded by a regular officer of the army, detailed for the purpose, and officered under him by cadets from the upper classes, who are appointed for general excellence in military deportment and studies, and accept the distinction as an honor. There is also a *cadet adjutant*, who is the highest cadet officer in rank except the four captains. It will please the readers of Capt. Charles King's delightful novels of military life to learn that during his cadetship he was promoted through various grades to this adjutancy, and was twice afterward returned to the Academy as an instructor. While "on duty," every point of military etiquette is observed by the students toward their cadet officers, but otherwise no distinction whatever is made between these and their fellows. The cadet officers are marked by chevrons of gold lace on their dress-coats, and of black braid on their "everyday" blouses. The awkward "squads" of each new class are drilled by these cadet officers, and after a month of it are scattered through the battalion, whose companies are organized regardless of class distinctions.

The Staff of the Military Academy consisted of the following officers on April 1, 1898.

SUPERINTENDENT.—Col. O. H. Ernst, Lieut.-Col., Corps of Engineers.

MILITARY STAFF.—Capt. Wilber E. Wilder, Fourth Cavalry, Adjutant of the Military Academy, Post Adjutant and Recruiting Officer, Commanding Band and Detachment of Field Music. Major William F. Spurgin, Twenty-third Infantry, Treasurer of the Military Academy, and Quartermaster and Commissary of Cadets. Capt. John B. Bellinger, Assistant Quartermaster, U. S. A., Quartermaster of the Military Academy, Post Quartermaster, and Disbursing Officer. Second Lieut. Harold P. Howard, Sixth Cavalry, Commissary, and Post Treasurer; in charge of Post Exchange. First Lieut. William Weigel, Eleventh Infantry, Assistant to Post Quartermaster, and Officer of Police. Major Geo H. Torney, Surgeon U. S A., Post Surgeon. Capt. William L. Kneedler, Assistant Surgeon, U. S. A. Capt. Francis A. Winter, Assistant Surgeon, U. S. A. Rev. (Capt.) Herbert Shipman, Chaplain.

ACADEMIC STAFF.—*Department of Natural and Experimental Philosophy.*—(Col.) Peter S. Michie, Professor (14th February, 1871). Capt. William B. Gordon, Ordnance Department, Assistant Professor. First Lieut. Henry C. Davis, Third Artillery; Second Lieut. Joseph T. Crabbs, Eighth Cavalry, Instructors Second Lieut. Harold P. Howard, Sixth Cavalry, in charge of Observatory and Astronomical Calculations.

Department of Drawing.—(Col.) Charles W. Larned, Professor (25th July, 1876). Second Lieut. Horace M. Reeve, Third Infantry, Assistant Professor. Second Lieut. Walter C. Babcock, Eighth Cavalry; Second Lieut. Charles H. Paine, Thirteenth Infantry; Second Lieut. Jens Bugge, Third Infantry, Instructors.

Department of Mathematics.—(Col.) Edgar W. Bass, Professor (17th April, 1878). (Capt.) Wright P. Edgerton, Associate Professor (1st July, 1893). First Lieut. Charles P. Echols, Corps of Engineers, Assistant Professor. Second Lieut. George Blakely, Second Artillery; Second Lieut. William M. Cruikshank, First Artillery; Second Lieut. D. M. King, Fourth Artillery; Second Lieut. William P. Pence, Fifth Artillery; Second Lieut. Charles W. Castle, Sixteenth Infantry; Second Lieut. Thales L. Ames, Third Artillery; Second Lieut. Joseph Wheeler, Jr., Fourth Artillery, Instructors.

Department of Chemistry, Mineralogy, and Geology.—(Col.) Samuel E. Tillman, Professor (21st December, 1880). First Lieut. Edgar Russel, Fifth Artillery, Assistant Professor. First Lieut. George F. Landers, Fourth Artillery; Second Lieut. Palmer E. Pierce, Sixth Infantry; Second Lieut. William R. Smith, First Artillery, Instructors.

Department of Tactics.—Lieut. Col. Otto L. Hein, Captain First Cavalry, Commandant of Cadets and Instructor of Tactics (15th June, 1897). Capt. James Parker, Fourth Cavalry, Senior Instructor of Cavalry Tactics. First Lieut. Granger Adams, Fifth Artillery, Senior Instructor of Artillery Tactics. First Lieut. John H. Beacom, Third Infantry, Senior Instructor of Infantry Tactics, Commanding Company of Cadets. First Lieut. John J. Pershing, Tenth Cavalry, Assistant Instructor of Tactics, Commanding Company of Cadets. First Lieut. Samson L. Faison, First Infantry, Assistant Instructor of Tactics, Commanding Company of Cadets. Second Lieut. Julian R. Lindsey, Ninth Cavalry, Assistant Instructor of Cavalry Tactics. First Lieut. Jay E. Hoffer, Third Artillery, Assistant Instructor of Tactics, Commanding Company of Cadets.

Department of Modern Languages.—(Lieut. Col.) Ed. E. Wood, Professor (1st October, 1892). First Lieut. Charles H. Hunter, First Artillery, Assistant Professor of the Spanish Language. First Lieut. Peter E. Traub, First Cavalry, Assistant Professor of the French Language. Second Lieut. Samuel C. Hazzard, First Artillery; Second Lieut. William R. Smedberg, Jr., Fourth Cavalry; Second Lieut. Edward B. Cassatt, Fourth Cavalry; Second Lieut. James M. Williams, First Artillery; Second Lieut. F. Le J. Parker, Fifth Cavalry, Instructors.

Department of Law.—(Lieut. Col.) George B. Davis, Deputy Judge Advocate General, U. S. A., Professor (20th August, 1895). First Lieut. Walter A. Bethel, Third Artillery, Assistant Professor. Second Lieut. Frank G. Mauldin, Third Artillery; Second Lieut. Matthew C. Smith, Second Cavalry; Second Lieut. Samuel Hof, Sixth Cavalry, Instructors.

Department of Civil and Military Engineering.—(Col.) Gustav J. Fiebeger, Professor. First Lieut. Thomas H. Rees, Corps of Engineers, Assistant Professor. First Lieut. Chester Harding, Corps of Engineers; First Lieut. F. R. Shunk, Corps of Engineers, Instructors.

Department of Practical Military Engineering.—Capt. James L. Lusk, Corps of Engineers, Instructor (31st March, 1893). First Lieut. E. Eveleth Winslow, Corps of Engineers, Asst. Instructor.

Department of Ordnance and Gunnery.—Capt. Lawrence L. Bruff, Ordnance Department, Instructor (17th August, 1891). First Lieut. John T Thompson, Ordnance Department; First Lieut. Henry D. Todd, Jr., First Artillery, Assistant Instructors.

Sword Exercise.—Herman J. Koehler, Master.

Teacher of Music.— George Essigke.

Turning to the right, a few steps northward bring the visitor to **The Plain**—an open, level plain of some forty acres. The street keeps on straight across to the hotel. On the right of the street is a dusty expanse, where field-pieces are packed under canvas covers, and where the mounted drills of cavalry troops and the light-battery take place. At the left is a beautiful lawn—the *campus* of the Academy and *parade* of the Post. Here the infantry battalion drills and dress-parades take place; and it is the ball-ground of the students and general play-field of the children.

Let us *turn to the right*—toward the river—and walk around the plain.

The Chapel is the modest stone building, with a Greek portico, which is immediately on the corner at the right.

This chapel was built in 1836, and the Reformed Episcopal form of worship is conducted there by the Post chaplain. It is small and old-fashioned, but elegant, and peculiarly adorned, not only by the crimson silk hangings about the pulpit, but by a vigorous *wall painting*, occupying the arch of the roof above it, from the brush of Prof. Robert W. Weir, for many years teacher of drawing at the Academy, and father of John W. Weir, professor of painting at Yale. The most interesting objects in this chapel, however, are the cases of **captured flags**. Those upon the west wall are the *British colors* surrendered by Cornwallis at Yorktown, in 1781. They were given, by Act of Congress, to Washington, who left them to G. Washington Parke Custis of Arlington, who, in 1858, presented them to the Government, which sent them here for preservation.

The opposite case is filled with *Mexican flags*, trophies of the Mexican War, in which the graduates of West Point had the first opportunity to distinguish themselves; and where they proved, in the most satisfactory manner, the great advantage to the country of such a school of soldiery.

The tablets on the wall commemorate the names of prominent American officers; those on the west wall are all the generals of the Revolution, except one; and the blank is to be filled—in silence—by the name of Arnold. Those on the east wall are officers of the Mexican War. The remaining space has but a single occupant—the tablet to Lieut. Casey, who was killed in the Sioux war of 1891, and who had been an instructor and exceedingly popular comrade at West Point. Admission to the chapel, when not open, may be gained by application to the adjutant of the Post in the Administration Building.

The Library is the building next beyond, at the southeast corner of the plain—a building of dark stone, in the Elizabethan style, erected in 1840. It is crowned by a dome in which the astronomical instruments were formerly placed. The tunneling of the Point by the West Shore Railroad Company, and the consequent jar of its trains, made this building untenable for instruments of precision; and in compensation for its privileges the company paid for the erection of the new observatory. The library now contains about 39,000 volumes, mainly devoted to military science and history, but including many general books.

Turning *northward*, upon leaving the library, the visitor will walk along the eastern side of the plain, where is now rising the Cullum Memorial Hall, a legacy from Maj.-Gen. G. W. Cullum. It will be of stone, in Neo-Greek style, will contain a spacious auditorium, an assembly room for the alumni, and many bedrooms, and will form a hall for social occasions and a sort of club for visiting officers. Beyond this building is the *camp-ground* of the cadets, where they live in tents, with all the routine of a field campaign, from graduation day in June until September. The black railings are set there as a more convenient and secure method of tying the tent-ropes than pegs afford. Beyond this shady camp-ground the rambler finds himself confronted by the grassy parapet of

Fort Clinton.—A stairway at the nearest corner leads to its top, but, before ascending, the visitor will do well to walk a little way along the carriage road, and observe the old masonry of the wall on that front, which is a part of the ancient structure. The present fortification, a simple form of earthwork, more or less star-shaped, without cannon, and covering, perhaps, two acres of ground, is a restoration, made in 1857, of the revolutionary fortress, and is not only a historical monument, but an object lesson in the science of field fortification. Within its interior, lessons are given in the construction of such structures, and in the making of gabions, fascines, abatis, chevaux-de-frise, and other elements entering into defenses of this nature. The fort is chiefly interesting, however, as a reminder of the history of West Point, which is purely military. To sift correctly from the mass of revolutionary record and tradition which belongs to this small, though momentous, spot, would require more judgment and labor than most of us have at command; those interested, therefore, owe a debt of gratitude to Capt. Boynton for his comprehensive *History of West Point,* the whole scene of which is under the reader's eye as he strolls along this grassy parapet.

Historical Sketch.—This whole neighborhood was part of an early grant to an English gentleman, John Evans, who, curiously enough, was a captain in the Royal Artillery; but his patent was vacated in 1669, and the lands then passed into the hands of several proprietors. No one seems to have actually settled here in pre-revolutionary times, however, the rocky character of the place inviting only the camping hunter and wood-cutter. When the war for independence broke out, the defense of the Highlands attracted the first attention, as has been pointed out; and a scheme of fortifications for Constitution Island—the rocky eminence opposite West Point, northward, which is separated from the mainland by a space of marshes—was begun as early as the autumn of 1775, but was soon abandoned. A congressional committee found, among other faults, that the site was overlooked by the "West Point," and recommended that that elevated ground be made use of as the site of a strong fortification. This was the first official suggestion to that effect. Nevertheless, additional redoubts were built and many guns mounted on the island, until good judges declared the whole affair useless. The principal redoubt was *Fort Constitution,* from which the island derives its present name, and which was destroyed by the enemy when they passed up the river in 1777.

The British success of that year taught the Americans that they had put their earlier chain in the wrong place, at Fort Montgomery, and that the proper place to stretch it was from Gee's, or Stony Point—the extreme rocky projection of the West Point headland—to the rocky shore of Constitution Island. This was not only 300 feet shorter in distance than the width at Fort Montgomery, but here sail-vessels ascending the river lost their headway to a great extent in rounding the sharp turn in the river, and by reason of the baffling winds of this tortuous gorge, so that they would strike the obstruction with diminished force. Accordingly another chain was prepared and put into position in April, 1778. It was defended by a battery of guns at each end, and that upon the West Point side is still visible, and is called the *Chain Battery.*

Meanwhile, the fortification of "the West Point" had been busily prosecuted during the preceding winter (1777-78), in spite of the extraordinary severity of that famous season and the depth of the snow. Parsons' brigade furnished the workmen, and the engineer was a French officer, Lieut.-Col. Radière. His plans were not approved, however, and he was superseded by Kosciusko, the Pole—afterward to become a name for the oppressed to conjure by—under whose direction the work went steadily forward. The principal fort was this one at the northeastern corner of the plateau, with a water-battery at the end of the chain, and another on the cliff face, the present *Battery Knox;* but, as the whole situation was exposed to the fire of any guns planted upon the eminences that rose from the plain on the landward side, it was imperative that these summits should be included in the general plan. To the most commanding of them, Col. Rufus Putnam was sent with his regiment, and they toiled all winter in the forest, and frost and snow, throwing up as strong a redoubt as could be made of logs and stones and a little earth. Works somewhat less pretentious surmounted other hilltops. Between *Fort Putnam* and the river was *Fort Webb*, now the site of the new observatory; and another, *Fort Wyllis*, covered a rocky knoll a quarter of a mile farther south, at the extremity of the same ridge. A fourth was erected upon the round knob some distance north of Fort Putnam. All of these, however, were regarded as outworks defending the approaches to the main citadel here on the plain, which was sufficiently advanced by June of 1778 to receive its garrison and its name—*Fort Arnold.* This name, according to Boynton, was continued until Arnold's defection, when its title was changed to *Fort Clinton,* which it has since retained. About 1,000 troops occupied West Point during the winter of 1778-79, and the remainder of the northern army was not far away—a part of it just across the river, where strong breastworks were constructed upon Redoubt Hill and Sugar Loaf, in addition to batteries along the south side of Constitution Island. Washington himself resided here from July 25 to November 28, 1779.

The impregnability of these works was soon ascertained by the British, and after the failure of Arnold's treachery, West Point was never even threatened with an assault. Vigilance was not relaxed, however. The forts, and Putnam in particular, were made stronger and stronger, well garrisoned, and filled with war stores of every kind. Their admirable condition is testified to by the Marquis de Chastellu, who inspected them in November, 1780. "These magazines," he exclaims, "completely filled, the numerous artillery one sees in these different fortresses, the prodigious labor necessary to transport and pile up on steep rocks huge trunks of trees and enormous hewn stones, impress the mind with an idea of the Americans very different from that which the English ministry have endeavored to give to Parliament."

After the war, West Point was made the repository of the war material remaining, much of which was sold; and the redoubts were not dismantled of their guns until 1787. They were then allowed to fall into ruin, and the curious may now find them overgrown with trees. In 1805, Fort Putnam was partly demolished, and rebuilt of stone, after a somewhat larger design, but was speedily allowed to sink into the present condition of decay. Fort Clinton was itself restored in 1857. The presence of these fortresses and their stores determined the stationing here of the corps of engineers and artillerists and their cadets, and expla ns the present location of the Military Academy—an aptness of historical foundation which does not often occur.

The Cliffs, *below Fort Clinton*, are a part of "the Point" dear to the hearts of habitués. "Love at the first sight," we read, "is epidemic at West Point in June and July," and nowhere is the insidious malady more infectious than along these crags that look out upon the shining river. "Tender-hearted damsels, fresh from the boarding-school, and ardent cadets, whose sober-gray uniform is completely opposite to the warmth of their feelings, wander through the shady lanes, plighting everlasting troth, and quite forgetful of the awful fact that a cruel fate may impend in papa and mamma. There are romantic nooks, arbors, grottoes, and quiet lanes, overarched with intertwining foliage—all that a lover could desire."

It is asking too much, perhaps, that the casual visitor of uncertain age, and in broad daylight, should find *Flirtation Walk*, *Kosciusko's Garden*, with its arched spring and marble fountain-bowl, and the other nooks and corners, as entertaining as do the fledgling lieutenants and those sweetest of summer girls; but they are delightful paths in which to stroll and smoke a post-prandial cigar, all the same. A sad note is felt in one's meditations as he encounters a plain marble shaft—around which an eagle is twining a laurel wreath—and reads the name DADE inscribed upon its plinth. "It commemorates the bravery of a detachment of United States troops, under Maj. Francis L. Dade, in a battle with the Seminole Indians in Florida, when 105 men out of 108 in the command were slaughtered."

A little farther on is **Battery Knox**—a revolutionary relic kept in modern repair, and with the guns mounted, whose muzzles command the river channel. But these great guns are rarely, if ever, fired. Continuing the walk, you may scramble down to the old *Chain Battery* on Gee's Point, or—since that is scarcely worth while—may ascend to the carriage road at the northeast angle of Fort Clinton, where the parapet is crowned with the **Statue to Kosciusko.**

Thaddeus Kosciusko was born in Lithuania in 1746. He exhibited remarkable ability as a military student, and became a captain of artillery, but on account of an unfortunate attachment to the daughter of a nobleman, in 1777, he went to Paris, and then to

America with the French fleet. Washington gladly accepted his aid, and he displayed such intrepidity and skill that he rose to be a brigadier-general; and his scientific knowledge was utilized in the construction of this very fortress, which now bears the memorial shaft raised to his memory, in 1828, by the cadets, at a cost of $5,000. In 1786, he returned to Europe; and in 1789 was made a major-general of the Polish army. In the war with Russia which followed, he acted with remarkable, but unavailing, skill and valor; and when, in 1793, a part of Poland revolted, Kosciusko became leader, and but for the interposition of Prussia would have freed Poland from the Russian yoke. The result was defeat for the country and wounds and imprisonment for himself. After two years, however, he regained his freedom, and again visited England and America, after which he remained a prominent figure in European politics until his death in Switzerland in 1817. The whole world has united in esteem and admiration of him, not only as a soldier, but as a chivalrous patriot.

Continuing the walk along the north front, and past the *Sallyport* of Fort Clinton, the visitor reaches the **Hotel**, from whose balconies a magnificent view up the river is gained.

The West Point Hotel dates from 1829, and long ago became antiquated. It is leased by the Government at so high a rental that the proprietor feels obliged to charge $3.50 a day, but at graduation time the old house is crowded almost to suffocation.

Along the *north side of the plain*, many interesting objects claim attention, not to mention the charming river views this elevated outlook affords. The most conspicuous is the

Battle Monument.—This was erected in 1895–7, at a cost of $75,000, accumulated by subscriptions from the army since 1863. It commemorates all of the regular army (188 officers and 2,042 enlisted men) killed or mortally wounded in defense of the Union during the Civil War. Their names are inscribed in bronze letters on the plinth and globes.

The designers are McKim, Mead & White of New York, who have produced a monolith of polished granite, 41 feet in height and 5 feet 8 inches in diameter, resting upon a circular base, and surrounded by flights of steps. Surmounting this is a winged figure of *Victory*, modeled in bronze by Macmonnies, whose feet are perched upon a globe. While this noble monument, whose total height is 78 feet, is placed with special reference to its aspect from the plain, its magnificent site will make it visible from a long way up the river. It was dedicated in 1897.

A curious round depression in the edge of the campus, which has been felicitously described as "the dimple in the face of the plain," will attract attention just here, and perhaps you will linger a moment to watch the playing in the tennis-courts that occupy it; but in the days of the revolutionary garrison it was *Execution* or *Gallows Hollow*, and no guide-book is needed to tell why. The gun upon its brink is that by which the flag is saluted when, at sunset, the band, or drum corps, plays "down the colors," and evening parade is dismissed. Just beyond, in a grove of fine trees, and with a grand outlook up the Hudson—past Cro' Nest and Storm King on the left, and the Beacons on the right—is

Trophy Point (once *Fort Sherbourne*), crowded with cannons and mortars captured in Mexico. Each bears an engraved legend. In the center of the array, supported upon iron posts, and inclosing some guns captured from the British in the Revolution, is a section of the great **Chain** which was stretched across the river here in 1778. In front of this chain was a heavy boom of logs, a description and pictures of which may be found in Ruttenber's *Obstructions of the Hudson River*.

This chain was forged at the Stirling Iron Works in Orange County, hauled piece by piece to New Windsor, and put together at the military smithy of Capt. Machin. It was then floated down as a whole, and placed in position without delay or breakage. Each winter the chain and boom were unmoored, taken up to the beach, in the cove now crossed by the railroad tracks, and piled up out of reach of the moving ice until ready to be replaced in the spring. Boynton gives the following particulars:

"The chain and boom were fastened, when in position, to cribbage blocks, the remains of which are yet" [1863] "visible in the little cove, just above the boat-house, on Constitution Island, and directly across from the 'Chain Battery,' yet in existence, and near which the south end was secured. Sixteen links of the chain yet remain united, at West Point, including a swivel and clevis. Two of the largest links weigh, respectively, 130 and 129 pounds, while the medium weight is 114 pounds. The whole chain is said to have weighed 186 tons. In removing the boom finally, a portion of it became detached, and the logs, being water-soaked, sank to the bottom of the river, where, after being washed by the tide for eighty years, they have been, in part, recovered."*

---

* These portions are preserved at The Headquarters, Newburgh.

Just below Trophy Point is the **Seacoast Battery,** whose guns point up the river. The name comes from the "Seacoast" guns with which the battery was first armed, and with which the cadets practiced in firing at the target visible upon the face of Cro' Nest. But these old-fashioned cannon have been replaced by rifles of large caliber, mounted upon modern carriages. A battery has occupied this commanding site since the Revolution; and below it is another, the Water Battery.

The buildings surrounded by a castellated wall, on the western side of Trophy Point, form the *Ordnance and Artillery Laboratory*, and were built in 1840, when artillery and cavalry drill were first added to the military curriculum of the Academy. They are used for making and storing ammunition, and for instruction in the fabrication of arms and projectiles, and are not open to the public. Beyond are seen the gas-works, the coal-hoisting apparatus, the excellent public *restaurant*, and the wide flats which have been recently filled in. All this low-lying part of the reservation, which reaches northward to the base of the hills, is styled *Camptown*—not because a camp is, or ever was, there, but after the name of an early settler on that slope. Along the higher ground beyond stand various laboratories, storehouses, soldiers' barracks, and the residences of the families of enlisted men, laundresses, etc., extending to the *Cemetery.*

Resuming his walk, the visitor comes speedily to the *northwest corner* of the plain, and stops to admire Launt Thompson's vigorous **Statue of Sedgwick**—a bronze presentment of the commander of the renowned Sixth Corps of the Army of the Potomac, erected by that corps "in loving admiration." It is a noble figure, with the steadfastness of the man's character and the excitement of battle in its pose.

An *obelisk* to the memory of *Lieut.-Col. E. W. Wood*, who was killed at Fort Erie, in Canada, in 1814, formerly stood near here, but was moved to the cemetery in 1885.

Officers' Row has now been reached—a line of comfortable, plain residences, built, for the most part, more than fifty years ago, in which many tenants whose names are bright on the rolls of the American army have succeeded one another. The house near this corner, having somewhat larger grounds, and distinguished by the super-solemn and extra-elegant sentry pacing before the gate, is that of the commandant of the Post. These

VIEW UP HUDSON RIVER, FROM HOTEL, WEST POINT.

residences continue northward for some distance around the curve in the road, which will take you directly to the gates of the

Post Cemetery, half a mile distant. If you have an hour to spare, this cemetery is well worth a visit. Among its many monuments, the most notable is that erected by the cadets to their comrade, Vincent M. Lowe, who was killed by the premature discharge of a cannon in 1817. It is known as the *Cadets' Monument,* bears the names of several other officers more lately inscribed upon it, and overshadows the grave of Miss Susan Warner, the novelist. To no one, however, can this lovely "bivouac of the slain" appeal with the sensation that it does to an old resident. The latest addition is the monument to Keyes.

"West Point," exclaims Prof. Bailey, in his *Reminiscences,* "is the saddest place in the world. When I go back, I feel like Rip Van Winkle after his sleep in those mystic mountains dimly seen up the river. Here is the old routine of long years ago; precisely the same calls, the same parades, and in precisely the same places; but the actors, where are they? Go out to the cemetery yonder; that peaceful, silent spot, so pathetic with the names of the dead. . . . Where is there a spot more sacred? Here lies the trusty Anderson, with the simple record: 'Fort Sumter, 1861.' Brave officer, simple-hearted gentleman, all honor to his memory! Near by is the tomb of the great commander, Gen. Winfield Scott. . . . Here is buried Quincy A. Gillmore—his grave, this last summer, still covered with the memorial flowers of the Grand Army. The dashing Custer lies here; Buford, the true and brave; Alonzo H. Cushing, 'faithful unto death at Gettysburg'; Gen. Cuvier Grover; Sykes, that glorious hero of a hundred battles—his monument is 'erected by loving comrades.' These, and many more no less worthy, here 'sleep their last sleep'! In this final repose there is no distinction of rank. We note the names of many enlisted men, true in their station, as I am proud to say those regulars always were. Old Twiggs could play the traitor himself, but not a man did he tempt over with him."

In front of the officers' quarters, a line of iron benches extends along the east side of the campus, beneath noble elms. This is the proper place to watch the infantry drills, and to see the dressparades, which, on gala days, are formed facing this row. Passing along it, the visitor sees before him, on the south side of the plain, the *Thayer Monument,* the new *Gymnasium,* the great *Cadet Barracks,* and the new *Academy Building.*

The Monument to Col. Thayer, "Father of the Academy," whose early influence has been described, is a granite figure, draped in a military cloak, which merits the admiration it receives, and is finely placed amid the trees.

The Gymnasium is an imposing double-towered structure of stone, after designs by R. M. Hunt, first occupied in 1893. It stands upon ground formerly occupied by a dwelling-house, some of whose early occupants were Gens. Keyes, McDowell, and McClellan. It is equipped with the best of apparatus, and the gymnastic training here given, including fencing, sword-play, and swimming, is regarded as a most important part of cadet training, especially in the earlier years of the course. Dancing is also taught systematically. The building behind it is the Cadet Quartermaster Store.

The great quadrangular, castellated, Tudoresque structure of the **Cadet Barracks** comes next. It was completed in 1849, and is 360 x 60 feet in dimensions, with a wing 100 x 60 feet. The four stories hold 176 rooms, 136 of which are cadet quarters. *Every one* is prohibited from entering the building during study hours, and it contains little, if anything, to interest the casual visitor.

The *corps of cadets* may include 371, but rarely exceeds 300. They present themselves for examination in June, and if passed and admitted are quartered in the barracks, and undergo preliminary "setting-up" exercises and drills while the upper three classes are in camp. At the end of summer, they are assigned rooms and places in the battalion, and constitute the fourth class. "Two persons are assigned to each room, and the entire furniture consists of two iron bedsteads, chairs, tables, and a few other necessary articles. The cadet is not allowed to have a waiter, a horse, or dog, but is required to make his own bed and keep his quarters tidy. He is aroused at 6 o'clock in the morning by the drums. At twenty minutes past 6 his room must be in order, bedding folded, and wash bowl inverted. Woe betide him if he be dilatory! He is visited by a superior, who reports his delinquency, or, as he would more vividly say, 'skins' him. At half-past 6 he goes to breakfast, returning shortly before 7; then an hour for recreation, and then five hours for recitations, class parades, and other duties. The time between noon and 2 P. M. is allowed for dinner and recreation. Academic work is over at 4 o'clock, and the rest of the day is occupied by drills, amusements, and dress-parade. Lights are extinguished in quarters at 10, and the embryo soldier is supposed to go to sleep."

It is to be feared that he does not always do so. Stories of stealthy midnight expeditions intent on the "hazing" of some unfortunate youngster, or to enjoy that mysterious edible compound, mixed in a wash-basin, known as "cadet hash," form a part of all the traditions of the Point. But these offenses against discipline are less frequent than formerly. The young men nowadays seem more enlightened and steadier, and even the wildest spirits appreciate thoroughly their privileges and responsibilities. A better sentiment has grown up as to hazing, which is nearly extinct. The "reduction of a plebe to his proper level of absolute insignificance" is brought about soon enough in the course of drill. The restriction of the cadet to "limits," which by no means include the whole of the reservation, and his total lack of money, are other powerful obstacles to forbidden pleasures and contraband indulgence of the appetite. He is paid $45 a month, but never handles a penny of it, all being spent for him by the quartermaster and commissary officers; and he is permitted to receive no money whatever, from home or anywhere else. He even has no pockets in his trousers! Moreover, the cadet is watched by some sort of superior every moment. He awakes, and dresses, and goes to meals; eats and drinks, and marches back again; studies and recites; says his prayers, goes to bed, and attunes his dreams to the word of command, the notes of the bugle, and the tap of the drum. There is scarcely a moment when he is not under eye and liable to correction of deportment by some one who has the power to enforce his hint, or punish the slightest sign of revolt; yet it is all done in so rulable and kindly a way, and is so much a part of the very air they breathe, that a jollier lot of fellows can not be found at any institution in the United States.

The Academic Building, first occupied in 1895, is from the designs of Richard M. Hunt, and was finished by the erection of an imposing clock-tower at the northeast corner. It replaces the fine old structure erected in 1838. It is used wholly for instruction, containing recitation rooms, laboratories, drawing-rooms and other apartments required in the actual college work of the institution. It is not open to visitors, though an officer is permitted to show the ordnance museum, etc., to any one especially interested in such matters.

The *circuit of the plain* has now been completed, and but one thing remains to be done by the conscientious tourist — the visit to

Old Fort Putnam. This ruined fortification, the history of which has already been given, crowns the summit of *Mount Independence*, 495 feet above the river. It is reached by a winding carriage road, which leaves the main street between the Academic Building and Grant Hall, and overlooks the plain, as it ascends, until hidden in the woods of the rocky hillside. Halfway up, the road *crosses* the upland road to Highland Falls; and at that point another road leads off to the left and ascends to the new *Observatory*, which stands upon the site of old Fort Webb, and is furnished with a 12-inch telescope and other high-class instruments for astronomical work. Continuing, certain short cuts may be taken advantage of by pedestrians, and Fort Putnam is finally reached and entered at the old sally-port.

No explanation is required here. One may wander about the ruinous ramparts, peer into the broken casemates, and speculate upon the difficulty of capturing by assault this castle, whose walls are perched upon the very brink of cliffs. It must be remembered that its purpose was to defend the garrison of the Point from a *landward* attack, and not to guard the river, though doubtless some of its guns would have shelled passing vessels very effectively. The view here is said to extend along fifteen miles of the river; but it is more commendable for its picturesque variety than for its breadth, combining in a most winning manner a savagery of nature that has resisted cultivation through two centuries with the perfection of civilization of art upon and along the beautiful river, which here, as everywhere else, is the lodestone that irresistibly attracts back to itself the wandering gaze.

The distance to Fort Putnam is not less than half-a-mile, and the climb is rather steep, so that not less than an hour should be given to this excursion.

The road to Cranston's leads along the edge of the bluff, past the *Hospital*, the residences of officers, and the old Kinsley estate. The last has now been bought by the Government, extending the Military Reservation almost to Cranston's Hotel. There is no interest for the casual sightseer in that direction, beyond the view of the river; but the first of all local traditions lies somewhere down at that end of the present reservation—the shrine of the tutelar saint of West Point, *Benny Havens*.

"Benny Havens," declares Prof. Bailey, "among army men, is a name to conjure by, for even those who never frequented his house, or toasted Gens. Brady or Worth or Scott beneath its roof, or sang *Petite Coquille* in memory of O'Brien, know by tradition of that old haunt and its well-bred keeper. Benny must have been much above the ordinary run of contraband dealers, or barkeepers, to have inspired such esteem in the hearts of our bravest and best. All the old fellows, after graduation, and sometimes after fame had come to them, would find their way back to that secluded spot. What a ring and joy there is to those old verses! How they survive the shocks of time! How we rise to our feet and shout to hear them, as the Frenchman does to his Marsellaise!

> "To our regiments now, fellows, we all must shortly go,
> And look as sage as parsons when they tell of what's below!
> We must cultivate the graces, do everything 'just so,'
> And never talk to ears polite of Benny Havens, O!"

WEST POINT TO NEWBURGH.

Rounding West Point, the steamer turns sharply to the left, bringing into view the two great mountains of the Highlands— *Cro' Nest* and *Storm King*, on the west side of the river, with *Breakneck, Bull Hill*, and *The Beacons* continuing the range northeastward. The rocky eastern shore immediately upon the right, however, is *Constitution Island*, and across this narrow and bent strait in the river was stretched the *chain* that has been described. The guarding redoubts may still be seen at each end of its position.

Little of the military post is visible from the water level. Some dwelling-houses along the south bluff, the headquarters' offices, and the battlemented walls of the new Academy Building; the riding halls and stables on the bluff; the hotel on the point; glimpses of a monument or two, and some foliage-hidden batteries, with a view of the laboratories and soldiers' quarters of "Camptown," north of the parade; and, finally, the white monuments of the cemetery, serve only to give the traveler who passes in a steamer an idea of the attractive as well as strategic situation of this famous post in the Highlands. The passenger on the Hudson River Railroad cars sees a few more roofs than are visible from the steamer; but he who travels by the West Shore Railroad sees very little. It runs along the base of the south bluff, and then passes beneath the parade through a long, curving, smoky tunnel; and its construction here, as often elsewhere, has sadly marred the beauty of the banks.

Constitution Island is a mass of rocks, inclosing considerable arable land, and separated from the mainland by marshes over which the railway now passes upon a causeway. It was anciently known as Marteler's Rock, after a Frenchman named Martelaire, who lived there about 1720.* The change of name and the revolutionary history of the island have been recounted; and nothing would remain to say of interest, were it not that for

---

*So says Boynton, but other explanations of equal authenticity have been given.

many years this secluded place was the home of that Warner family, all of whom were literary, and one, Miss Susan B. Warner, attained to fame, thirty years ago, by the novel, *The Wide, Wide World.* It was long and "slow," but, in defiance of critics and canons, attained a popularity never reached by any other book by an American woman (or man, perhaps), except *Uncle Tom's Cabin*, over 250,000 copies having been sold. It was published in 1857, and followed by *Queechy, Say and Seal*, and many other stories and religious books, which had a varied success. Miss Warner died in 1885, and is buried, as she wished to be, near the Cadets' Monument at West Point. The house is on the southern shore of the island, and is still occupied, but is so ensconced by trees as to be nearly invisible. Miss Warner's sister *Anna* was also a novelist, and in the hills behind the island formerly lived another talented spinster—Clara Louise Kellogg.

Beyond Constitution Island, a deep cove penetrates the eastern shore. Into it flows a brook, at the mouth of which is the once famous, and still prosperous, *West Point Foundry*, while just beyond it the valley is filled with the cheerful village of Cold Spring.

Cold Spring is an old and inviting, but not very progressive, little town, which takes its name from a powerful spring near the railroad station, and its reputation from its great foundries, whose flaming chimneys often cast brilliant reflections, at night, far out upon the river, giving a startling appearance to the dark crags thus lit up.

"*Night in the Highlands*, indeed, is scarcely less lovely than the day. The river breaks with faintest murmur on the precipitous shore; the walls of the mountains are an impenetrable blackness, against which the starry path overhead looks the more lustrous. Trembling echoes strike the hillsides plaintively, as a great steamer cleaves her way up the stream, or a towboat, with a string of canalboats in her wake, struggles against the tide, while fleets of sailing-vessels drift past."

In 1828, Gouverneur Kemble brought here, from New York, the plant of an iron foundry, to which he gave the name "West Point." Later, his relatives, the Pauldings, came in, one of whom was that literary J. K. Paulding whose home will be seen at Hyde Park. Then Major Parrott, artillery officer, also connected by marriage, was introduced to the firm; and he gave the West Point foundry a world-wide reputation by the invention and manufacture, just before the Civil War, of the Parrott gun, the principle of which was the strengthening of the breech by shrinking upon it a broad tire of forged steel. Here, during the war, were cast cannons, shot, and shell, to the exclusion of almost everything else; but since then the casting of machinery has chiefly employed the 200 to 300 men constantly at work.

The village stretches mainly along a single street, reaching for half-a-mile up the glen; and it has one of the finest Episcopal churches in the whole Hudson Valley—a Gothic structure of gray stone, with a lofty spire, which cost half a million, and was the gift of a single parishioner. The population is about twenty-five hundred, and there is a comfortable hotel upon the dock, where minor steamers call.

The bold eminence just north of Cold Spring is **Bull Hill**, lately modernized into the more elegant *Mount Taurus*. It is the continuation of Cro' Nest, is over 1,500 feet high, and extends backward, parallel with the South Beacon. At "Undercliffe," in front of this hill, lived Col. George P. Morris, editor, fifty years ago, of *The New York Mirror;* but more widely remembered as the author of *Woodman, Spare that Tree*, and several other songs that touched the popular heart. It was one of the most spacious and elegant places of its day, and was built by John C. Hamilton, one of the sons of Alexander Hamilton. Its elevated position commands not only one of the most interesting river pictures in the Highlands, but overlooks the parade at West Point, so that the evolutions of the cadets at drill can easily be discerned from the piazza. F. B. James has a house near the river, just here; a little farther on live D. Heusted and E. A. Perkins, in the rear of the rocky cape called *Little Stony Point;* and just beyond Bull Hill, where a road zigzags down between it and the naked, purple cliffs of Breakneck, is *Storm King Station*, on the Hudson River Railroad, forming, in summer, the station, by ferry, for Cornwall.

Cro' Nest and Storm King.—All this time the massive, rounded crags of Crow Nest and Storm King mountains overshadow the river on the left, not leaving room even for the West Shore Railroad, which has partly hacked out a pathway along their bases.

The former, now usually written *Cro' Nest*, is an ancient name, probably borrowed from the red men, and simply notes the

VIEW NORTH FROM UPPER ROAD, WEST POINT.

abundance of crows on that eminence, as *Eagle Valley*, between Cro' Nest and Storm King, was noted as a breeding-place of eagles—a bird once extremely abundant all along the Hudson, and still often seen. The name *Cro' Nest* is applied to the whole massive ridge fronting the river for two miles or more, and attaining a height at one point of 1,416 feet.

"Here, as elsewhere in the neighborhood, crack-brained speculators have searched for Capt. Kidd's buried treasure, and the river front of the Cro' Nest is called *Kidd's Plug Cliff*, on the supposition that a mass of projecting rock, on the face of the precipice, formed a plug to the orifice where the pirate's gold was hidden."

THE CULPRIT FAY.

Cro' Nest is linked in English literature with Joseph Rodman Drake's fairy story in verse, *The Culprit Fay*. It was written in a spirit of bravado, when the author was only twenty-one years old, to sustain his contention that it was just as possible to place the scene of a romance among the unstoried American hills as among those of Europe, where every pinnacle, slope, and valley was a memento of suggestive deeds. This discussion happened during a memorable walk through the Highlands, in 1816, of a party in which were Drake, Washington Irving, Fitz-Greene Halleck, and J. Fenimore Cooper; and, to confute his elders, the audacious young poet wrote, in three days, one of the most charming poems in the English language. Drake, who became a physician, and lived only until 1820, published some other good things, notably the poem to the American flag, beginning:

> When Freedom, from her mountain height,
> Unfurled her banner to the skies;

but *The Culprit Fay* is that by which he is, and will long be, remembered. "It was a sudden and brilliant flash of a highly poetical mind, which was extinguished before its powers were fully expanded." Its action and sentiment have been admirably sketched in the following language:

"The story is of simple construction: The fairies who live on Cro' Nest are called together at midnight to sit in judgment on one of their number who has broken his vow. He is sentenced to perform a most difficult task, and evil spirits of air and water oppose him in his mission of penance. He is sadly baffled and tempted, but at length conquers all difficulties, and his triumphant return is hailed with dance and song.

"These Cro' Nest fairies are a dainty and luxurious race. Their lanterns are owlets' eyes. Some of them repose in cobweb hammocks, swung on tufted spears of grass, and rocked by the zephyrs of a midsummer night. Others have beds of lichen, pillowed by the breast plumes of the humming-bird. A few, still more luxurious, find couches in the purple shade of the four-o'clock, or in the little niches of rock lined with dazzling mica. Their tables, at which they drink dew from the buttercups, are velvet-like mushrooms, and the king's throne is of sassafras and spicewood, with tortoise-shell pillars, and crimson tulip-leaves for drapery. 'But the quaint shifts, and the beautiful outfit of the Culprit himself,' says a writer on Drake, ' comprise the most delectable imagery of the poem. He is worn out with fatigue and chagrin at the very commencement of his journey, and therefore makes captive a spotted toad, by way of steed. Having bridled her with a silk-weed twist, his progress is made, rapidly, by dint of lashing her sides with an osier thong. Arrived at the beach, he launches fearlessly upon the tide, for, among his other accomplishments, the Fay is a graceful swimmer; but his tender limbs are so bruised by leeches, star-fishes, and other watery enemies that he is soon driven back.

"'The cobweb lint and balsam dew of sorrel and henbane speedily relieve the little penitent's wounds, and, having refreshed himself with the juice of the calamus-root, he returns to the shore, and selects a neatly-shaped mussel-shell, brilliantly painted without, and tinged with a pearl within. Nature seemed to have formed it expressly for a fairy-boat. Having notched the stern, and gathered a colen bell to bail with, he sculls into the middle of the river, laughing at his old foes as they grin and chatter around his way. There, in the sweet moonlight, he sits until a sturgeon comes by, and leaps, all glistening, into the silvery atmosphere; then, balancing his delicate frame upon one foot, like a Lilliputian Mercury, he lifts the flowery cup and catches the one sparkling drop that is to wash the stain from his wing.

"'Gay is his return voyage. Sweet nymphs clasp the boat's side with their tiny hands, and cheerily urge it onward.

"'His next enterprise is of a more knightly species, and he proceeds to array himself accordingly, as becomes a fairy cavalier. His acorn helmet is plumed with thistle-down, a bee's nest forms his corselet, and his cloak is of butterfly-wings. With a ladybug's shell for a shield, and a wasp-sting lance, spurs of cockle-seed, a bow made of vine twig strung with maize silk, and well supplied with nettle shafts, he mounts his firefly, and, waving his blade of blue-grass, speeds upward to catch a glimmering spark from some flying meteor. Again the spirits of evil are let loose upon him, and the upper elements are not more friendly than those below. A sylphid queen enchants him by her beauty and kindness. But though she played very archly with the butterfly-cloak, and handled the tassel of his blade while he revealed to her pitying ears the dangers he had passed, the memory of his first love and the object of his pilgrimage kept his heart free. Escorted with great honor by the sylph's lovely train, his career is resumed, and his flame-wood lamp at length rekindled, and before the sentry-elf proclaims a streak in the eastern sky, the culprit has been welcomed to all his original glory.'"

Next north of Cro' Nest, the rocks rise to an even greater height in a rounded pile which some of the early Dutchmen called *The Klinkenberg* (meaning "Echo Mount," and usually misspelled "Klinkerberg"), and others *Butter Hill*. The country people still hold to the last name, indeed, explaining that the height resembles a market-roll of butter in its dome-like roundness—a notion that dates back to very early times. N. P. Willis, however, succeeded in fastening upon it the new name *Storm King*, as a term befitting its dignity, not only, but expressive of the fact that it is an unfailing weather-gauge to all the country north of it. The highest point of Storm King is somewhat inland, and may easily be reached by a plain path which ascends from near the Mountain House, in Cornwall. Next southwest of this mountain is the still loftier eminence *Black Rock*, whose round poll can be seen peering over the crest of Storm King from the south, and stands out in plain view from the north.

The straight space of river in front of these mountains used to be known to the old-time sloop captains as Vorsen's Reach; and to the rugged headland opposite, whose precipices are too steep to bear much vegetation, was given the name *Breakneck*, so long ago that the time and the reason are both forgotten, for the modern yarn about some old Dutchman chasing a runaway bull over Mount Taurus, until it hurled itself off the crags of the next mountain and broke its neck, is nonsense. A century ago it was known as *The Turk's Face*, owing to a remarkable image of a human countenance, formed by projecting rocks on the south side, where now a huge purplish wall of bare rock testifies to the ravages of stone-quarrying; but this was long ago tumbled down by the operations of blasting. This Turk's Face, or Breakneck Mountain, is the counterpart of Storm King, and the range continues northward in a chain of summits that form the water-shed between the Hudson and the Croton rivers, in Dutchess County—which begins at this point on the river.

These mountains are very rough, and quite uninhabited and wild. A road creeps around their base, however, and paths ascend to their summits, which align themselves into a very prominent and handsome range, as the steamer sails out of this "northern gate of the Highlands into the ampler breadth called Newburgh Bay."

With the help of **Pollopel's Island**, an outlying projection of Breakneck—passed just here—this "northern gateway of the Highlands" was obstructed in 1779 by the *chevaux de-frise*, fragments of which may be examined in the museum at the Headquarters in Newburgh. They consisted of massive iron-pointed pikes, about thirty feet long, secured at the bottom in cribs filled with stones, and slanted so that their points came just at the surface of the water. The British sailors found little difficulty in passing this obstruction under the guidance of a deserter, after their capture of the Highland forts, and the cribs were gradually destroyed by ice, or removed. Later, Pollopel's Island was probably used as a place of confinement for prisoners of war, and it is now an occasional picnic resort.

Cornwall appears, as the steamer gets farther on, thickly set along the base of Storm King, which extends backward in a lofty ridge. Here, fifty-three miles from New York, is a busy landing and railway station, where the *New York, Ontario & Western Railway*—whose trains run between this point and New York (Weehawken) over the tracks of the West Shore Railroad—leaves the river for the interior of the State, and to a connection with the Canadian Pacific's transcontinental system on the St. Lawrence River.

The extensive pier which this company built in 1892, to form a tide-water terminus for the delivery of coal and other freight, is seen a few rods northward. Nearly all of the minor lines of steamboats stop here; but the Albany day-line does not do so, landing only at Newburgh, two miles beyond. Great quantities of small fruit are sent away from here, in spring and summer, to New York, and the place is the most populous summer resort upon the river.

Cornwall-on-the-Hudson lies along the sloping base of Storm King, the best houses and hotels occupying a table-land that overlooks the Hudson and the pretty valley of the Moodna. Nathaniel P. Willis styled this plateau the Highland Terrace, and said that the curving mountains bent about it seemed "like a waving arm, like a gesture from Nature, and an invitation to come and look around you." Willis himself made his home here in a many-gabled cottage designed by Calvert Vaux—since celebrated as an architect, and the designer of Central Park, New York—who was then a young man in Newburgh. It is now occupied by William A. Hudson, and has many nearer neighbors than when Willis lived and wrote there during the last fifteen years of his life, and loved it for its real remoteness, although within sight of "the thronged thoroughfare of the Hudson." Nearer the mountain, and perhaps a mile from the landing, is the home and fruit farm of the late *Rev. E. P. Roe*, who was, perhaps, the most popular and influential American novelist of his day. Somewhat beyond his estate, on the slope of *Deer Hill* —the small foot-hill projecting conspicuously into the valley— still dwells another well-known novelist—Mrs. Amelia E. Barr— in a locality distinguished as Cornwall Heights.

The vicinity of Cornwall is a little literary Parnassus in itself. Edward W. Bok, in a chatty article in the Chicago *Herald*, thus described the authors' homes there:

"It is now nearly forty-five years ago since Nathaniel P. Willis first made known his 'Idlewild' retreat, and more than twenty-five years have passed since he left it to be taken to Mount Auburn, near Boston. The 'Idlewild' of to-day is still green to the memory of the poet. Since Willis' death the place has passed in turn into various hands, until now it is the home of a wealthy New York lawyer, who has spent thousands of dollars on the house and grounds. The old house still stands, and here and there in the grounds remains a suggestion of the time of Willis. The famous pine drive leading to the mansion, along which the greatest literary lights of the Knickerbocker period passed during its palmy days, still remains intact, the dense growth of the trees only making the road the more picturesque. The brook at which Willis often sat still runs on through the grounds as of yore. In the house, everything is remodeled and remodernized. The room from whose windows Willis was wont to look over the Hudson, and where he did most of his charming writing, is now a bedchamber, modern in its every appointment, and suggesting its age only by the high ceiling and curious mantel. Visitors are now denied the grounds—a forbidding sign announcing to the wanderer that the 125 acres of 'Idlewild' are 'Private Grounds.' This restriction was found necessary, one of the occupants informed me, because of the liberties taken by visitors, who still come, almost every week, to see the place made famous by 'the dude poet of the Hudson,' as he is still called by the old residents of Cornwall. Only a few city blocks from 'Idlewild' is the house where lived E. P. Roe, the author of so many popular novels, as numerous, almost, in number as the several hundreds of thousands of circulation which they secured. The Roe house is unoccupied, and has been since the death of the novelist. For a time, the widow and some members of the family resided there, but Mrs. Roe now lives in New York, and the Cornwall place is for sale. There are twenty-three acres to it in all, and, save what was occupied by the house, every inch of ground was utilized by the novelist in his hobby for fine fruits and rare flowers. Now nothing remains of the beauty once so characteristic of the place. For four years the grounds have missed the care of their creator. Where once were the novelist's celebrated strawberry beds, are now only grass and weeds. Everything is grown over, only a few trees remaining as evidence that the grounds were ever known for their cultivated products. A large board sign announces the fact that the entire place is for sale.

"Away up on the mountain-side, flanked on the right by Storm King Mountain and on the left by Deer Hill, is the pretty roadside cottage home of Amelia E. Barr. The place is a mute testimony of the novelist's success, it having been bought by her, last spring, from the profits of her literary work. It stands some 600 feet above the Hudson, with a view of landscape that stretches to the Catskills. Here, where one feels closer to his Creator and farther from his fellow-men, Mrs. Barr writes the stories which bring her an income of over $8,000 a year, and make her one of the most successful novelists of the day."

The beauty of its situation renders Cornwall a fashionable resort during the summer, when its many beautiful residences are the scene of a constant round of gaiety. The entertainment of summer visitors has become the characteristic business of the town. About 5,000 persons annually take their summer abode here, and the permanent population has increased, within a few years, to about 3,000 souls. The hotels and boarding-houses do not reach the magnificent proportions of some of the Saratoga hotels, but are neat and convenient. There are several schools and churches, a savings bank, public library and reading-room in the village.

The neighborhood abounds in varied and interesting drives over good roads, which wind about the broad valley of the Moodna, where almost every house, glen, and hilltop has some memory of the patriot army and the war for American independence. Especially noteworthy are "the Montana drive, which is one of the most romantic and picturesque in the district; the Moodna drive, traversing the bed of the glen through a labyrinth of groves and sylvan grottoes; and also the drive to Orange Lake through one of the most fertile valleys in the State, the road leading through a continuous chain of stock farms and waving fields of ripe golden grain." A new road has just been completed across the mountains to West Point, but is said, by impartial travelers, to fall far short of the praise that it has received. It is no better than the old road from Cornwall to Cranston's and West Point, and that is dangerous for light vehicles in several places, and utterly useless for bicycling. Country lanes and by-paths invite those who enjoy rambling afoot to explore the shaggy heights of Storm King and the Schunemunk, whose blue height is seen inland, broadside on; or to wander into valley nooks, away from the dusty highways. (Read Roe's *Nature's Serial Story* for the local scenery.) One needs only to be a student of colonial history, and a reader of Willis, to find here a parallel to the peculiar attractiveness more widely felt toward Tarrytown. The camp of the Continental army, in 1782–83, spoken of farther on, is just as accessible from here as from Newburgh.

One sees nothing of Cornwall from the West Shore Railroad, which follows the beach; and not much is learned of it from the boats, or the distant eastern shore; but a grand mountain view develops as the Highlands are gradually left behind. The mouth of the *Moodna* (another of Willis' names—it was always *Murderer's Creek* before his time), *Plum Point*, and *New Windsor* are passed in succession.

New Windsor became prominent in revolutionary annals, when it was the home of the Clintons, and the birthplace of De Witt Clinton, the famous "canal" governor of the State in after years.

From the campaign of 1777 on, these broad valleys on both sides of the river, along the northern base of the Highlands, were the scene of constant musterings of soldiers and war-like operations; and in June, 1779, Washington came to reside at New Windsor, taking Thomas Ellison's, on the hill immediately south of the village, as his headquarters; while his generals, Knox, Lafayette, and others, were nearer their respective commands, up the Moodna valley, on the Fishkill shore, or in the mountains. Here he and Wayne planned the capture of Stony Point, and here he himself was nearly captured by treachery. This house was undermined not long ago and destroyed by the digging of the clay-pits. Washington left New Windsor the following winter and summer, but returned in the autumn of 1780, and made ready for the southern campaign of the next summer—which resulted in the capture of Cornwallis—and from which the army returned to encamp for the winter in the valley of the Moodna, above New Windsor, while Washington resided at Newburgh, as we shall presently see.

The City of Newburgh has already attracted the attention of all travelers, since it covers the slope of a wide hillside along the western bank of the river, with a long water-front crowded with shipping, and tier upon tier of business and residential streets rising to the crest of the ridge. On the opposite (eastern) shore of the river (*Newburgh Bay*) is *Fishkill*.

Newburgh is beautiful for situation. The site rises from the margin of the river, here 1¼ miles wide, in a series of terraces that well display the city from the water, and make it a brilliant spectacle when lighted up at night. Its *water-front* is crowded for two miles with wharves, warehouses, factories, and railway structures, which hide to some extent the business streets; but these are mainly narrow, and irregular, and unattractive. Higher up are the residences, standing in tiers along the hillside, where broad, well-shaded, and smoothly graded avenues are modern and most pleasant in appearance, and are studded with the churches and schools whose spires are conspicuous from the river. There are two parks, and *capital roads for driving* in all directions. Water is pure and abundant, and the drainage is natural and thorough; the city is lighted by gas and electricity, has street cars in all directions, a capable police and fire brigade, and a watchful Board of Health. Its seven public schools are of a high order. One among them, the *Glebe School*, in Clinton Street, is the regular successor of a series of schools, which began in 1752, and was sustained by a part of the revenues of the Glebe lands, appropriated by the Government for the support of divine service and teaching in the infant colony. Another is the *Newburgh Academy*, which also grew out of the Glebe funds, about 1790, and was the first institution of higher learning in all this region. It is now the city's high school, and occupies a new and commodious building on Montgomery Street. To these must be added three schools under the care of the Roman Catholic churches, and eight private schools, notable among which are

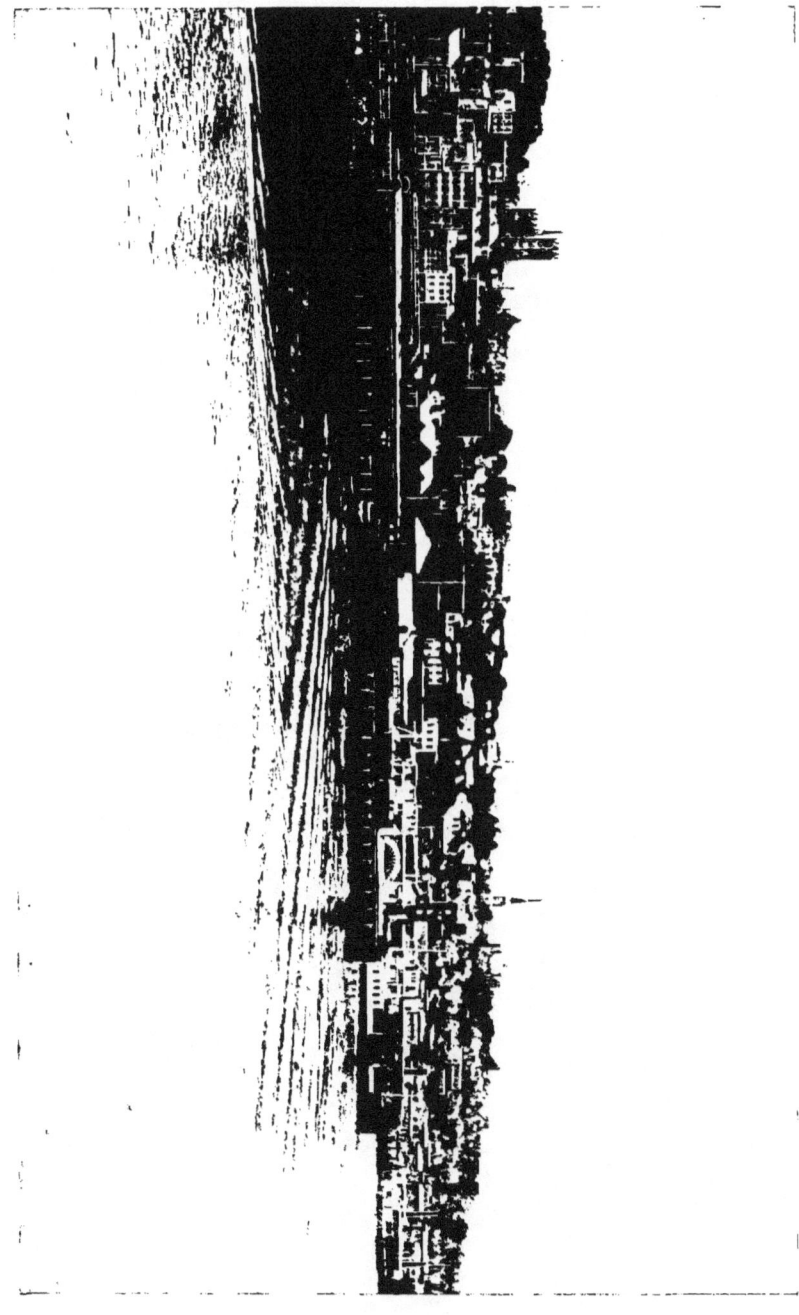

Mount St. Mary's Academy and Miss Mackie's for girls, and Siglar's preparatory school for boys. Besides this, the city well supports a *Free Library and Reading-room*, with over 17,000 volumes—one of the most admirable public libraries in the eastern United States; it is at No. 100 Grand Street. Music also receives a large amount of attention, and there is a pretty theater.

Newburgh is the home of many wealthy and refined families, and the amenities of life are cultivated.

Among her citizens of wide repute were *Joel T. Headley*, the author of many works of history, biography, and travel—written in a popular manner—and one of the earliest exponents of the beauty of the Upper Hudson and the Adirondacks. Mr. Headley lived here over thirty years, and died at the age of ninety-five. Other citizens of note have been Henry Kirke Brown, the sculptor; Charles and Andrew Downing, pomologists and landscape gardeners; Judge J. Monell, the jurist, and many others.

The *City Club*, at Grand and Third streets, is the leading social club; while the extraordinary local interest in outdoor sports, and particularly those of an aquatic kind, has led to the organization of several clubs for yachting, rowing, canoeing, etc. The *Palatine*, on Grand Street, is the newest hotel, and one of the finest in the Hudson Valley. The old United States is near Fishkill ferry.

HISTORICAL SKETCH.—Newburgh occupies almost the only spot upon the western shore of the river, between Kingston and Jersey City, where a great town could be situated, accessible by passable wagon roads to the interior. It has therefore excelled, from the first, as a trading town. Settled in the beginning (1709) by refugees from the Palatinate, who were given lands along Quassaick Creek by Queen Anne, these were gradually outnumbered by Dutch, Scotch, and English accessions, forming a community "diligent in business." Before the Revolution, the farmers of all the back country brought hither their produce for sale or shipment; the lumber and stave trade became important; ships were built that engaged in the Liverpool and West Indian trading, and the town was even a whaling port of some account. During the latter part of the Revolutionary War, Newburgh and Fishkill were the center of the most active operations. This meant an increase of trade and wealth for both farmers and citizens; and, as the place escaped direct devastation by the British, after the fall of the forts in the Highlands, it was in better condition than many other of the river villages to go ahead when peace presented the opportunity. With the opening of this century, Newburgh became a village separate from the township—the third in the State to receive that distinction. It then had some 1,500 inhabitants, and contained several churches, an academy, a post office, newspaper (the *Packet*), a fire company, and was filled with enterprise. Its citizens promoted and mainly built the Cochecton turnpike, which brought them a large amount of trade from the west which theretofore had gone to New Windsor, and that ambitious rival was forever left behind. The opening of other turnpikes followed, and Newburgh speedily became the most important trading and export point on the river, where the shipping was steadily increased to meet the growing demands of both passenger and freight traffic. Until 1830, sailing-vessels, chiefly sloops, carried the produce to New York, and returned with merchandise to be forwarded to the interior or sold in the local shops; but after 1830 steamboats took their place for all local traffic, and those of the Newburgh lines were the crack boats of the day. The streets leading to the docks were frequently blocked for hours with farmers' and freighters' wagons, coming in long processions from the interior of the State, and even from Northern New Jersey and Pennsylvania, to deposit and renew their loads at the wharves; and the turnpike resounded with clattering coaches, which ran thence to many interior towns, and connected through them to the West; for the shortest route from New York to Buffalo at that time was by way of Newburgh and Ithaca.

"But the completion of the Erie Canal diverted most of this great trade through other channels; and on the night when the waters of Lake Erie mingled with those of the Atlantic, in the harbor of New York, with beacon-fires blazing on the headlands along the Hudson, Newburgh rolled up and laid away its map of the Southern Tier. Considerable travel by stage-coach continued until the opening of railroads through the center of the State, and a large trade remained with the southeastern portion of this State and neighboring portions of New Jersey and Pennsylvania; but the Delaware & Hudson Canal at length penetrated this region, and cut off another source of wealth. Efforts were made to repair the loss thus sustained, by the organization of a company to engage in whale-fishing, and by endeavoring to secure the establishment here of a Government navy-yard. The former enterprise, however, met with limited success, and the proposal to establish a navy-yard did not receive the favor of the Government. The construction of the Erie Railroad from Goshen to Piermont, and its subsequent extension in other directions, took away the last vestige of the ancient trade of Newburgh, and the old stage-coaches, and the long lines of farmers' wagons, with their stores of butter and pork, became but a memory."

"But," adds the author of *Newburgh**—from which the pre-

---

* NEWBURGH: *Her Institutions, Industries, and Leading Citizens.* By JOHN J. NUTT. Quarto, Illustrated, pp. 335. Newburgh: Ritchie & Hull, 1891.

ceding words were quoted—"another change has come; a new era has dawned; the tidal wave of prosperity that swept over the village 100 years ago has returned. The old turnpikes have been paralleled with railroads, stretching to us from every direction; and the river, too, gives communication with the Atlantic Coast and all the world."

In *sport*, Newburgh has always taken a prominent place. The first general rowing regatta on the Hudson was held there in 1837, succeeded by others in 1840, 1841, and 1842, which excited great public interest. By this time, special oarsmen had been developed, and the gay popular contests among amateurs degenerated into races between professionals, among whom were such leading men as the Wards, the Donoghues, and others of international repute. Walter Brown was also a Newburgh man; and the great sculling race between him and Hamill, run here in 1867, will be recalled by boatmen. Yachting never reached so far, but in the '70's some good races were seen in the bay, and here, in 1877, catamarans were first admitted as a class. Speed-skating, as a sport, originated here, where June, Shaw, the Donoghues, and other famous skaters won their first laurels, and then went forth to compete successfully with Canadian and European champions; and here is still the headquarters of professional skating.

Newburgh is a station on the West Shore Railroad, and a terminus of the Erie and of the New York, Ontario & Western Rd., which connect, by ferry transfer, with the New York & New England Railroad on the other side of the river.

The town has electric cars, which run from Balmville, north of the city, to the southern extremity, and out Broadway to *Orange Lake*, a picnic and fishing place seven miles west, and on to *Walden*, on the Walkill Valley Rd., fourteen miles from Newburgh. This line has cars, in summer, every half hour, and offers a pleasant excursion through charming scenery.

The driving excursions possible in the neighborhood of Newburgh are among its special attractions. Excellent roads run in every direction through a district of country-seats and neat dairy farms, here descending into some romantic glen, there coming out upon a knoll where the river and the mountains are displayed in some new aspect of beauty. Northward, two lovely roads extend parallel for several miles, lined with well-kept estates, some of which are remarkable for effects in landscape gardening and scientific horticulture. Passing the site of *Wiegand's* old log-house, where Wayne had his headquarters, and *Hathaway Glen*, the road comes to "the balm-of-Gilead tree"—an immense and aged landmark, giving the name *Balmville* to the suburb. Here several roads diverge to New Paltz, Plattekill,

Modena, and other fruit-growing villages inland; to the up-river towns, and down along the shore past the convent of the Sacred Heart and Roseton.

Southward from Newburgh extend several other broad highways, with many connecting cross-roads. One traverses the manufacturing district along Quassaick Creek, and gets a glimpse of the deep *Vale of Avoca*, where a treacherous attempt to capture Washington at the house of a farmer was frustrated by the man's daughter and the general's cool precautions. "A mile below the vale," says Nutt, "we pass through the ancient village of New Windsor—a little collection of houses on the river shore. The place is now given over to brick-making, but before and during the Revolution it was an important trading village. Its importance then exceeded Newburgh's, and it was predicted it would become the chief city of the central Hudson Valley. A large town was mapped out, and the work of the projectors may be traced in the few remaining streets; but it has its principal existence in old maps of record. In this little hamlet, Gen. James Clinton lived after his marriage, and here his son De Witt was cradled. . . . A mile below New Windsor village is *Plum Point*, a wooded promontory at the mouth of the Moodna, approached over a natural causeway. On Plum Point, in the early part of the war for independence, was erected a battery of fourteen guns, designed to assist in maintaining obstructions to the navigation of the river, which at this point consisted of a *chevaux-de-frise* stretching across to Pollepel's Island. It was known in official orders as Capt. Machin's battery. Outlines of its embrasures are still visible. In the vicinity of the battery are the remains of the cellar of the first dwelling-house in this county. Its owner was Col. Patrick MacGregorie, a Scotch gentleman of fortune, who was chosen leader of a company of persecuted Presbyterians, who emigrated from Scotland, and settled on this beautiful spot."

The northern side of Plum Point is washed by the waters of Waoraneck, or *Murderer's Creek*, to which Willis has fastened the prettier name Moodna. One of its tributaries falls from the grounds of his home, "Idlewild," which is in full view from the point where the road crosses the stream, at the mouth of a deep glen. This road continues southward to Cornwall, and on over the mountains; or one may turn up the Moodna Valley, visit the former headquarters of Lafayette, see the place at the foot of Forge Hill where the chain that crossed the Hudson at West Point was partly put together; and, ascending to the old continental road, on the table-land of New Windsor, visit the famous *Ellison House*, a partly stone, partly frame mansion, built in 1754 by Col. Thomas Ellison (whose earlier residence, near the river, has been mentioned as Washington's headquarters in 1779), in which Gens. Knox, Gates, Greene, and other officers had a military residence at different periods during the active operations here, between 1779 and 1783. It is an excellent example of a substantial, old-fashioned rural home of the better class, and remains very much as it appeared when the brilliant Mrs. Knox gave a party there at which the highest officers of the Continental army and all the sparkling belles and gracious dames of this countryside were entertained. Not far above was the great cantonment of the army during the winter of 1782-83, where, in the large public building on *Temple Hill*, peace was proclaimed to the soldiers, and whence they marched home on furloughs which became perpetual. Many traces of that eventful occupation still remain upon the ground, which is skirted by the Erie Railroad's branches (with a convenient station at *Vail's Gate*); and a large field-monument has been erected by the people of the neighboring towns, under the guidance of the learned local historian, E. M. Ruttenber. All this historic ground is within five miles of Newburgh or Cornwall, and the vicinity of Fishkill is scarcely less interesting.

This fitly introduces the object of chief interest to the stranger in Newburgh:

WASHINGTON'S HEADQUARTERS.

This building, which now forms a *historical museum* of great value, is situated in the southern-central part of the city, and derives its interest from the fact that it was occupied by George Washington, as the general headquarters of the Northern army, from April, 1782, to August, 1783. It stands in plain view from the river, or the Fishkill shore, upon an eminence, the brow of which is adorned by the new *Tower of Victory*, sheltering a statue of the commander-in-chief. Liberty Street trolley-cars pass the gate.

This house was the home of Jonathan Hasbrouck, a farmer, miller, merchant, and leading man in the community; and here, in the early days of the Revolution, many meetings of supervisors and committees of safety were held, and the militia assembled whenever called upon for local service, as often happened. The northeast corner of the building is the oldest portion, and was erected by Hasbrouck in 1750; the southeast corner was added in 1760, the west half in 1770, and the whole embraced under one roof, the structure of which, as shown in the attic, will interest all builders. The west, or southwest, view is said to give a better idea of the house as it appeared at the time of its occupation by Washington, the west being the true front of the building on Liberty Street, then "the King's highway," or old public road. As described by men who were familiar with the premises from boyhood, there was a front yard on Liberty Street, while immediately south of the house were the barns. East was the family garden, beyond which, between the house and river, was the family burial-plot in which Col. Hasbrouck was buried.

The property was bought by the State of New York in 1849, and placed under the care of a board of trustees, to be preserved as a memorial. It was dedicated in 1850, with impressive ceremonies, Maj.-Gen. Winfield S. Scott formally raising the flag, while an ode was sung. The house has been restored, and maintained in repair, as closely like its original condition, within and without, as possible, and is stored with a large and exceedingly interesting collection of furniture, accouterments, documents, and miscellaneous historical relics, mainly belonging to the revolutionary period. It is under the care of a superintendent, and is open, free, to the public every week-day.

A *descriptive catalogue*, prepared by Dr. E. M. Ruttenber, is sold (price 25 cents), from the preface to which the following facts are selected; it should be purchased by all visitors (the bound copies, 50 cents, contain a historical appendix), not only because of its intrinsic value, but as a modest contribution to the funds for maintaining the museum.

On the 4th of April, 1782, Washington made this building his headquarters, and remained here until August 18, 1783. "While here, he passed through the most trying period of the Revolution—the year of inactivity on the part of Congress, of distress throughout the country, and of complaint and discontent in the army, the latter at one time bordering on revolt among the officers and soldiers; but a period, nevertheless, marked by victories more substantial than those which had been won in the field, as well as by the successful culmination of the long and heroic struggle for national independence."

The general and his family occupied the entire house. The large room entered from the piazza on the east was Washington's dining-room; the northeast room was his bedroom, and the one adjoining it on the left was his private office. The family room was in the southeast, the parlor in the northwest, the kitchen in the southwest corner. Though one of the largest houses of the region, it was so small that a guest could only be accommodated by placing a camp-bed in the parlor, as was done on special occasions. Such a guest, in December, 1782, was the Marquis de Chastellux, one of Rochambeau's officers, who has left the only authoritative account of the domestic life and hospitality of Gen. and Mrs. Washington under these cramped conditions. This officer was struck, moreover, by the admirable discipline at headquarters. "When one sees," he remarks, "a battalion of the general's guard encamped within the precincts of his house; nine wagons, destined to carry his baggage, ranged in his court; a great number of grooms taking care of very fine horses belonging to the general officers and their aids-de-camp; when one observes the perfect order that reigns within these precincts, where the guards are exactly stationed, and where the drums beat an alarm and a particular retreat, one is tempted to apply to the Americans what Pyrrhus said of the Romans: 'Truly these people have nothing barbarous in their discipline.'"

The papers and relics within and without the house are worthy of special examination. The credit for their collection is largely due to the late Enoch Carter of Newburgh, but many accessions have been the gift of others. The printed catalogue gives a particular description of each, and most objects are intelligently labeled.

The *block of brownstone* near the entrance is a monument over the grave of Uzal Knapp, the last survivor of Washington's Life Guard, who died in 1856, ninety-six years old.

The Life Guards were stationed a few rods northwest of Washington's headquarters. They were all native Americans, "sober, young, active, and well made," the pick of the army, and none less than five feet nine inches tall. Their uniform consisted of a blue coat, with white facings, white waistcoat and breeches, black stock and black half-gaiters, and a round hat with blue and white feather. The motto of the corps was, "Conquer or Die." Their number was about sixty. William Colfax was the captain commandant.

The **Tower of Victory** is a memorial monument of artistic interest, standing on the northeast corner of the Headquarters' ground, and overlooking the river, from which it is well seen. It is the result of a movement the design of which was to mark not only that spot, but also the encampment grounds at New Windsor and Fishkill. The final decision was to erect here a single monument, and the matter was placed in the hands of a committee of Congress and the Secretary of War, who approved plans submitted by Maurice J. Power of New York, drawn by John H. Duncan, architect.

It is a stone tower, fifty-three feet high, with four large archways that open into an atrium, and stairways leading into a belvedere. In the center of the atrium is a bronze statue of Washington, copied from Houdon's celebrated model by O'Donovan. Resting in niches in the walls are four bronze figures representing four arms of the service in the army of the Revolution—the dragoon, the artilleryman, the rifleman, and the line officer—dressed in costumes of the times. Four large bronze gates, bearing seals and coats-of-arms of the thirteen original States, guard the approach to the atrium, and are raised and lowered by portcullis. A bronze tablet is set on the exterior east wall, with a figure of Peace in relief. It bears this inscription: "This monument was erected under the authority of the Congress of the United States, and of the State of New York, in commemoration of the disbandment, under proclamation of the Continental Congress of October 18, 1783, of the armies by whose patriotic and military virtue our national independence and sovereignty were established." The total cost was $67,000.

The view from the belvedere of this tower well repays the exertion of climbing the stairways. It extends up-river to where the New Hamburgh shore bends out of view behind Low Point. Now the eye sweeps along a sparsely settled shore, down past Fishkill (opposite), and follows the rampart of the Beacon Hills to where the rough ridges of Breakneck Mountain fall steeply down, opposite the precipices of Storm King. The gap between the two is half filled by the ugly little heap of rocks and brush forming Pollopel's Island, and beyond it the eye sees, far down the stream, the promontory of West Point; and still farther, the curving eastern shore behind Anthony's Nose. The rounded bulk of Storm King is here lifted up to the best advantage, with the houses and gardens of Cornwall scattered like some quaint inscription along its base, and the massive front overhead, "scarred by a hundred wintry water-courses," rounding down with simple dignity to where the Hudson rolls against its deeply buried base. Beyond is Cro' Nest, equally massive, and the two are like the paired paws of some colossal sphinx crouching upon

WASHINGTON'S HEADQUARTERS AT NEWBURGH.

the bank, while its head towers invisible into the vault of heaven. Beneath, pigmy ships go sailing, and over them whirl the clouds, but their passive majesty is unruffled. Inland from these noble headlands, lofty and rugged summits stretch southwestward into Orange County, and the blue rampart of Schunemunk Mount rises across the head of the valley westward, with 'Chattoes Hill as a landmark nearer the city.

Fishkill is a term which applies in a general way to all the shore opposite Newburgh, and to the whole valley of the Matteawan, or Fishkill Creek, along the base of the Fishkill Mountains. The visible settlement at the ferry and railway station is *Fishkill Landing*, or, in the more high-sounding modern phrase, *Fishkill-on-Hudson*. Two miles inland, this village blends with the pleasant manufacturing town *Matteawan*, and three miles farther up-stream is the ancient settlement which was the original "Fishkill," and is now distinguished as *Fishkill Village*. The two last named are stations on the Newburgh, Dutchess & Connecticut Railroad, which connects with the Hudson River Railroad at *Dutchess Junction*, two miles south of Fishkill Landing. There are also electric cars to Fishkill village.

The railway station and landing of the steam ferry to Newburgh (fare 9 cents), at Fishkill Landing, are in connected buildings. Here, also, the line of electric street-cars may be taken, which will carry the passenger through Matteawan to Fishkill Village. Fishkill Landing and Matteawan together contain some 12,000 people, and are busy in trade and manufactures, especially at Matteawan, where the water-power of the picturesque stream is utilized by factories that are overshadowed by elms, and look out upon lovely landscapes that must go far to compensate for confinement at desk and loom within their walls.

Historically, Fishkill is full of interesting associations. The district was purchased from the Indians toward the end of the seventeenth century, and the earliest pioneers of Dutchess County were living at the mouth of Fishkill Creek previous to 1700. By the time of the opening of the Revolution, however, the whole Piedmont district was well-cultivated, populous, and prosperous, with a community mainly Dutch and English.

"*Fishkill Village,*" Ruttenber writes, "was then the largest and most important place in Dutchess County, and most favorably situated for communication with the Eastern States, while its proximity to the forts in the Highlands rendered it not only one of convenience, but one that could readily be covered against marauding attacks by the enemy. These considerations led to its selection (August 28, 1776) . . . as the place to which should be removed the treasury and archives of the State, and as the place for holding the subsequent sessions of the Provincial Convention " [which had been driven out of New York]. " Almost immediately following (August 14th), it was resolved to quarter troops here, establish hospitals, depots for provisions, etc., and convert the place into an armed encampment. From that time until the war closed some portion of the army was constantly here, and its invalid-camp was never without occupants." The two old churches—the Reformed Dutch and the Episcopal—remain, as well as many of the old residences, including the *Wharton House*, where the Committee of Safety held its meetings; the *Verplanck House*, headquarters of Steuben, who used the level plateau near the river, at the foot of the mountains, as a drilling-ground; the *Brinckerhoff House*, headquarters of Washington; the *Brett* (or *Teller*) *House*, which was built in 1709 as the manor-house of the great Rumbout patent; and other historical buildings are still preserved.

At that time, the present Fishkill Landing was represented by a small wharf at *Denning's Point*, the shady little peninsula—with a white house among the trees—jutting out from the shore a mile south of the present long steamboat wharf. Denning's Point was then owned and occupied by Capt. William Denning, an influential patriot and army officer; and it was there the original Newburgh ferry (which had existed under charter for many years previously) made its landing. Two great oaks stood on the point, widely known as *the Washington oaks*, as a reminder of that time; but one of them was blown down a few years ago. In early times the present main road up the hill did not exist, but the road from the landing was that which leads inland north of the present station. The *Verplanck House* still stands, with some additions, on the turnpike to Poughkeepsie, about 1½ miles north of the railway station, and half-a-mile back from the river. It was not only occupied by Baron Steuben, but within its walls was framed the constitution of the Society of the Cincinnati, which was practically organized at Newburgh.

The Beacon Hills.—The finely sculptured range of elevations extending northeastward from here, and forming the front of the Highlands on this side, are known as the Fishkill Mountains, or Beacon Hills. The last name is due to the fact that in the Revolution some of their peaks were prominent stations for the beacons, or signal-fires, which were intended to give warning of any approach by an enemy.

The beacon-pyres were pyramidal in form, made of logs filled in with brush and inflammable materials, and carried to a height of thirty feet; and that upon Butter Hill gave the first signal, to which the others were subordinate. The lofty peak beyond Matteawan, and south of the deep gap in the range there, is still known as the *North Beacon*. South of it, three-quarters of a mile distant, is *South Beacon*. The latter is the higher of the two (1,685 feet), and is the big overtopping hill seen directly west from the railroad or river when at, or opposite, Denning's Point and Dutchess Junction; it is not visible from Fishkill or Matteawan, being hidden by the long ridge of North Beacon. It can be ascended without much difficulty almost anywhere, but most easily from near the terminus of the electric road in Matteawan. Here a road leads up the gulch separating North Beacon (on the right) from Fishkill Mountain. About a mile from the village it forks, and the right branch (which is to be followed) crosses the brook and ascends a side valley dividing North Beacon from Lamb's Hill. Half-a-mile more, in the course of which one gets some very interesting outlooks eastward over the Hudson, Newburgh, and the adjacent country, brings the walker to the reservoir of the Fishkill and Matteawan Water Company, and to "Beacon Inn," the house of the guardian, who sells materials for a mountain luncheon, edible, potable, and fumaceous, and is very accommodating in respect to information. North Beacon is the height behind the cabin, and the road curves to the right, and leads directly to its top. South Beacon is half-a-mile away, across the reservoir, but will repay the climber with a much wider view. Thus far, a stout carriage can come with little difficulty in good weather. The path to South Beacon follows the shore around the south side of the reservoir to its farthest point, where there is a clearing made by wood-cutters, and then, turning to the right, goes straight up to the summit—a steep but not hard climb. The peak is a cap of bare rocks, and overlooks not only a long stretch of the Hudson Valley and the Newburgh region, but a large part of Dutchess County northward, and almost the whole of Putnam County southward, with a big patch of the river near Peekskill. Watchers here could therefore see more than at any other point in the Highlands east of the river. A cool day should be chosen for the ascent, as shade is deficient.

NEWBURGH TO POUGHKEEPSIE.

The Hudson above Newburgh is a scene of quiet beauty and interest for many miles, with the landscape astern taking on a new charm as distance mellows the picture. The river gradually narrows, and the channel is once more in the center of the stream. At *Low Point*, or *Carthage Landing*, is a village and railway station on the east side, with a straight road to Fishkill Village. Opposite is the small brick-making settlement of *Roseton*, or *Middlehope*, a mile above which the house of Bancroft Davis may be seen, close above the railway, with the Armstrong mansion a little beyond. Here the boat's course follows the river, in a bend to the right, around Low Point; and there appears ahead, upon the left, a rocky headland with wall-like fronts of white rock. This crag has long been known as the *Danskammer*, or Devil's Dance-hall—a name going back to the voyage of Henry Hudson. The "devils" referred to are Indians, who were accustomed to meet here for councils, merrymakings, etc., always accompanied by dancing about the camp-fire, when they seemed fiends incarnate to the witch-fearing Calvinistic Dutchman. This point was the boundary-line between the jurisdictions of New Amsterdam and Fort Orange (Albany); and *Hampton Point*, half-a-mile above, is the place where now the northern boundary of Orange County comes to the river and the southern border of Ulster County. No county crosses the river; and on the east, Dutchess continues as far north as Tivoli.

Having passed the Danskamer, the pretty vale of

New Hamburgh—one of the old Palatinate settlements—opens to view on the right, where Wappinger's Creek, named after the powerful Wappinger Indians, comes in from the northeast, and is crossed by the Hudson River Railroad upon a drawbridge. This valley is the home of many summer residents of wealth and social station. Resuming here the more truly northward course, the steamer is soon passing the bluff shores of *Marlborough*, whose spires can be seen at the head of the gorge of the Maune-

butterfield

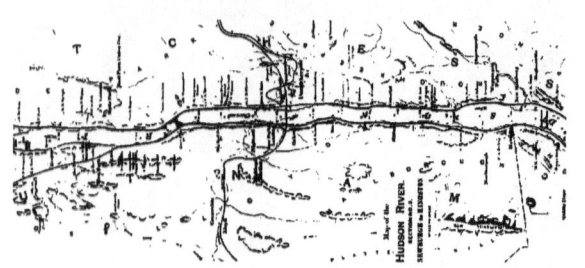

kill, in the opening of which is the railway station and steamboat landing. This was one of the towns bombarded when the British went up the river. It is now a thriving village, which sends a great quantity of fruit to the city, and welcomes summer boarders. The hilly bank opposite, for two or three miles above New Hamburgh, is dotted with the fine country-houses of the Van Rensselaers; S. W. Johnson at "Uplands"; J. F. Sheafe at "High Cliff"; Irving Grinnell, on the river brink, at "Netherwood"; Dr. J. Lenox Banks at "The Cedars"—the house with a square white tower—and many others. Still farther north, the tower of "Elkhorn," the residence of Prof. R. H. Bull, will attract attention.

A few miles farther brings the traveler to *Milton*, another little fruit-yielding port and village, among the hills on the western side. The West Shore Railroad has a station here, and the Hudson River Railroad one opposite, whence a traveler may be set across by boatmen. Milton is coming to be a great favorite with summer residents. Readers of the illustrated magazines will be glad to know that this village was the early home of Mary Hallock Foote, the artist-author, who learned among the old Quaker families the facts and local color of those stories of primitive life among the Friends which have delighted her readers. Milton's wharf is piled high with the crates in which strawberries, raspberries, currants, grapes, and other small fruits are sent by steamboat to the city.

Off westward may be seen the serrated summits of the *Shawangunk* Range (pronounced "Shawngum"), trending northward at the headwaters of the Wallkill.

ICE AND THE ICE HARVEST.

It is in this part of the Hudson River that ice-houses begin to attract attention, that at Marlborough being the first of a long line of immense storehouses that line the banks of the river, especially on the western side, all the way to the head of navigation, and which form a feature of the scenery more conspicuous than ornamental. These are the storehouses in which the garnered harvest of the river is stored, to be sent to New York and other cities, in barges, as it is needed; and the Hudson is the great highway to the market.

"No man sows," writes John Burroughs, "yet many men reap a harvest from the Hudson. Not the least important is the ice harvest, which is eagerly looked for and counted upon by hundreds, yes thousands, of laboring-men along its course. Ice or no ice sometimes means bread or no bread to scores of families, and it means added or diminished comfort to many more. It is a crop that takes two or three weeks of rugged weather to grow, and, if the water is very roily or brackish, even longer. It is seldom worked till it presents seven or eight inches of clear-water ice. Men go out from time to time and examine it, as the farmer goes out and examines his grain or grass, to see when it will do to cut. If there comes a deep fall of snow, the ice is 'pricked' so as to let the water up through, and form snow ice. A band of fifteen or twenty men, about a yard apart, each armed with a chisel-bar, and marching in line, puncture the ice at each step with a single sharp thrust. To and fro they go, leaving a belt behind them that presently becomes saturated with water. But ice, to be first quality, must grow from beneath, not from above. It is a crop quite as uncertain as any other. A good yield every two or three years, as they say of wheat out West, is about all that can be counted upon. When there is an abundant harvest, after the ice-houses are filled, they stack great quantities of it, as the farmer stacks his surplus hay. Such a fruitful winter was that of '74–75, when the ice formed twenty inches thick. The stacks are given only a temporary covering of boards, and are the first ice removed in the season.

"The cutting and gathering of the ice enlivens these broad, white, desolate fields amazingly. My house happens to stand where I look down upon the busy scene, as from a hilltop upon a river meadow in haying time; only here the figures stand out much more sharply than they do from a summer meadow. There is the broad, straight, blue-black canal emerging into view, and running nearly across the river; this is the highway that lays open the farm. On either side lie the fields or ice meadows, each marked out by cedar or hemlock boughs. The further one is cut first, and, when cleared, shows a large, long, black parallelogram in the midst of the plain of snow. Then the next one is cut, leaving a strip or tongue of ice between the two for the horses to move and turn upon. Sometimes nearly two hundred men and boys, with numerous horses, are at work at once, marking, plowing, planing, scraping, sawing, hauling, chiseling; some floating down the pond on great square islands towed by a horse or their fellow workmen; others distributed along the canal, bending to their ice-hooks; others upon the bridges, separating the blocks with their chisel-bars; others feeding the elevators; while knots and straggling lines of idlers here and there look on in cold discontent, unable to get a job.

"The best crop of ice is an early crop. Late in the season, or after January, the ice is apt to get 'sun-struck,' when it becomes 'shaky,' like a piece of poor timber. The sun, when he sets about destroying the ice, does not simply melt it from the surface —that were a slow process; but he sends his shafts into it and separates it into spikes and needles—in short, makes kindling-wood of it, so as to consume it the quicker.

"One of the prettiest sights about the ice harvesting is the elevator in operation" [lifting the ice into the storehouse]. "When all works well there is an unbroken procession of the great crystal blocks slowly ascending this incline. They go up in couples, arm in arm, as it were, like friends up a stairway, glowing and changing in the sun, and recalling the precious stones that adorn the walls of the celestial city. When they reach the platform where they leave the elevator, they seem to slip off like things of life and volition; they are still in pairs, and separate only as they enter upon their 'runs.' But here they have an ordeal to pass through, for they are subjected to a rapid inspection, and the black sheep are separated from the flock; every square with a trace of sediment or earth-stain in it, whose texture is not the perfect and unclouded crystal, is rejected and sent hurling down into the abyss; a man with a sharp eye in his head, and a sharp ice-hook in his hand, picks out the impure and fragmentary ones as they come along, and sends them quickly overboard. Those that pass the examination glide into the building along the gentle incline, and are switched off here and there upon branch runs, and distributed to all parts of the immense interior."

This business is one of the largest and most remarkable industries of the Hudson River and vicinity, the tonnage alone amounting in storage capacity to nearly three millions of tons yearly. Of this immense quantity, the Knickerbocker Ice Company of New York—to whose treasurer, Mr. S. O. Reeves, the writer is indebted for these statistics—stores fully one-half. The industry affords employment during the ice-harvesting season to great numbers of men, and that mainly in the season when no other occupation is available to the laboring classes in the river counties, as many as 15,000 or 20,000 men being employed at times, when the harvesting is active, and the work goes on uninterruptedly. The time occupied in gathering this enormous quantity is necessarily lengthy, averaging thirty days in the season, much of the time being needed for snow-scraping and "cultivating" the ice, preparatory to housing it. The revenue thus derived from the ice dealers forms an important factor in the general interests of trade along the Hudson Valley, where no worse disaster, commercially, could happen than a failure of the crop. The business in this section was inaugurated in 1831, when ice was first taken to New York City from Rockland Lake, as has already been stated.

"The hole in the ground, in which the beginners tried to keep their ice from melting, has given way to these immense storehouses, holding variously from 7,000 to 70,000 tons, and upward. The hand-wagon has given way to the large and expensive spring-wagon, over 600 of which are in daily use by the Knickerbocker Ice Company alone, and probably as many more by the rest of the ice dealers in New York City and vicinity; the freighting by sloop has given way to a wonderful fleet of ice-barges, especially built and adapted for the carrying and preservation of ice *in transitu*, and many tugs whose ponderous tows render the scene on the river picturesque, night and day. The capital has grown from the first $2,000, invested in 1830 at Rockland Lake, to upward of $5,000,000, in New York City, Brooklyn, and adjacent places. From such small beginnings has the ice industry augmented until it now challenges comparison with the tonnage importation of all other foreign or domestic commercial industries whose mart is the great metropolis of the New World."

Long before this, the **great cantilever bridge** spanning the river at Poughkeepsie has excited admiration in every eye, for its delicate lines do not disturb the beauty of the landscape.

The corner-stone of this bridge was laid as early as 1873, but construction proceeded no farther at that time. It was re-begun in September, 1886, and was finished January 1, 1889. The builder was the Union Bridge Company. It is entirely for railway service, and has a double track, with a foot-path which is not yet open to the public. The bridge is 12,608 feet, or about 2¼ miles, long, reaching from highland to highland, at an elevation of 212 feet above the water. One or two athletes, seeking money and notoriety, have allowed themselves to drop from its center, and survived the foolhardy feat. The breadth of the river under the bridge is 6,767 feet from pier to pier. The cost was about $3,500,000, and the present owner is a company operating in the interest of the Philadelphia & Reading Railroad Co.

Presently the spires and southern suburbs of Poughkeepsie appear on the eastern shore; and here, one house, standing between the river and the highway in a fine open spot where its square central tower is readily perceived, should not be overlooked, since it is "Locust Grove," once the home of *Prof. S. F. B. Morse*, who made practicable for us the invention of the electric telegraph. The great *Kaal Rock* is passed, where tradition says the early burghers of the town used to sit, and hail the sloops for news as they drifted by, and which is now crowned with the old

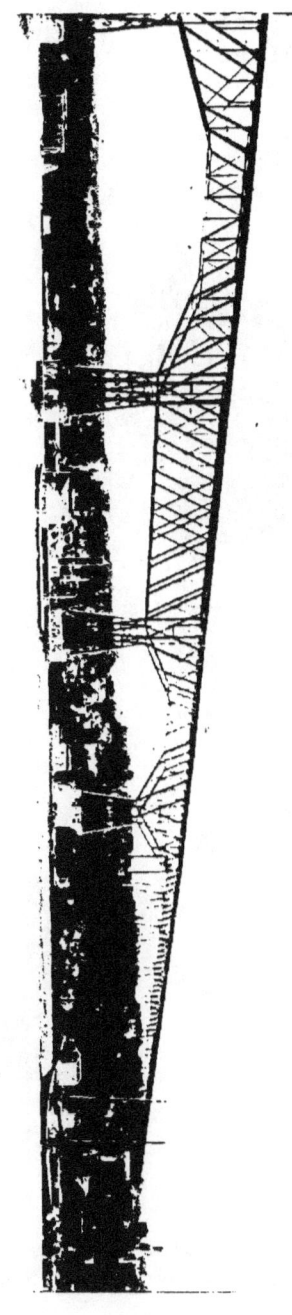

THE POUGHKEEPSIE BRIDGE.

The Leading Hotels of the Hudson Valley

The Palatine

NEWBURGH, N. Y.

H. N. Bain & Co., Proprietors.

Nelson House

POUGHKEEPSIE, N. Y.

H. N. Bain, Proprietor.

These Hotels are modern and up-to-date, and are the leading homes between New York and Albany.

brick buildings of Matthew Vassar's first brewery, whence, after a while came the hospital, the young ladies' college, and other good works of that genial philanthropist; and the steamer slows up under the shadow of the great bridge at the bustling wharf of

Poughkeepsie.—Poughkeepsie (pronounced *Po-kip-sie*), situated advantageously about half-way between New York and Albany, is referred to by local chroniclers as the "Queen City of the Hudson." Its population is reported at about 24,000, which is said now to be a trifle less than Newburgh's. From its foundation by the Dutch as a village, at the end of the last century, Poughkeepsie has always been a leading point on the river as a business and social center. The State Legislature met in it in 1777 and 1778, when the British held New York; and here also the State Convention for the ratification of the Federal Constitution met, holding debates in which Gov. Clinton, John Jay, and Alexander Hamilton took part. It is the shire town of Dutchess County; and it has attracted to it, and maintained, an average quality of citizenship and sociality that is not surpassed by any other town in the State. In fact, the society has been of so high an order, and so secure in wealth, or competence, that at times its preference for home-like ease over dashing activity has been thought a barrier to the rapid business progress the town might have secured; but this tendency is not so apparent now. The community in some directions was never laggard, however. It was early at the front in the educational line, and has always been noted for the number and character of its different schools. Among those which now exist are *Vassar College*, the first institution which gave to girls the advantages of a complete liberal education, and *Eastman College*, a pioneer in the commercial field. Both these schools hold their high rank and celebrity undiminished, both for the number of their students and for the fact that almost all the nations of the world contribute to the names on their catalogues.

Vassar College, named after its munificent founder, Matthew Vassar, is, indeed, the most widely known fact in connection with the city. It occupies a series of large brick buildings in the midst of an extensive and beautiful park, on high ground, two miles back from the river; and can not be seen from either the boats or railway, the imposing building on an eminence in the rear of the city, usually supposed to be its building, being a former school-house, now otherwise occupied. The Main Street trolley cars go out to the college every 12 minutes (fare 5 cents). Apart from the general interest of the institution, its library and natural history and art museums are well worth a visit. The zoölogical collection, mainly the work of the late Prof. James Orton, is unusually large and instructive; it is strong in ornithology, more especially in the birds of South America, where Orton became famous as a scientific explorer, and wrote one of the foremost books upon the Amazon region.

Eastman Park—beautiful gardens open to the public—is an ornament to the city which should be seen. The city also possesses a capital **Public Library,** for both reference and circulation, with a reading-room attached, and an annex devoted to law books. It occupies a beautiful new marble building on Market Street. There are also a Young Men's and a Young Women's Christian Association, in the former of which the reading-room is a popular feature. *Vassar Brothers' Institute* is a worthy foundation endowed for scientific and literary culture. There are also a number of clubs and club-houses, of which the *Amrita*, the Duchess, and the Bicycle Club are the most conspicuous. Other institutions are various religious and benevolent organizations, and the *Vassar Hospital*, conspicuous from the river upon a hillock in the southern part of the city, which is described as "one of the most completely equipped and liberally endowed in the country." The churches are numerous, and represent all the chief denominations. There is an opera-house accommodating 2,200 people—which John B. Gough called the most interesting audience-room of its size he had ever seen—and other public halls. The militia have a fine armory.

Journalism has always flourished in Poughkeepsie. Four daily newspapers, which also issue weeklies, are now published, and one semi-weekly and two Sunday papers.

The street-railway system connects the railroad stations, steamboat landing, and Vassar College, reaches the northern suburbs, and extends south along Broadway to Wappingers Falls (see page 136). These trolley cars pass the court-house, the post-office, the public library, and the principal hotels — Nelson and Morgan houses (single fare, 5 cents).

The water of the city is taken from the Hudson, far out from shore, is thoroughly filtered, and is believed to be as good as any city can hope to procure. The sewerage system, owing to the topography of the city's site, is absolutely perfect, and much care is taken to keep it so. Consequently, Poughkeepsie is a very healthful town. The city is lighted by electric lamps at intervals of 500 feet in all the streets, and has incandescent lights and gas for in-door service. Within a few years the erection of a *Driving Track* and the removal of the Dutchess County Fair from the center of the county to this city has added a new and welcome feature. Driving for amusement is, indeed, one of the foremost pleasures of life here, as in other towns on this side of the Hudson, where the splendid roads are suitable for speeding; and inspiring landscapes and the sight of fine estates lend a varying interest to any excursion, especially on the Hyde Park and the Fishkill roads. In the winter this place is the headquarters of *Ice Boating*, and its craft in that line are unsurpassed for beauty and speed. The free space on the river here, and the extended view one obtains of it—both to the north and south—are aids in making it a select place for this sport. Thirteen miles east of Poughkeepsie, and a station on the Newburgh, Dutchess & Connecticut Railroad, is *Millbrook*, a summer resort of people of note and wealth, which has made the farm land there worth in many places $3,000 and upward an acre. It is fast becoming another Lenox.

Poughkeepsie has a considerable wholesale trade, and its manufactures are constantly increasing. This is due to its favorable situation as respects both water and land lines of transportation. Four steamboat lines furnish passage to New York, two to Albany, two to Newburgh, and two to Kingston. The river is navigable to these wharves for the largest vessels, and the river freight-boats have always been well patronized. Small steamboats make frequent trips between Poughkeepsie and the various little landings along the river, northward to Rondout and southward as far as Newburgh. A *steam-ferry* connects the city with Highland, opposite, where country roads concentrate at an old village landing and the West Shore Railroad Station.

Poughkeepsie is the principal station, between New York and Albany, on the Hudson River Railroad, all express trains stopping here, and many of them for that 10-minute lunch in the station restaurant so familiar to travelers. The completion of the great bridge has brought here a branch of the New England Railroad, while the Philadelphia, Reading & New England Railroad runs trains across the bridge between Hartford, Conn., and Eastern Pennsylvania. By means of this bridge and the connecting railroads, coal has been reduced to the lowest figure, many new markets have been opened to Poughkeepsie's merchants and manufacturers, and a great impetus given to the city's growth and prosperity.

The Buckeye Mower is perhaps the most famous article made here, and it is sold all over the world. Added to this great factory, are the Phœnix Horse-Shoe Works, an iron works, a glass works, two large shoe factories, Lane Bros.' door hangings and coffee-mill concern, the Fall Kill Knitting Works, a silk thread factory, and a large number of small miscellaneous shops, including that of the De Laval Separator Company, which makes a peculiar machine for the separation of cream from milk, and also a somewhat remarkable churn; it came to Poughkeepsie from Sweden, and is giving much enterprise to its new work here.

The city contains six excellent banks and one savings bank, and long-distance telephones connect it with Albany and New York.

Wappingers Falls.—A delightful excursion from Poughkeepsie in summer is a trip in an open trolley-car over the electric railroad to Wappingers Falls. The distance is about seven miles (south), and the whole route is along the old Albany Post Road, which is known here, as usual, as Broadway. It winds about in pleasant irregularities, between stone walls and rows of ancient shade-trees, and past fine suburban estates and cozy farm houses. The suburbs of Poughkeepsie are interesting in all directions. The road lies too far back from the Hudson to permit the river itself to be seen, but the hills on its further shore form a beautiful background to the nearer picture. In the outskirts of the city a park and rural cemetery are passed. Wappingers Falls is a large old-fashioned village on both sides of Wappingers Creek (see page 128) at a point, some two and a half miles above its mouth at New Hamburgh, where the stream falls over a series of high ledges and dams, behind which is a considerable lake. The steep walls of the ravine, the arched stone bridge, the mill races that have been carved out long ago, and the ruins of some ancient mills lend picturesqueness to a spot already highly endowed in that respect. Many factories line the stream below the falls, and the village is also of importance as a market town, and interesting socially and historically. The run is made in about thirty-five minutes, and the fare is 15 cents each way.

POUGHKEEPSIE TO KINGSTON.

As Poughkeepsie is left behind, the huge red buildings of the *Hudson River State Hospital* become conspicuous upon the hills along the Hyde Park road, north of the city. Here are received those of unbalanced minds, to be kept and nursed until restored to health or else proved incurably insane. It now shelters several hundred inmates; yet, large as it is, this is only the beginning of what must finally be one of the largest asylums in the world. The estate in front of it is that of Thomas Newbold. The pumping station of the city waterworks is seen near the river bank, whence the water is forced into a reservoir in the park on College Hill.

The bank opposite Poughkeepsie is very high and precipitous, but it is broken just above the bridge by a narrow wooded ravine, at the mouth of which is the railway station of **Highland**, and a ferry and steamboat landing. A little above, some warehouses mark the position of the old New Paltz Landing, where the farmers of the Wallkill Valley were wont to come in former days to cross to Poughkeepsie or meet the sloops and steamboats. Up the ravine goes the old road to *Highland Village*, a thriving settlement on the plateau, which is thronged with visitors in summer, and is the terminus of a trolley line to New Paltz, in the Wallkill Valley, nine miles along rural roads. It is a pleasant walk up to the village along the ravine, down which the creek comes in one long, winding rapid, with here and there a tall waterfall over some dam, which turns, or once turned, a small mill-wheel. Milling is still one of the chief industries of the pretty little town, where there are two small but comfortable hotels. Trolley cars (fare, 5 cents) run between the village and the riverside stations, meeting all trains and boats. Highland is also a station on the Connecticut, New York & New England Railroad, near the western terminus of the big bridge. The large yellow building seen upon the brow of the bluff overlooking the landing is Hasbrouck's *Bellevue Villa*, a summer hotel.

The Eastern Shore is much less steep and high than the western, and for the next thirty miles in particular it is dotted with old estates and costly, handsome, and often historic residences. To this purpose the shore is well adapted, for it rises, not too abruptly for effective landscape gardening, to a plateau about one hundred feet above the water, where the houses stand upon a uniform level. It is upon this plateau, too, that the villages are situated, out of sight, along the old post road, with insignificant railway stations and landings down by the water-side, a fortunate disposition of things for the scenery of the noble river.

The roughness of the western bank culminates ahead, as Poughkeepsie is left behind, in bold and shaggy headlands, forming a promontory around which the river bends just far enough westward to cut off the view. This slight bend, eighty miles from New York, the river men call Krum Elbow (the original Dutch name was *Krom-me Hoek*—a rounded point), and, as the steamer imperceptibly swings around it, a broad reach gradually opens almost as far as Rhinebeck, and there appear, in blue silhouette ahead, the eastern peaks of the **Catskill Mountains**, some thirty miles distant. They will rarely be out of sight, henceforth, for several hours; but, before reaching their base, many things of nearer interest will engage the attention, always with that beautiful background made by the heights of Rip Van Winkle's story.

Here on the right, five miles above Poughkeepsie, comes **Hyde Park**, the road from the station leading up the gorge of Krum Elbow Creek to the village, half-a-mile inland. It is an old place, named in honor of Sir Edward Hyde, one of the early English governors of the province; and years ago there was here, where now stands the railway station, a horse-power ferry for the accommodation of the people on the western shore.

The heights of Crum Elbow having been passed, the *Western Shore* becomes more habitable, and the fine river-road is lined with handsome places that face the water. The woods disappear, too, and the sloping shore is cultivated in vineyards and fruit orchards. Behind this gracious forefront towers the saddle-backed eminence called *Mount Hymettus* by John Burroughs, "an author and naturalist of pleasant fame" (whose cottage will presently come into view), because of his success in finding upon it bee-trees and stores of wild honey. Mount Hymettus stretches northward in lessening elevations, all wooded to their summits, and known as the *Esopus Hills*. At its base is seen, among private residences, the tall white *Manresa Institute*, formerly a Roman Catholic theological seminary, but now an orphanage. North of this, there intervenes between the hills and the river a broad space of arable lands holding several villages. The first of these is **West Park,** from whose pretty river-landing (*Frothingham's Dock*), directly opposite Hyde Park, a most romantic lane leads up to the turnpike. This is a stopping-place of the steamer between New York and Saugerties, and is a West Shore station.

West Park is a delightful spot, where a village is gradually arising. The old post road runs along the brow of the terrace between ranks of grand shade-trees, and bordered by fine country places. The little Episcopal Church of the Ascension—a stone building overgrown with vinery—fitly recalls the rural churches of England; and a queer little mill brings out the sketch-book of every artist who strays near it. One of the oldest of the neighboring estates is that formerly occupied by the Astors—a large house of the English style, in spacious grounds, now owned and occupied by a New York maltster. This road is good for bicycles, though somewhat hilly, and is admirable for walking or driving.

The Hudson is here very beautiful and interesting. Looking backward, one can still obtain a glimpse of the spires of Poughkeepsie, and of a small section of its bridge, traced in hair-lines upon the pale blue front of the Fishkill Mountains, twenty miles away. Ahead, the Catskills are coming more and more plainly into the perspective, and each bank attracts the roving eye with competing charms. My own impression is, that this section from Poughkeepsie to Catskill is the most pleasing part of the whole river, even though it lacks the majestic scenery of the Highlands.

Conspicuous just above Hyde Park landing, standing upon the smooth, grassy terrace, between ancient oaks and elms, is the palatial residence of F. W. Vanderbilt — one of the most costly in the long line of noble river-side properties. Next above it is the *Drayton House*, the old Kirkpatrick estate; and directly opposite, on the West Park shore, and behind and slightly above some enormous ice-houses, is seen the stone cottage of *Mr. John Burroughs*, the writer of such familiar out-door books as *Wake Robin, Birds and Poets, Pepacton, etc.*, and many acute and pleasing essays in literary criticism. Many acres of vineyards and orchards lie in front of the house, as along all this western side of the river; and Mr. Burroughs and his neighbors ship great quantities of table grapes, currants, and small fruits to New York and Boston. A mile above, on the same side, is the immense and much-advertised orchard (said to contain 25,000 trees) of the late R. L. Pell, who sent apples to Queen Victoria—canny man!—and so made a good market for his fruit in Great Britain. His wharf (*Pelham*) is distinguished by its big stone warehouse with iron gates.

Opposite it, on the eastern bank, and about a mile above Hyde Park, a quaint, chalet-like house appears among the trees on the distant terrace. This place is called "Gros Bois" by its present proprietor, Robert T. Ford; but it derives a greater interest from the fact that years ago it was "Placentia," the home of the gifted James K. Paulding, a literary man who published many and varied books, until his death in 1860. He was one of that coterie of bright minds that clustered about Washington Irving, and was his associate in the publication of *Salmagundi*.

The little island met here, usually animated in summer by the camps of canoeists or fishermen, is *Esopus;* and just above it, on the western bank, is the landing (*Brown's Dock*) for *Esopus Village*, an old-time cross-roads hamlet a mile and a half back. It stands on the shore of Black Creek, whose outlet, here at the landing, is almost hidden in lily-pads and masses of blossoms of the spiked loosestrife—a tall water-weed, naturalized from Europe, which sprouts densely in the shallow coves all along the Hudson, encircling their margins with bands of bright magenta pink, amid which glow here and there the more fiery standards of the cardinal flower.

Black Creek is a lively little river that merits its name, for its water is stained with the roots and bark of hemlock and cedar until it looks like an outlet of the juniper jungles of the Dismal Swamp. It rises down beyond Marlborough, and flows north, behind Mount Hymeltus, expanding into a pond which the Dutch called Grote Binnewater ("Big Pond") and the moderns name Black Pond, and frets its way down innumerable waterfalls and through deeps and shadows until it escapes here at Esopus Village. It contains a fair quantity of black bass, perch, and sunfish, harbors a good many copperheads, and still turns the wheels of small mills, hidden away in the brush, as it used to do in the good old days of the Dutch. The road which leads back over the hills from West Park strikes it in its most picturesque part.

KAATERSKILL FALLS

The name "Esopus" is one that is met with often and rather confusingly in this part of the country. The hills on the west take the appellation, and the island opposite, but the marshy Esopus Meadows are some three miles north of Esopus Lighthouse. Esopus Village and landing are here at the mouth of Black Creek; while Esopus Creek empties into the Hudson twenty miles north at Saugerties; and Rondout Creek, at Rondout, used to be called the Little Esopus.

This confusion arises, as will be clear when the history of Kingston is read, from the fact that in early colonial days the whole district on the western side of the river, of which Kingston was the center, was known as Esopus—a Dutch and English corruption of an Indian word, the earliest spelling of which was *Desopus*.

By this time, Krum Elbow has blotted out the Poughkeepsie bridge and the southern highlands, Mount Hymettus is well behind us on the west, and its continuation, the *Shaupeneak*, and *Hussey's Mountain* are becoming prominent. The eastern shore is lower than heretofore and better cultivated, and the Hudson River Railroad disappears behind a bluff where the little village of *Staatsburgh* is hidden from view; D. O. Mills is its principal resident. Just beyond, *Esopus Light-house* marks the outer edge of the weedy shoals called *Esopus Meadows*, opposite which, on the eastern shore, is *Dinsmore's Point*, with the large yellow mansion of the late William B. Dinsmore behind it. Just above it the river indents the shore with the wide shallows of Vanderberg Cove. Immediately upon this cove, in a house on the end of the ridge, dwells the brewer, Jacob Rupert; and next above him another New York brewer, Finck, occupying a great white stone mansion overlooking an immense lawn. This is "Wildercliffe," formerly the estate of Edward R. Jones. A little farther on, and nearer the river, is the house of Robert Suckley; and next beyond, just above the railway tunnel, is "Ellerslie," once the residence of the Hon. William Kelly—long prominent in political life—and now the summer home of ex-Vice-President Levi P. Morton. His estate contains about six hundred acres, much of which is devoted to gardens. The newest resident here at Staatsburgh is Ogden Mills, whose house cost $500,000 in 1897.

A magnificent view of the Catskill Mountains is now presented. The passenger sees here the whole eastern series, from Overlook to where the Mountain House gazes down from its storied ledges. They are too far away and misty to exhibit details, but the lofty and well-chiseled outlines culminating in *High Peak*, the stately grouping beyond the foreground of water, and the long sweep of swelling outlines, cumulative contours leading the eye artistically to the center of the picture, with the dull red and gray of Rondout's buildings in the middle distance, make a composition as pleasing in arrangement as it is vivid in color. Nor is the element of "life" wanting, for the shimmering foreground is dotted with boats, sailing-craft and steamers, from some natty sloop-yacht or huge "day-liner" to a laboring old steam canalboat bound for Buffalo or bringing coal from Scranton. Sometimes a dingy little steam launch may be seen, loaded fore and aft with eatables—a regular floating market. Piled high on top of the pilot-house may be cabbages and corn, or other green truck, while the entire space in front is often filled with loaves of bread, and the space amidships, sheltered by an awning, may contain a heap of ice. A shelf runs along the low bulwarks, and it will perhaps be covered with fruits and vegetables whose trailing leaves ripple the water as the boat skims from shore to shore, or runs alongside a tow of canalboats, seeking for trade.

The rough crags of *Hussey's Mountain*, 1,000 feet high, are now at hand on the west, with the brick-yards and ice-houses of Port Ewen at its base; and there presently opens beyond it a river gorge crowded with shipping, and lined with buildings. This is Rondout Creek and harbor, and

The City of Kingston.—Originally, as will presently be noted, two flourishing towns grew up here in close contiguity—*Rondout*, at the river mouth, and *Kingston*, whose nucleus was three miles inland. Both increased in size until their borders nearly touched, whereupon they united (1878) as a corporate city, under the name of the latter.

Kingston has now a population of about 25,000, is growing steadily, and has a strong commercial foundation. It is the most important station on the West Shore Railroad between Weehawken and Albany, and the eastern terminus of the Ulster & Delaware Railroad, and of the Wallkill Valley Railroad, the latter connecting it with the Erie Railroad system at Goshen, N. Y. These three roads have a union station in the center of the town, one mile from the landing, besides which the Ulster & Delaware sends its trains down to the steamboat wharf at Rondout as the port town and local postoffice is still familiarly called. The steam-ferry (fare, 13 cents) to *Rhinecliff*, on the opposite bank of the Hudson, connects the town with the Hudson River Railroad and with the Hartford & Connecticut Western Railroad, which gives a direct line into Dutchess County and eastward. Rondout is also the terminus of the Delaware & Hudson Canal, and is the most important shipping-point on the whole river above New York. The *Albany Day Line* boats do not go into the river mouth, but receive and deliver passengers at the new wharves on Kingston Point, to which the railway has been extended. Kingston has, besides, several steamer lines of its own. This is the home and terminal port of that fast and favorite boat, *Mary Powell*, which has long been the queen of the Hudson. Here, also, are owned the steamers *James W. Baldwin* and *William F. Romer*, which are among the largest steamers on the river, and afford a daily night-line between Rondout and New York. The Newburgh day-line makes this a port-of-call, daily; and there are small steamers which pass back and forth between Kingston and Poughkeepsie, southward, and Saugerties northward, stopping anywhere, on both sides of the river, that passengers wish to land or embark, or any freight is offered. Lastly, this is the headquarters of the Cornell Steamboat Company, which owns about forty-five towboats and tugs, and is one of the largest concerns in the towing business.

Kingston Point is a steamer landing a mile north of the ferry landing, and has lately become a popular summer pleasure resort. The Day Line and other boats stop there, and the Catskill Mountain trains of the Ulster & Delaware Railroad meet the boats on the wharf. A pretty park has been made, a long promenade on the edge of the water, boats, bathing, and various means of quiet amusement are maintained. Excursion trains from the interior and from various river towns bring large pleasure parties almost daily, and in the evening crowds of citizens resort there for coolness and recreation.

These varied means of transportation have made Kingston-Rondout a place of much commercial importance, and are encouraging the rise of manufactures. Three great industries are prominent: *Cement-making, bluestone, and coal-shipping.*

CEMENT AND CEMENT-MAKING, BLUESTONE, ETC.

The mining and manufacture of *hydraulic cement*, known more especially as Rosendale cement, from the suburb up the Rondout where it was first produced, is the peculiar industry of the locality. One can not fail to notice the openings of great caverns, picturesquely overhung with vines and shrubbery, in the cliffs above the harbor, and along the high banks of Rondout Creek. They reach far underground, and out of them, in hot weather, pours a draft of air as strong and chill and damp as that blown from the cavernous cheeks of old Boreas himself. Out of these old excavations, and from newer mines, Kingston has dug, and continues to dig, a large part of its wealth, and has built up an industry which brings in $3,000,000 annually, and furnishes employment to more than 3,000 men, besides the army of coopers, boatmen, etc., indirectly benefited.

This cement is water-lime, or the material for hydraulic mortar—that is, a mortar which will harden under water. It is made from a magnesian limestone, containing more or less sand and clay, thus approximating it to the European artificial mixture of 23 per cent carbonate of lime (chalk) and 77 per cent silicate of alumina (clay), which is called Portland cement. When, about 1828, the Delaware & Hudson Canal was building here, the engineers, casting about for a cement suitable for use in constructing locks, discovered that a better kind existed right here than was then known in the western part of the State; and the mining of it upon the outcrop for immediate use soon developed into a general industry. Since then a similar cement-rock has been discovered and worked in the neighborhood of Buffalo, opposite Louisville, Ky., and near Allentown, Pa. At Allentown, in addition to the natural product, they are making an artificial "Portland" cement. In all these localities the rock is the very ancient Upper Silurian limestone. Here at Kingston, the particular geological horizon is the Tentaculite, or water-lime, division of the Lower Helderberg series, which overlies the great Niagara group of limestones. The beds are massive, varying from fifteen to thirty feet in thickness, and more or less interstratified with non-cementitious layers. They have been much disturbed, lie at all sorts of angles, and are broken here and there by faults.

For the most part, only the edges appear at the surface, so that the rock must be removed by methods of mining similar to those pursued in excavating coal, rather than by quarrying, and many of the tunnels and shafts penetrate to the heart of the hills, and are sunk more than 100 feet below tide-water. The rock is somewhat harder to mine than coal, but there is no danger from liberated gases, and the roof is firm, requiring little timbering.

The Upper Silurian rocks everywhere, as a rule, are crowded with the fossil remains of invertebrate sea life, as corals, crinoids, and a great variety of shellfish. In the series to which the cement-rock belongs, as it appears elsewhere, tentaculites (fossil pteropods of the molluscan family *Tentaculitidæ*) are especially numerous, and give their name to the subdivision; but, curiously enough, the cement-beds here are almost entirely barren of these or any other fossils, although the adjacent, and even the intercalated, strata are highly fossiliferous.

The rock itself, no matter how finely crushed, will not act as a hydraulic cement, or even as a good mortar; it needs preparation to impart to it its valuable quality. This preparation consists in roasting or calcining it. The area of the beds is about ten miles in length, extending along a ridge from the northern part of Kingston, or its suburb Rosendale, southwestward, with a width varying from forty feet to five miles; and fifteen mills are now in operation, of which those of the Lawrence and Newark companies are the largest. At each of these establishments the rock is brought from the mines in cars, crushed into small pieces, and then placed in huge kilns, mixed with fine coal. The kilns having once been fired, the process of roasting the mass goes on continuously, new supplies being poured into the top as the calcined stone is removed at the base. When cooled, crushed, and placed in barrels the cement is ready for use.

The process and character of the change, presumably chemical, which the stone undergoes in turning into cement are not clearly understood. Many theories have been advanced, but none are satisfactory. Beyond the fact that the calcining drives off the water, little is really known about the matter; and the hydraulicity of this substance is another one of the many facts of practical experience and utility which remains unexplained.

This cement is sold all over the Atlantic States, and the extent and variety of its service are increasing. Not only is it required for all masonry exposed to water, as sea-walls, canal-locks, bridge-piers, and the like, but it is used almost entirely for every sort of underground masonry. It is the principal constituent of "concrete." The foundations of all the great buildings in New York are laid on it, and it is extensively applied in fortifications. Its strength and tenacity are far superior to that of the best mortar. When treated with water in the mass, it forms a stone more cohesive and trustworthy than ordinary sandstone.

The 3,000,000 or so of barrels annually required by this industry are made largely in this neighborhood, and cost only 10 cents apiece; they are formed mainly of spruce-wood, and are usually thrown away when emptied.

Coal at Kingston.—The total amount of coal reaching tide-water here, from the canal, now averages about 900,000 tons during the season of navigation, nearly all of which is immediately reshipped. All of it comes from the anthracite fields in the Wyoming Valley of Pennsylvania, and its transshipment here gives employment, on the average, to 350 men, with a large increase of that force at certain times. The storage docks for coal are the largest in the State.

Bluestone is the name given to a more or less argillaceous sandstone of a bluish color, extensively quarried at various points along the Hudson River, and used for building purposes and for flagging. The quarries are scattered throughout the Catskills and along their base, and are in rock of Lower Silurian Age (Hudson River group), and the stone is brought in, rudely shaped, by railway and by teams. The double line of stones set like a tramway in many of the country roads and some town streets on this side of the river, are to enable the horses to draw these loads of stone without sinking irretrievably into the mud; and they are as deeply rutted as the old chariot-tracks in Pompeii. The bluestone is to a great extent prepared for architectural or pavement use here in Rondout, and then reshipped by water, some of it going direct to Southern coast cities, the West Indies, etc. This industry involves a large capital and employs many men.

The *Rondout* end of the city, apart from the picturesqueness of its river-mouth, is not very interesting. The queer little chain-ferry that plies between the city and Sleightburgh, on the southern bank, is quaint and ingenious, and gave Jervis McEntee a subject for a well-known painting. Huntington's brush has studied here, too, his painting, "On the Rondout," being considered one of his best. A little steam launch runs up the river and canal some miles, offering an interesting excursion to the visitor. Rondout's best street lies along the top of the river's high southern bank; the leading hotel is the new Mansion House.

The northern part of the town, or *Kingston proper*, is more attractive. It is a handsome, well-kept little city of itself, where every street and square can tell some story of the past which somehow seems longer ago than the seige of Jerusalem. Its streets give glimpses of the Catskill and Shawangunk mountains, or of sweet valley lands in all directions, and from its suburban eminences pictures may be obtained that are among the most charming in the Hudson Valley.

One point of view is especially recommended, and may form the objective point of a delightful afternoon's walk. This is the *Kuyckuyêt* (a Dutch word pronounced kake-out, and meaning "the lookout"), the summit of a hill south of the city. It overlooks the broad valleys of the Rondout and Hudson, and gives one the best local picture of the mountains. The abrupt heights surrounding Lake Mohonk, in the northern Shawangunks, are plain in the southeast; then comes the hilly valley of the Rondout, northward, rising again, directly west, into the magnificent heights of the southern Catskills, where Slide, Cornell, and the Wittemberg dominate the range. The break occupied by the valley of the Esopus cuts this lofty group off from the main mass, northward, where dozens of well-known summits may be recognized around to the headlands of High Peak and South Mountain in the northern horizon.

Manufactures, etc.—Kingston has many small factories (one of cigars employing 700 hands), and does a very large business in

the manufacture and sale of brick, though many of its yards are
elsewhere along the river. The wholesale and jobbing trade of
the town is good, and its streets are animated. The city contains
five national banks and three savings banks; issues three daily
newspapers; has a public hospital, well-equipped fire and police
departments, and water brought from a mountain stream with a
pressure sufficient for fire purposes without the aid of steamers.
The city hall is a florid brick building, of the aldermanic school
of architecture, midway between Rondout and old Kingston, in
front of which is a "manufactured" soldier's monument not
much better. Electric street-cars extend from the river side in
Rondout to Kingston by two routes, and thence into the outskirts
of the village. A line is about to be built northward along the
Albany road to Lake Katrine.

HISTORICAL SKETCH OF KINGSTON.—Few towns in the State
were more patriotic than this, and none have a more thrilling
story, or so many substantial relics of the beginnings of the commonwealth; and the visitor may find along its streets the actual
buildings where many of the momentous incidents occurred that
have been so fully recorded by Schoonmaker in his *History* of the
town.

It was in 1609 that Hudson sailed up the river; in 1610, the
first trading-ship followed; and in 1675, the New Netherland
Company chose the mouth of the Rondout Creek as the site of
one of their three fortified trading-posts. No proper settlement
was made, however, until the level-headed Stuyvesant had come
as governor to New York to correct the abuses of his greedy
predecessors, and disentangle the Dutch colonists from the Indian
troubles which they had brought upon themselves. In 1652,
quarrels arose in Rensselaerwyck over lands, the aristocratic
Patroons claiming too much for the "common people" to endure;
and it must not be forgotten that these Dutchmen, as well as the
English Puritans, were, to a great extent, refugees from oppression, political and religious, in the Old Country; and were as
deeply imbued with the spirit of liberty as their Protestant brethren in New England; nor that, if it had not been for the unswerving patriotism and self-sacrificing co-operation of these Hollanders
along the Hudson, the English-born colonists could never have
won in their struggle for independence with Great Britain; and
this spirit and help were nowhere more active and serviceable
than here.

In consequence of this quarrel with the Patroons, a band of
trader-colonists, led by Thomas Chambers, an Englishman, moved

down to the level prairie lands which the Indians called *Atkarkarton*, lying along the Esopus between the mountains and the Hudson (see map), where the red men at first gave, and later sold, lands to them. Settlers rapidly followed, disagreements and fatal conflicts with the Indians speedily arose, and, in 1658, Governor Stuyvesant thought it worth while to visit the place, and advise with the people as to the future. He at once ordered the scattered farmers to come together and erect a stockade large enough to contain all their buildings, into which they were to concentrate each night. With a military eye, he selected a level bluff of land on the southern border of the meadows, where the banks fell steeply away on three sides, and there was just room enough for the intended fort. Here a strong stockade was built with great rapidity, and it inclosed the ground now occupied by the business part of old Kingston. A name was officially given to the stockade and community by Governor Stuyvesant, when a charter was granted in 1661; this was *Wildwyck*. "Wild" was the Dutch term for Indians, meaning simply wild, or savage, and "wyck" denotes "a place," so that, literally, Wildwyck signifies "Indian place." The name was changed to Kingston on September 25, 1679, in honor of Kingston Lisle in England, the place from which Lovelace, the colonial governor of the moment, had come. It is a great misfortune that the change was made, and it is worth mention that "Wiltwick" still survives as applied to a portion of the city.

The early history of the colony differs little from that of most others in those days. The burghers and farmers behaved badly toward the Indians, who revenged themselves, and years of border warfare ensued, in which both sides suffered. These were the "Esopus wars," during which, nevertheless, the colony increased and flourished, having a good road to the redout* at the "strand," or river-mouth (present Main Street), and a little outpost at Hurley, with a large area of grain and corn lands under cultivation. This post, indeed, was regarded as the garden of the Dutch possessions; and from the first devoted itself almost wholly to farming, paying little attention to the trading which engrossed Fort Orange and New Amsterdam. Finally, the wars culminated in an adroit seizure of the stockade by the redskins, who massacred a great many men, women, and children, and burned down all the houses. Then troops were sent from below, an active campaign was instituted against the Indians, who were hunted and punished far and near, and no more such disasters occurred; but many years elapsed before the district was safe from occasional inroads. Meanwhile, the country went into English hands, and the name was changed to Kingston, but otherwise there was little alteration, and the settlement grew steadily

---

*It is asserted that the name *Rondout* is a corruption of this word "redout" (there was another there in revolutionary times); but that seems (re)doubtful, and its origin is still obscure.

for a century, until it had become the most important place between New York and Albany. Then again its peace and prosperity were disturbed by the discontent among the Indians, that finally swelled into the French and Indian wars, in which the American colonists were trained to a soldier's life, taught their strength, and given self-confidence for the impending fight with Great Britain.

Many of the houses still standing and occupied in Kingston date from this period. The monumental old *Senate House*, to be more particularly spoken of presently, is such an one. A part of the present *Court House* (Kingston is the shire town of Ulster) was built for that purpose long before the Revolution. Another relic is the *Coonradt Elmendorf Tavern*, on the southeast corner of Maiden Lane and Fair Street, which bears the date of its erection (1723) upon its gable; it witnessed memorable political deeds during the Revolution. At the lower end of Wall Street stood, until 1898, the *Van Steenburgh House*, an example of the old Dutch cottage, noteworthy as the only building which escaped at the burning of the town by the British in 1777. The present home of the Hon. Augustus Schoonmaker, the large square building at John and Crown streets, formerly the *Kingston Academy*, and other antiquated but still servicable structures may be pointed out, whose heavy walls withstood the historic conflagration. Another object of interest is the *Dutch Church*, now remodeled out of all resemblance to the original structure, but standing on the same spot.

Here was organized, in 1657, the oldest congregation holding an unbroken line of services on the same spot that can be found in the State of New York, and probably in the United States. It was, of course, Protestant Dutch Reformed, and the present structure is the fourth that has stood on the spot, not counting the log building which temporarily was used by the settlers in the beginning. The foundations, greatly extended to meet the growth of the congregation, have included part of the surrounding grave-yard. The families whose past generations filled the first graves still worship in the church, and in the last reconstruction of the edifice their pews were placed over the tombs of their ancestors, each family over its own dead. When the old Middle Dutch Church on Nassau Street, New York City, was torn down, the stones bearing the inscription in Dutch were taken to Kingston, and set in the walls of this church, where they now are. The church has the two original communion cups that were, according to tradition, presented by Queen Anne. The communion table is said to have been used by the Prince of Orange, whose coat-of-arms is over the church door, and the walls are covered with tablets commemorating the early pastors and distinguished citizens who sat in the congregation.

THE SENATE HOUSE.

But the particular object of historical interest and curiosity in Kingston is the **Senate House**, which is well worth examination, not only for itself but for what it contains.

It stands upon Clinton Avenue just around the corner from the postoffice and both of the principal hotels—*Eagle* and *Clinton*—and derives its distinction from the fact that here the first sessions of the State Legislature were held. Originally built by Wessel Ten Broeck, in 1676, it later became the dwelling-place of that sturdy patriot Abraham Van Gasbeek, and was the gathering-place of the patriots of "the time that tried men's souls." It shared in the burning of the city by Vaughan, but its wall remained firm, and it was repaired and afterward became the home of Gen. John Armstrong, Madison's Secretary of War, and, later, United States Minister to France. A few years ago the property was bought by the State, to be preserved as a memorial of the past. With great propriety it has been placed under the care of the historian, Marius Schoonmaker, a descendant of one of the oldest and most prominent local families; and is gradually being furnished and filled up as a museum of the heroic past of the town and county. The Kingston branch of the Daughters of the Revolution is especially interested in this laudable undertaking, and holds each year an anniversary celebration which keeps public interest alive.

The **Museum** contains documents, books, pictures—including many studies and portraits by John Van der Lyn—costumes, furniture, military equipments, etc., calculated to illustrate the story of the past. The collection is especially interesting as an exponent of the daily life and condition of the Dutch burghers, whose real character, manners, and customs have been so obscured by the veil of drollery that Washington Irving threw over them, that few understand the practical good sense and sterling virtue which characterized these excellent and patriotic founders of New York.

This building was chosen as the first State House under peculiar pressure. During the summer of 1776 a constitution and form of State government had been formulated. The meetings of delegates who had accomplished this preliminary work had been held at Fishkill; but that village was too small and exposed, and after considerable search Kingston was selected as the proper place for subsequent meetings. The Provincial Convention therefore gathered at Kingston in March, 1777, and held its sessions in the Court House until April 20, 1777, when the constitution was finally agreed upon and signed. This occurred on Sunday. The exigencies of the times admitted of no delay on account of the sacredness of the day. Two days afterward, on April 22d, the constitution was formally proclaimed from the front door of the Court House with great pomp and rejoicing, the elections followed, and George Clinton was chosen governor.

The first Legislature got together on September 10th, and on the preceding day the first court ever held in the State of New York, under the constitution, convened at the Court House at Kingston, and was presided over by the newly appointed Chief Justice, John Jay—scholar, statesman, diplomat, and jurist—equally distinguished for his virtues and his talents, who had been a member of the Constitutional Convention, and was the principal draughtsman of that instrument.

This first Legislature consisted of seventy members of the Assembly and twenty-four Senators. The Assembly convened at a house which then stood on the corner of Fair Street and Maiden Lane, and the Senate sat in this building. The joint body continued its deliberations until October 7th, when, on account of the threatened invasion of British troops, it adjourned. This, however, was not the last session of the Legislature in Kingston. It met again in 1779, and sat from August 18th to October 25th. It was at this session that the famous act was passed confiscating the property of adherents to the British side, or Tories, as they were termed. The Legislature again met in Kingston in 1780, and sat from April 22d to July 2d. It met for the fourth time here in 1783, and sat from January 27th to March 27th.

THE BURNING OF KINGSTON BY THE BRITISH.

After the capture of the Highland forts, the British fleet sailed up the river, firing at almost every prominent house on the shores as it went along. On the evening of October 15, 1777, the vessels came to Esopus Island and anchored there. The next morning, about 9 o'clock, they reached the mouth of the Rondout, where small earth-works, armed with light cannon, had been erected upon high ground overlooking the northern extension of the present city along the Hudson River front called *Ponhockie*. These opened fire, but were soon silenced and captured by assault, but the little garrison escaped. In the harbor lay an armed galley and a hulk which had been used as a military prison. These and some sloops were captured and burned, together with several houses in the neighborhood, after which the British troops, led by Vaughan in person, and guided by Jacobus Lefferts, a resident Tory, marched up from the "strand" to Kingston, encountering no more resistance than a stray shot now and then from some exasperated American, and arrived at the village to find it deserted by almost every one except a few slaves. The villagers, who had not men enough to make even a show of resistance, had fled, taking away such valuables only as they could hastily stow into wagons, while some had left nearly everything in their houses, refusing to believe that the town would be burned. The soldiers were immediately scattered about the town, looting and firing the houses and barns, filled with the stores of the harvest. This done, they hastily withdrew, not daring to wait until the American troops, hurrying from New Paltz, should come up, and the enraged people should gather in force. Clinton's advanced guard reached the Kuyckuyt in time to witness the expiring conflagration, and to see the last of the redcoats hastening back to their vessels; and the general relieved his feelings by hanging on the spot that spy, Lieutenant Taylor, who had been captured at New Windsor, some days before, with the silver bullet in his gorge.

Here are the reasons which account for the unexampled and entirely needless destruction of this town in 1777. One of the distinct objects Howe had in view, in his expedition up the river in that year, was the devastation of Esopus, and General Vaughan wrote a falsehood when, to justify his act in the eyes of the neutral world, he alleged in his dispatches that he was fired upon from the houses of the village. Quoting Augustus Schoonmaker:

"In no part of the United Colonies did the fires of liberty burn more brightly, or the spirit of patriotism animate more manly breasts, than in the new State of New York and in the little hamlet of Kingston. The best evidence of this is found in the report made by General Vaughan, the British commander, on October 17, 1777, in which he denounces the place as 'a nursery for almost every villain in the country.' . . . Lord North, the Prime Minister of George III., complained to Sir William Howe, then commanding the royal forces in New York, of 'the pestiferous nest of rebels clustered about the banks of the Esopus.' Howe had already been stung by the signing of the Articles of Association by the inhabitants of Kingston and Marbletown, and by the fact that the Committee of Safety found refuge at Kingston when driven from New York and Fishkill."

A few words more will complete the story of Vaughan's marauding expedition, which was so noteworthy an incident in the war-history of the Hudson Valley. The vessels proceeded up the river a few miles, landing to burn the houses of several Whigs, among which was the manor of Robert R. Livingston, notwithstanding the fact that Mrs. Livingston was then entertaining two or more British officers (prisoners on parole) who were ill or wounded. The surrender of Burgoyne was now known, however, and Continental troops were hurrying to the river to cut off and destroy the invaders, if possible. The redcoats therefore turned back, and on the 24th of October passed through the Highlands, and returned to New York.

The record of Kingston since those days has been one of prosperous but uneventful growth. The town broadened its acres and extended more and more widely its streets. In 1805 it was incorporated as a village, and remained so until it consolidated with Rondout as a city in 1872. The town has always been ambitious and progressive. It founded a school of higher learning as early as 1664, and for many years the Kingston Academy was the only institution of its kind north of New York, graduating many men of note. One of its principals was that John M. Pomeroy who became a standard authority upon international law. It is now the city high school. Earnest efforts were made to found here a State university; and also to make this town the capital of the United States. Among its citizens have been many of eminence in State affairs, and some who have acquired world-wide reputations. Here was born (October 15, 1775) **John Van der Lyn,** the painter of *The Landing of Columbus* in the rotunda of the capitol at Washington—a picture still more widely popular as the ornament of the back of the United States five-dollar note, and of the two-cent postage-stamp in the Columbian memorial issue of 1893.

Having early exhibited a decided taste and talent for drawing, Van der Lyn spent some months, under the patronage of Aaron Burr, in the artist Stuart's studio at Philadelphia, where, among other things, he made a copy of Stuart's Washington, which now hangs in the Senate House. Burr also enabled him to go to Paris in 1798, where he studied four years. In 1801 he returned to the United States, but in 1803 went again to Europe, and painted his first historical sketch, *The Murder of Jane McCrea*, an incident of the Saratoga campaign. In 1805 he moved to Rome, and there painted his master-piece, *Marius on the Ruins of Carthage*, for which he was awarded the first gold medal by Napoleon at an exhibition in the Louvre. He remained in Europe until 1816, during which time he painted his figure-pieces *Ariadne* and *Cleopatra*. The former is in the gallery of the Academy of Arts at Philadelphia, while his *Cleopatra* is owned in Kingston. He painted a full-length portrait of Washington for the United States House of Representatives, for which the House had appropriated $1,000; but when it was unveiled in the House, such was its merit that the House immediately and unanimously voted an additional compensation of $1,500. In 1839 he received the commission for his rotunda painting above mentioned, the studies and primary sketches for which are preserved here, as also is the principal part of his panorama of the *Garden of Versailles*, painted here in 1816, from sketches made by him when in Paris.

At Kingston, too, lived and studied the landscape painter *Jervis McEntee*, whose brush was much occupied in this truly picturesque region; and literature is now represented in the city by *Henry Abbey*, whose poems have given his name an enviable notoriety.

Kingston is a favorite place of residence for summer visitors from the city, and the excellent Eagle Hotel, near the square, entertains many such. Its streets and the surrounding roads are excellent for cycling and driving.

THE TOUR OF THE CATSKILLS.

The writer has yet to appear who, taking the Catskill Mountains as his theme, shall adequately and truthfully deal with the group in all its aspects.

The magic of Washington Irving's pen, by the relation of the tale of *Rip Van Winkle*, has endowed the whole region with poetic charm, and has given us the impression that every glen must be haunted by the "little people," and each peak have some story. The fact is, on the contrary, that the legendary lore of the Catskills is scanty, and historical incidents of popular interest are almost as scarce.

Again, if one were to believe wholly the perfervid pictures contained in the books issued annually by the local railway companies—excellent and trustworthy as these pamphlets are coming to be in many respects—he must conclude that nowhere else in the world were such grandeur and beauty of scenery, such perfection of hotel and boarding-house accommodation, such supernal excellence of air and water; but these must not be taken literally.

The Catskills are not mountains, of course, in any proper sense—only big hills. Not to suggest the contrast between them and the Rockies or the Alps, they will not compare in mountainous size, nor in their approach to mountainous scenery, with the White Hills of New Hampshire, nor with the Smoky or Black ranges of the Carolinas; nor are their hotels better or worse than the average along the whole line of Appalachian summer resorts, from Moosehead Lake to Chattanooga.

Nevertheless, it is a wholesome and beautiful region, easily accessible, offering opportunities for an outing, either in the wilderness in some secluded hamlet, or amid the holiday-keeping crowd, in a manner costly and luxurious, or simple and cheap, as you prefer; and the Catskills are year by year attracting not only more holiday visitors, but more home-makers. The tendency, indeed, of late years has been decidedly toward the building of cottages and the increase of villages, rather than the patronage of great hotels, many former patrons having purchased extensive tracts of land and built upon them cottages for permanent occupancy. In these associations, the houses and their surrounding grounds are owned individually, of course, yet are mutually connected by some simple regulations, which enable the community, as a whole, to say who shall and who shall not be admitted to the neighborhood, and to make rules of local police. Such are Onteora, Sunset, Twilight, Schoharie, Elka, Santa Cruz, and other "parks," Fleischmann's pretty village, and similar aggregations of friendly summer residents. The striking beauty and salubrity of this part of the mountains has contributed to the prosperity of these parks, and the pleasantest social intercourse prevails among the cottagers, many of whom own their forest homes, and return to them year after year. To those who are in search of health and vigor, no more promising place of sojourn can be found, within the same distance from New York, than on or near the summit of its highest points. People who are weary of noisy, restless city life may be reasonably certain of peaceful and comfortable living among the tree-clad hills and fertile valleys of the famous Rip Van Winkle country.

An alphabetical list of hotels will be found on pages 227-232. A complete list of boarding houses may be secured by addressing the general passenger agent of the Ulster & Delaware Railroad at Rondout, also from the general passenger agent West Shore Railroad, 5 Vanderbilt Avenue, New York City.

Two principal entrances to the Catskill Mountains exist, but both admit to the two lines of valleys in which the tourist may find nearly all of the hotels, and the great body of summer travel and residents. One of these entrances is along the route of the Ulster & Delaware Railroad from *Kingston* west across the southern part of the group; the other is from *Catskill* by rail to the resident parks and Tannersville, and thence down Stony Clove, just behind the line of peaks which form the eastern front of the range. The latter (see the next chapter) is the older approach, but the former comes first in our progress up the river.

The Ulster & Delaware Railroad has a terminal station in Rondout, at the water-side, where passengers arriving or depart-

HAINES' FALLS.

ing by the Rhinebeck ferry, can change to and from the cars without trouble. It skirts old Rondout on high ground, giving a good view of the old town, and stops at the junction station of the West Shore Railroad, a mile inland, where passengers from that line are received in the union station. A third halt is then made at Fair Street, the upper city, or Kingston station proper. The railroad then finds its way across the southern part of the mountains, through the valley of the Esopus on the east and the headwaters of the Delaware on the west. Its devious course gives as good an idea of the scenery of the range as can easily be obtained. The Hudson-Delaware divide is crossed near the summit of Pine Hill, at Grand Hotel station, 1,886 feet above tide-water, after which the line bends northward along the watershed of the Delaware and ends at Hobart, seventy-eight miles from Kingston. From Hobart to Bloomville, nine miles beyond, a little road has been built, which is leased and operated by the Ulster & Delaware, so that, practically, the line and its trains extend to Bloomville, eighty-seven miles from Kingston. A gap of less than twenty miles remains between Bloomville and the Cooperstown & Charlotte Railroad; but as this would bring this company into connection with the railway system of the interior of the State, subject it to competition, and compel it to share through rates, and reduce its present large, non-competitive charges, the gap will probably not be bridged. At present the charges on the main line of the Ulster & Delaware road are at the rate of 3 cents a mile; and on its branches at the rate of 10 cents a mile!

Leaving Kingston, finally, at the upper city station (*Fair Street*), the train crosses the Esopus, or Kingston Creek, and ascends the valley called Stony Hollow. At *West Hurley*, nine miles west, 540 feet of altitude have been gained, and a broad farming valley is opened to view.

The mountain on the right (northward) is *Overlook* (altitude, 3,500 feet). At its base is the village of Woodstock, five miles distant; half-way up stands Mead's "Mountain House," one of the oldest resorts of the region; and two miles farther brings one to the **Overlook House,** near the top, and having an observatory upon the very crest. The breezes are always cool, the surroundings are wild, and the view is truly an "over-look," reaching far away across the Hudson, and north and south for a long distance, including, it is advertised, parts of seven States; but the long stage-ride for passengers, and the necessity of hauling supplies over a rough road from this station, or from Tannersville, have proved too large a handicap, and the hotel was closed with the season of 1891.

Stages from West Hurley leave daily, except Sunday, throughout the year: For Woodstock, 5 miles, fare 50 cents; Bearsville, 7 miles, fare 60 cents; Lake Hill, 10 miles, fare 75 cents. During the summer months only, for Mead's Mountain House, 8 miles, fare $1.00; Overlook Mountain House (when open), 9 miles, fare $1.50.

Olive and one or two small stations in this broad valley having been passed, *Esopus Creek* is again reached and crossed at Broadhead's Bridge, where the line turns up the stream and keeps close to its western bank almost as far as the source. This is the principal easterly stream of the middle Catskills, collecting all the water from the Pine Hill summit, Big Indian, Stony Clove, Beaverkill, Woodland, Shokan, Woodstock, and Platterkill valleys. It is divided from the Catskill and Schoharie, on the north, by the water-shed range that extends from High Peak to Hunter, and from the Rondout, on the south, by the peaks of which Slide Mount is the highest; and in old times was known as the "Little" Esopus, while the Rondout was "Big" Esopus.

The next two or three stations, Shokan, Boiceville, Mount Pleasant, etc., as far as Phœnicia, are quiet little villages, each provided with a small hotel and surrounded by farmers who keep boarders. A continuous line of hills on the right cuts off the view of the mountains proper with the exception of a distant glimpse of the Overlook from Olive Branch, above that portion of the hills called Little Tonche. The central and highest point is named Ticetenyck, and the most western, near Boiceville, Tonche Hook. In approaching Shokan, the beautiful High Point Mountain, 3,100 feet in height, is seen at the left side of the cars, in a southerly direction.

At Shokan the hills shut in rather closely, and nowadays the place is invariably referred to as "at the gateway of the Catskills"—a phrase originating in the title of a magazine article by the present writer in *Harper's* for February, 1876. The region has not greatly altered since that time, such changes as have occurred being a loss of rusticity in the people which is accompanied by the loss of a picturesqueness that it will be interesting to recall. Following is an extract:

The valley [of the Esopus, here] is several miles long and irregularly broad, but with a level surface. The soil is coarse drift-bowlder material, and water-worn stones from an ounce to a ton in weight are everywhere to be seen. Stone walls, consequently, almost entirely take the place of fences. These become browned by exposure to the weather, embroidered with varicolored lichens, entangled in thickets of briers, where lightly rests a mantle of snow-blossoms, or droop rich clusters of delicious berries, or glow sunburned masses of foliage; and they tumble into piles exceeding picturesque the year round. They are the favorite resort of sparrows and wrens, whose lithe bright forms dodge in and out of hiding-places with ceaseless activity, or choose some taller bush near by as a pedestal for joyous song. On every side rise hills to the height of 1,500 or 2,000 feet, culminating at Shokan in the two mountains Ticetenyck and High Point, that stand over against one another at the head of the valley, like two giant warders guarding the portal to the mysteries of the Catskills, which the far blue summits beckon feet and imagination to explore.

Through this huge gate and down the valley winds the Esopus, . . . a brawling mountain stream, such as the painters go to Scotland to find; or rather, it was before the forests on its banks were felled, and its waters were befouled by refuse from the tanneries, mills, and villages which, attracted by its bark and lumber, have grown up on its banks. But to follow up any of its small tributaries, like the Little Beaverkill or the Bushkill, or to work your way to its source, is to penetrate the primeval forest, where, now that the bark-peelers have departed, rarely wanders any but the trapper or trout-fisher, or an occasional tramp like the writer, who would seek for love of them the inmost recesses of the wilderness.

Through this gateway, about the beginning of the century, passed many of the settlers of Delaware County—which lies thirty miles to the northwest—coming from Long Island, Connecticut, and from the counties beyond the Hudson. Down through it now comes a large part of the produce, mainly butter, from that county to market. The settlers beyond the mountains have also sent back a man or two into the world, who emerged from these mountain portals. . . .

If searching varied scenery nearer the village of Shokan, you must not fail to walk two miles down to Bishop's Falls, to which I alluded a moment ago, where the Esopus leaps into its little cañon. To get the complete picture, you must climb down to the foot of the falls, cautiously, for the rocks are slippery with spray and slimy confervoid growths. Beside you is the deep dark pool where the fish love to lie; over your head, the long, covered, age-colored Olive Bridge, spanning the chasm from abutments of living rock; in front, the rock amphitheater, raised still higher by a log dam at the top, down whose steps rushes the tumultuous water, white with the foam of its mad leap and hoarse with the thunder of its breaking waves. On your right is an old tannery, on your left a still older mill. This ancient mill is historic. Through its decayed and moss-grown flume the water has flowed to grind a hundred harvests. Could its walls repeat the stories they have listened to, tell the events they have seen, no other chronicle of the neighborhood were needed, for there have been few inhabitants within a circle of a dozen miles who have not driven under its roadway shed. . . .

About a century ago a man named Bishop, with a baker's dozen of children, came down from Delaware County—curiously enough—to settle here. The space about these falls was all "commons," and Mr. Bishop bought a large tract on one side of the river for a few cents an acre. His first move was to take advantage of the magnificent water-power, and erect a small mill, building so well that the solid oaken timbers stand to-day as firmly as when first put up, but browned by the lights and shadows of the long years which have soaked into their pores. The first machinery, an undershot wheel and simple gearing, was made entirely of wood whittled out by Bishop himself; where he got his buhr-stones, or whether he had any, I do not know. These contrivances lasted some years, but one winter were torn away by ice. Then a workman from Kingston made a wooden tub-wheel. This also stood a long time, but a few years ago was replaced by a turbine wheel, and the primitive gearing by the iron shafts and cog-wheels in present use. Meanwhile, under the ceaseless turning of the stream of life, the owner wore out along with his wheels, and Mr. Bishop was laid aside. Some would think this pioneer might have said, "My life is one dem'd horrid grind"; but we have no record that he even thought of his stay on the earth thus harshly.

The old mill, in its stability, regularity, and slow movement, is not a bad type of the men who bring their harvests to be crushed; and while waiting, grind between the stones of each other's comments the grist of neighborhood gossip. They differ mainly in the cut of their coats from those who came when the old mill was new, for they have preserved the traditions and customs of their forefathers with great tenacity. Their faces show the mixture of Yankee and Dutch blood which flows in their veins, and the thrift in their farming and their incessant whittling further attest the double parentage. All the farms have been in the families of those who now own them for several generations, but still yield abundantly. The aged orchards, the pieces of large second-growth timber, the occasional ruin where once stood a homestead, the many low, old-style, tumble-down houses, show how long the va'ley has been under the plow.

Thus far, these paragraphs remain a fair account of life all along this and the neighboring valleys and mountain slopes, but the following picture can no longer be realized by a visitor to the Esopus Valley, where the old self-sufficiency has been replaced by worldly notions, ambitions, and materials, introduced by the summer boarder and the fast mail.

"The simplest mechanical arts," I recorded in the Centennial year, "never had much foot-hold here, for every young man learns all the trades as well as the methods of agriculture, and by the time he is twenty-four is supposed to be proficient in every handicraft likely to be of use to an independent farmer. He is a wheelwright, a blacksmith, a house-carpenter, a stone-mason, a shoemaker; can patch his harness, repair his gun, or intelligently tinker the few pieces of machinery which have forced their way from the outside world of labor-saving inventions into these quiet precincts. You find a workshop on every farm and a more or less complete set of tools for each of the trades. The cutting and splitting of hoop-poles occupies profitably many a rainy day, after the farmer has seen that his hoes lack no handles and his ox-yoke does not need a new bow.
"On the other hand, the women are skilled in all those household industries which were considered the accomplishments of the Puritan maidens, and are slow to displace the spinning-wheel by the sewing-machine. Of course the testimony of their proficiency as cooks is 'new every morning and fresh every evening.' In the long August afternoons, when the mellow sun glances upon the circles of ruddy cider apples under the broad orchard trees, and the cat drowses on the door-step, guarding the immaculate kitchen from the invasion of the chickens, is heard the loud rhythmic purring of the spinning-wheel, rising and dying away like the droning of the giant bee. Watching the plainly attired woman walking back and forth beside her whirring wheel, guiding with dextrous hands the fleecy lengths she holds, one can easily think himself back in the 'good old colony times,' when the maidens paused in their spinning to chat of the news brought in the last ship from England, or guided their yarn with tremulous hands and beating hearts while their lovers were silently watching them through the misty spokes of the flying wheel. The carding-bee has been outgrown, but the idea remains, and the people still find their pleasures in combining play with work; husking-bees, quiltings, and raisings are yet the enthusiastic occasions of tremendous labor and equal fun. In the fall there is an occasional nutting party, or hunt for wild honey by 'lining' the bees home to their treasure. Hundreds of pounds of fine honey are thus got every year out of these woods."

The mountains which now appear grandly in the south and southwest are the *loftiest of the Catskills,* and the wildest and most picturesque part of the group lies in and about them—a region almost uninhabited, and penetrated by only a few old wood roads usually ending in nothing, or continued by some grown-up bark-peeler's track of long ago, or an obscure footpath known only to the local mountaineers, who tramp it once or twice late in the fall and winter to hunt bears and foxes, and to gather wild honey. These peaks are about four miles distant, and form a half-circle with long converging spurs. The central one of this group is *Slide* (4,220 feet), the highest and most Alpine of all the Catskills, and next to it are *Peakamoose* (altitude, 3,875 feet) and *Table Mountain* (altitude, 3,865 feet); but none of these three is to be seen from here. Their two great companions, visible on this side, are *Mount Cornell*, 3,920 feet in altitude, and crowned by a circle of cliffs, and *The Wittenberg* at its right, 3,824 feet high. Both are rough, densely wooded, and rocky, but they can be climbed from almost any approach. Mr. John Burroughs and the present writer once walked to the top of the Wittenberg from Boiceville, with no great difficulty, by ascending *Traver Hollow* from Boiceville, and keeping *along the ridge of Cross Mountain*, that long spur which reaches down almost to the railway. The ascent was very steep near the top, and the descent into the head of Woodland Hollow, on the other side, was a continual scramble down rocky ledges. Not a path was seen the whole trip; and its adventures, which included a night spent on the summit under an extemporized hut of hemlock boughs, formed the subject of two articles in *The Christian Union* for June 18 and 25, 1891, in which some details may be found of service to any one who cares to repeat the ramble. These mountains show grandly from this side, but as the train advances beyond Shokan presently become hidden by the nearer mass of *Mount Pleasant* at the mouth of the *Beaverkill*, which comes in from the northeast, and up whose valley you see Sugar Loaf, Roundtop, High Peak, and other heights that look down on the Kaaterskill Clove. Here is the Mount Pleasant station, and from it a road runs up the Beaverkill and through to the populous Sawkill Valley, and so down to Saugerties, passing many farms and little villages.

Phœnicia is the next stopping-place, important mainly as the junction of the Ulster & Delaware and Stony Clove railroads.

The valley is here closely environed by shaggy mountains, which are broken northeastward by a great gulch called *Stony Clove*— the latter term an old Dutch word meaning a ravine, still in use all along the Hudson River, and appearing commonly in South Africa in the modified form *kloof*. As you face the Clove, *Tremper Mountain* is close overhead on the right, its spurs forming the right-hand wall of the Clove, and *Mount Sheridan* (2,490 feet) is opposite on the left; while *Mount Garfield* (2,650 feet) is directly westward, and *Mount Romer* southward, behind the observer. Esopus Creek and the Ulster & Delaware Railroad, therefore, come down to Phœnicia between Mounts Garfield and Sheridan, and continue southward between Tremper and Romer. Looking westward, between Romer and Garfield, one sees some ten miles distant the bulky mass of Panther Mountain (3,800 feet) and the "giant ledge" reaching southward from its shoulder at the head of Panther Kill. *Panther Mountain* is a vast elevated plateau of dense rough forests, abounding in big game, and utterly destitute of roads, paths, or people. Those in search of a wilderness, and desirous of "roughing it," can be recommended to go thither, and work their way along to Slide and the head of the Rondout until they get enough of it.

Phœnicia contains, besides several boarding-houses, the great Tremper House, the first large hotel to be built in this part of the mountains. Its elevated situation above the surrounding plain gives it perfect drainage; accommodates 300 guests. A good path leads to the great out-look-ledge on Mount Sheridan, and a carriage road ascends to the summit of Mount Tremper, while just over the hills, at the left, is the pleasant Woodland Valley, as they now call Snyder Hollow, which is some nine miles long, and reaches backward, parallel with the railroad, to the very foot of the Wittenberg.

STONY CLOVE, HUNTER, AND TANNERSVILLE.

Stony Clove is a deep and narrow ravine, where many ledges of bare rock break the monotony of the steep and wooded mountain-sides. A little stream comes cascading down its cleft, and the old wagon road still climbs beside it. It is perhaps true that it "has long been regarded as one of the great scenic attractions of the Catskills"; but it is by no means so interesting as Kaaterskill Clove, nor does it compare with some of the railway passes in the mountains of Virginia or East Tennessee. The railway, built about 1880, is a narrow-gauge line called *Stony Clove & Catskill Mountain Railway*, leased by the Ulster & Delaware Co. All passengers must change cars, but freight-cars are lifted from their wheels, balanced upon the little narrow-gauge trucks, and hauled through without unloading. The terminus is Hunter. Three miles below Hunter a connecting narrow-gauge line called *Kaaterskill Railroad*, and the property of the Ulster & Delaware Co., diverges to the east five miles, to a terminus at Otis Summit station, at the head of the Otis Elevating Ry. The fare on these lines is 10 cents a mile; and on many of the trains are run open cars similar to those between Brooklyn and Coney Island.

Three small stations, two of which are little more than chair factories, are passed in the ascent of the cañon, where an elevation of 1,273 feet is gained in ten miles, and in some places the grade is as high as 187 feet to the mile. One of the stations, Chichester's, is at the mouth of a side ravine called Ox Clove. The summit is reached in an especially narrow pass named *The Notch*, where there is scarcely room in the bottom for the wagon road and railroad together, and the rocky walls are steep but beautifully overhung with vines and shrubbery. Four miles beyond, and around at the left, is the village of **Hunter**, forming a long street along the base of Hunter Mountain, next to Slide the highest of the Catskill peaks. It is an old place, and has churches, factories, a weekly newspaper, etc., but has become prominent as a summer resort since the completion of the railway, and has several large hotels and so many boarding-houses that "nearly 2,000 visitors can be entertained in this locality." *Mount Hunter* (altitude, 4,038 feet) and *The Colonel's Chair* (altitude, 3,165 feet) overshadow the town, and are ascendible by good paths.

Stages leave Hunter daily, except Sunday, for Lexington, 9 miles, fare 75 cents; Hensonville, 7 miles, fare 75 cents; Windham, 9 miles, fare $1. These are pretty villages along the Schoharie, of which Windham is the best known, and has long been a favorite with the migrants who scatter through these mountains in summer. The vicinity is especially noted for its excellent and shady roads, especially that to the cleared summit of Mount Pisgah, whence a landscape of unusual breadth and variety is spread before the gaze.

Five miles east of Hunter, by the turnpike, or six by the railroad (Kaaterskill branch), is **Tannersville**, which is distinctively a summer resort. It abounds in small hotels and boarding-houses, as well as a great number of small cottages, scattered over a wide area of uplands, pretty thoroughly cleared of trees, so that there is a lack of shade and a plenitude of dust. Able and willing to accommodate anybody vying with other places in point of cheapness, and accessible by rail and stage from both Kingston and Catskill, Tannersville has become the resort of a very mixed and rapidly moving summer population, and is a great resort, in particular, of our Israelitish brethren, who love to gather where they can be together. A great circle of high mountains surrounds the town. On the east are North and South mountains, *High Peak* (or Mount Lincoln), and *Roundtop;* on the south, Sugar Loaf, half hidden by *Clum Hill* (the ascent of which is a favorite walk, and about as much mountaineering as the visitors there care to undertake, or would better try, if they depend upon their fanciful imitations of the alpenstock); and westward rise the bulky masses of Plateau and *Hunter* mountains; while northward is Mount Parker (or Spruce Top), and more distant, and the only really interesting peaks of the lot, are *Black Dome* and *Blackhead*. If one goes to the mountains simply to join a rollicking, highly varied crowd, which is bent upon having a "good time" without much expense or attention to conventionalities, the Tannersville district will suit him; but it is not the place for quiet folk, who seek in the hills something else than a cheap copy of the noise and amusements of the city they have left behind.

Tannersville is the station for several of the elegant and exclusive of the associations of cottagers that are annually becoming more numerous in the Catskills, including Elka Park, Schoharie Manor, and Onteora Park.

Onteora Park is a preserve of some 2,000 acres on a hill-slope a mile or more north of Tannersville, and separated from it by a valley which was selected originally as a summer homestead by Mrs. F. B. Thurber of musical fame, and the wife of one of New York's leading merchants, with Mrs. Candace Wheeler and Miss Dora Wheeler, the artists, as neighbors.

It was a place, we are told, where daisied meadows rolled away from their feet, and fir forests climbed the heights behind them;

where little brooks trickled through the shadows of the woods, and away to the left the hills stood aside to show a glimpse of the silver Hudson, beyond which rolled again blue billows of distant hills, which were the Berkshires. "Here is our home," they said, without more ado, and began to build mountain lodges of unhewn spruce logs, with pillars of the silver-skinned birch, having within great low-timbered rooms with wide fireplaces, floors strewn with the skins of bear trapped in the forest behind them, and furnished and fitted in the rustic fashion suiting such a dwelling.

Every autumn there were collected here parties of well-known artists, littérateurs, and musicians. These began to take envious counsel among themselves—seeing all this uncostly pleasure and simple beauty—and to say: "Why can't we have the same thing?" A land company was organized, which purchased 2,000 acres of the mountain, so that no intruders might come in and spoil the lovely environments of the place. A rustic and picturesque inn was built, christened the Bear and Fox. A good road to the top of the mountain was made through the woods, and a number of charming little cottages sprinkled about at odd intervals, all of logs and rustic in character, but individual in design.

This club has a peculiar purpose. It is not meant for rich people, but for cultured and elegant ones. The land is sold, or cottages rented, or camping-places and board at the inn are offered to the right people at very low rates, and denied to unacceptable applicants at any price. Artists are numerous, and make it a point to leave in the club-house some brush memento of their visit. Says a happy guest: "Famous people whose names are on the backs of well-known books, down on the right-hand corner of beautiful paintings, or signed to musical scores, lounge about in flannels all day, reading, sketching, or simply 'inviting their souls,' and in the evening cluster about the great altar in front of the inn, where a huge log-heap blazes every evening, healthily weary with out-of-door sports, tossing brilliant fancies about or trolling minstrel songs to a banjo. There is Gilder, the editor of the *Century*, with his slender dark face and cavernous eyes lit by the firelight. . . . Hamilton Bell, the young Englishman who designs all Daly's gorgeous stage-settings and the Rehan's picturesque costumes, has his note-book on his knees explaining to the noted pianist who makes her home with Mrs. Thurber how Mrs. Potter's Cleopatra costumes are to look when he has finished them. It is the paradise of busy women. Whenever a clever, gifted girl is working for her living she finds the Onteora Club ready to make her entry here so reasonable that even her slender purse can afford it, and several of them have homes here already, simple as may be, but their own, where they can come and meet the most charming people in the whole of America, and yet not be overshadowed by the French dressmaker of richer women."

SCHOHARIE MANSION.

Elka Park is an organization of somewhat similar character and limitations which has lately purchased a large tract of land on Spruce Top, at the source of the Schoharie, and a mile or so beyond Onteora Park. Its members are mainly the gentlemen of the Liederkranz Society, and others prominent in German society in New York; and it will doubtless perfect an encampment of summer residences as interesting and beautiful as Onteora.

Schoharie Manor — having within its boundaries a large club house in the colonial style, termed the Schoharie Mansion — is a recent addition to cottage clubdom in the Catskills, occupying 300 acres adjacent to Elka Park.

Another association, originating in the Twilight Club of New York, has a tract of land called **Twilight Park,** at the head of Kaaterskill Clove, upon which an excellent club-house and many pretty cottages have been built among the trees, whose windows look across and down the Clove,

Still farther, along the steep acclivity of Roundtop, is a similar newer park, called *Santa Cruz,* nearly opposite the Hotel Kaaterskill. The station for both these parks and for *Haines' Falls* is *Haines' Corners,* a mile beyond Tannersville, and itself the center of a large number of small hotels and farm boarding-houses, mostly possessed by some member of the old and numerous Haines family, whose farms join one another in a sort of continuous tribal possession all around the head of the Kaaterskill Clove.

Two miles more brings the train to the *Laurel House* station, and just beyond to the station on South Lake, half-a-mile to the rear of the *Hotel Kaaterskill,* and less than a mile farther is the terminus (*Otis Summit*) at the head of the Otis Elevating Railway. This eastern group of hotels and lofty points of interest overlooking the Hudson belongs rather to Catskill (city) than to the present connection, and will be spoken of more particularly hereafter (see Chap. VI), and it is necessary now only to point out, as has been done, that they are accessible in the rear, as it were, by this all-rail route from Kingston or the interior mountain towns via Stony Clove; and that they can be seen, or made halting-places, upon an interesting round-trip from Kingston to Catskill (city), or *vice versa,* by way of the Ulster & Delaware, Stony Clove, Otis Elevated, and Catskill Mountain railroads. This can be done in a single day, at a cost of $5 to $7, by any one who can not afford more time, or whose curiosity will be satisfied by so rapid a glimpse; and it is well worth doing. The fare from the top of the Elevating Railway to Catskill city is $1.75.

From *Phœnicia westward* the Ulster & Delaware Railroad follows up the valley of the Esopus between Mount Sheridan on the right and Panther Mountain on the left, making its first stop at *Shandaken*, in a valley which already has many hotels and boarding-houses, and seems destined to grow rapidly in population. Its most prominent hotel is Goodheim's "Palace," formerly widely known as Lament's, at the entrance to *Deep Notch*, through which a road leads to the Westkill Valley, *Vinegar Hill*, and *Lexington* on the Schoharie.

Stages from Shandaken run daily, except Sunday, throughout the year: For Bushnellville, 3 miles, fare 35 cents; Westkill, 7 miles, fare 75 cents; Lexington, 11 miles, fare $1.

Making a sharp turn westward at that point, under the brow of Rose Hill (northward), the road winds its way through wild hills to *Big Indian* (station), at the mouth of Big Indian Creek, which is really the head of the Esopus, since it is a larger stream than that which comes more directly from Pine Hill and is followed by the railroad.

This name "Big Indian" has been accounted for by a variety of fantastic stories, of which one given by Van Loan is as follows: In 1832 Theodore Guigou, founder of the family so closely identified with the history of this district since then, settled at Pine Hill, and was shown a stump of a large pine tree, carved in the form of an Indian, near the present site of the Big Indian station. He was then told by one of the old settlers that an Indian whose height was eight feet was buried near the stump. The Indian was chased by a pack of wolves and killed near this spot. The beautiful and wild valley just beyond was then named Big Indian. A more recent and elaborate tale makes this red giant the hero of a love affair in which he was shot by his white rival, and found afterward standing dead, but erect, in a hollow tree, whither he had crawled after receiving the fatal bullet.

Big Indian Creek, or the Upper Esopus, rises high up on the northern slope of Slide Mountain, receiving the tribute of scores of springs and rivulets from Big Indian and Balsam mountains on the west, and from the Giant Ledge and Panther Mountain on the east, and it is a fine clear, cold Alpine stream, once alive

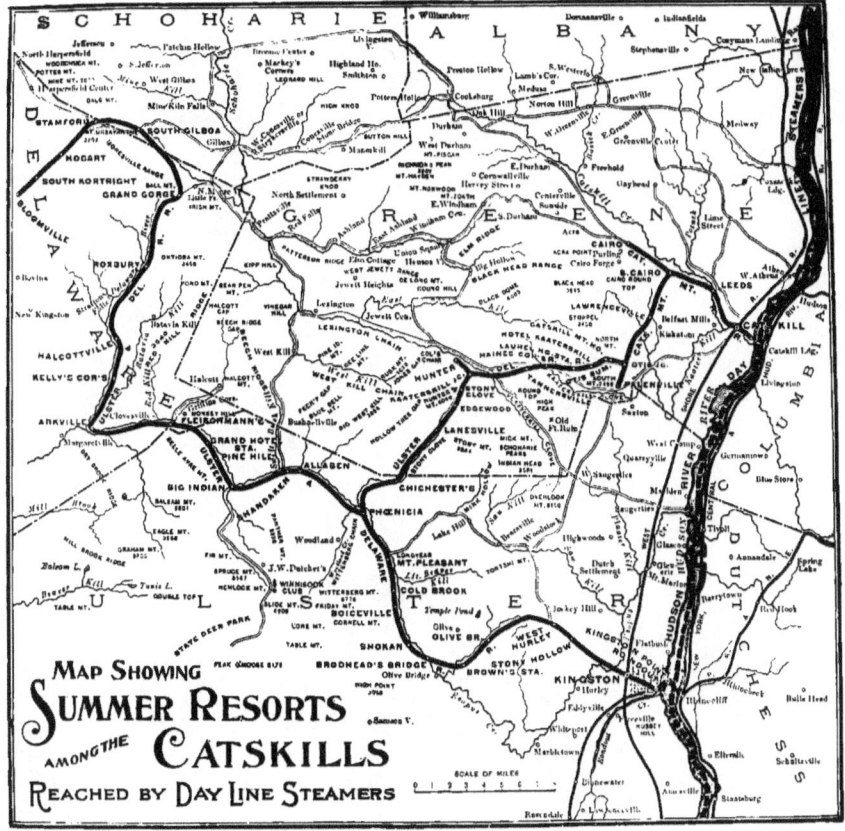

with trout, and still holding enough to give good sport to those who are skillful in angling.

Balsam Mountain is really a part of the summit divide intervening between the Big Indian and Dry Brook, and is interesting for the sake of the *Lost Clove*, a long valley which splits it in two, and opens here in plain sight of Big Indian station ahead on the left. The name refers to the mysterious actions of an educated, well-mannered man named Flint, who, about 1856, built a log cabin far up the Clove. He would occasionally go away for a month at a time, and return with a good supply of money, procuring provisions at the country store, after which he would disappear among the mountains again. He employed a woman to cook, who, with her child, remained with him four or five years. He eventually abandoned the place, and ten years afterward it was known that a man of the same name had died in Sing Sing Prison while confined there for counterfeiting United States coin. Van Loan, who notes the incident, remarks that the seclusiveness and all the mystery surrounding the movements of this man, among a people who are accustomed to know not only the movements but the motives of all their neighbors, have connected the Lost Clove with the counterfeiter; and the white smoke seen in those days rising above the tree-tops near the head of the Clove is thought to have come from the furnace used in preparing the spurious metal.

Up the Big Indian Valley lies the route to **Slide Mountain**, the summit of which is $10\frac{1}{4}$ miles by carriage road and foot-path from Big Indian station. Five miles from the station is a small hotel kept by J. W. Dutcher, where many stop over night so as to give themselves the whole of the next day for the ascent. Mr. Dutcher is an old resident who feels a sort of proprietorship in the mountain, and no one could be a more trustworthy or interesting guide than he.

The carriage road ascends three miles beyond Dutcher's, ending at the gates of Winnisook Lodge, a woodland preserve owned by a club, mainly of Kingston citizens. A novel and commodious club-house has been erected, and a bit of choice mountain water has been converted into a small lake; there are also two or three private cottages. About two miles beyond this, on the west branch of the Neversink, is the State Deer Park, which covers a portion of the 80,000 acres of State domain in the Catskills. It contains a fine herd of deer and some other wild animals, which are breeding successfully, and is well worth a visit. From here on ($2\frac{1}{4}$ miles) the ascent must be continued on foot, but there is a fair path, which is being made into a bridle-road by the State. The great land-slip, or "slide," to which the peak owes its name, and the scar of which is plain in a long, bare, vertical streak upon its face, is said to have occurred during a period of excessively rainy weather half a century ago; but history has recorded no particulars of the catastrophe.

"This crowning crag of the Catskills," says the intelligent writer of a recent pamphlet issued by the railway company, " is the grandest and most interesting of the whole group. . . . The view from this mountain transcends that of any other in the range, it being nearly 200 feet above the highest. Here the lordly Hudson, like a broad silver ribbon with an occasional fold hidden from view, is seen for about fifty miles, extending from the gate of the Highlands to near Hudson. The cities of Poughkeepsie and Kingston, and numerous villages in New York and Connecticut, are in sight. The Housatonic River also shimmers faintly far to the east, and portions of six different States can be identified. In the sublime sweep of vision from the observatory are streams, lakes, valleys, farms, factories, church spires, railroads, and mountains piled on mountains. To greet the rising sun from this crest on a clear morning, and watch again as it sinks over the rugged rim of mountains away to the west, is an experience that no description can portray or anticipate. A recent visitor was delighted with a most novel effect presented by the receding sun there on a remarkably clear afternoon. He says the huge lengthening shadow of the giant mountain, as it reached out toward the river, finally extended over the city of Kingston, and he plainly saw the whole city lying in the gloom of Slide Mountain. This is twelve or fourteen miles away through the air, and it is thus evident that the familiar characterization of Kingston as being "in the shadow of the Catskills" is not merely figurative, but real. A large portion of this mountain, including the crest, belongs to the State. The spruce trees on and near the top are very thickly branched, so that one can recline upon their tops with ease. An excellent spring of water has been found near the crest . . . [and] some choose to spend the night on this summit, which is indeed a decision fraught with varied possibilities, for which ample preparation in advance is peculiarly judicious. But the sublime experience fully warrants the risk of encountering the terrible atmospheric conflicts that at times culminate there. Plenty of food and an abundance of warm clothing and blankets should be provided. A convenient ledge of rocks will be found, under which a small party can secure shelter."

Stages from Big Indian run daily, except Sunday, throughout the season: For Olivera, 2½ miles, fare 25 cents; Slide Mountain P. O., 5 miles, fare 50 cents; Winnisook Lodge, 8½ miles, fare

75 cents; Branch, 12 miles, fare $1; Frost Valley, 15 miles, fare $1; Claryville, 22 miles, fare $1.25.

At Big Indian station is begun *the ascent of Pine Hill*, the summit dividing the watershed of the Hudson from that of the Delaware. Presently there appears on the sky-line ahead the broad white front of the *Grand Hotel*, which by the road is less than three miles distant. The railway, however, must take a more devious course in order to maintain its ascending gradient of about one hundred and fifty feet to the mile, and before reaching the top halts at *Pine Hill station*, beneath which, in the fair valley, lies the scattering and pretty hamlet of Pine Hill. Besides the many summer hotels and cottages, the village has churches, stores, a weekly newspaper, and other features showing a considerable permanent population.

For a charming valley tramp from Pine Hill, the reader is advised to follow up Birch Brook—in which, if you are keen-eyed, you may discover speckled trout lying in its deep, quiet pools—to Bushnellville; cross the divide into Deep Notch, with its summer ice-beds; follow Angle Brook down it to Shandaken, and then turn up the Shandaken Valley and follow the wagon road back to Pine Hill. It will take the greater part of a day.

In the mile and a half of long curve beyond, 226 feet of height are gained, at the end of which the train halts in front of the Grand Hotel, on the "summit," 1,886 feet above tide-level, and forty-one miles from Rondout.

Grand Hotel is an important summer station. A few rods distant is the hotel, the largest of this region, and opened in 1881. It has a frontage of 675 feet; is luxurious in its appointments, costly, and exclusive in its patronage. Every means of elegant amusement and fashionable mountaineering is provided for, and wealth and beauty find there the most congenial company and surroundings. The expenditures for fittings and appointments seem to have been practically without limit, and each season appears to bring a greater share of tourist patronage, many returning year after year. From the hotel piazzas, or, better, from the top of the isolated, bare-topped Summit Mountain, or *Monka Hill*, as it is now styled, just behind the hotel, and 1,000 feet higher, one gets a wide, unobstructed, and inspiring view, through the clear, bracing, balsamic air, of mountains and valleys, the more beautiful because on all sides the refinement of civilization mingles with the savagery of nature. "Southward, in the sky, is old King Slide, only slightly overtopping its aspiring neighbors; westward, the farms and hamlets of Delaware County, and far down under the projecting rocks on which you stand is the green, primeval, wooded, and far-extending valley." A carriage road reaches this eminence.

The range of high hills west of the line, and facing the Grand Hotel, is named *Belle Ayr*, and its slope, *Highmount*, has two hotels—the "Grampian" and "Belle Ayr"—in the center of a cottage community, where building-lots are sold only under certain restrictions. At the western foot of the summit, where was formerly the station called Griffin's Corners—an ancient farming settlement—a village of beautiful and costly houses has grown up around that of Mr. *Louis Fleischmann*, the great Vienna bread baker and restaurateur of Broadway and 10th streets, New York. Here have gathered many German friends of wealth and cultivation, including Anton Seidl, the orchestra leader. The station and park is now known as *Fleischmann's*.

In these swift-descending valleys springs one of the sources of the *Delaware*, and four miles below Fleischmann's the *East Branch* of that great river is encountered at *Arkville*, under the shadow of Pakataghkan Mountain (altitude, 3,000 feet), which is south of the station, across Dry Brook. This is a central point for many diverging roads up neighboring valleys. It is, in fact, one of the delightful features of all this part of the Catskills, and especially here in Delaware County, on the western slope, that one may drive in almost any direction over excellent roads and find the greatest diversity of scenery.

Seven miles southward, up Dry Brook, is *Furlough Lake*, where George J. Gould has erected a handsome summer residence, within sight of his father's boyhood home near Roxbury. *Alder Lake*, still farther south, is a private fish and game preserve, owned by a club of Kingston gentlemen, who sequestrate themselves and their families there in midsummer, and have trout every day. The streams which concentrate here have not only been long famous for fishing, but soon after the Revolution made the place conspicuous by a novel accident. One autumn a sudden and tremendous rainfall on the mountains created terrific freshets in all the streams. A Western man would now say, "There was a cloudburst and the creeks boomed." One old farmer was first made aware of the high water by hearing his

FURLOUGH LODGE, GEO GOULD'S SUMMER HOME.

children crying in the night, and reached out of his high four-poster to find their trundle-bed all afloat. It was before harvest, and thousands of ripe pumpkins were swept down by the flood, which was spoken of ever afterward as the "pumpkin freshet."

Stages run from Arkville daily, except Sunday, throughout the year: For Margaretville, 2 miles, fare 15 cents; Clark's Factory, 6 miles, fare 50 cents; Andes, 12 miles, fare $1; Delhi, 26 miles, fare $1.75; Lumberville, 8 miles, fare 50 cents; Union Grove, 12 miles, fare 75 cents; Shavertown, 15 miles, fare $1; Pepacton, 19 miles, fare $1.25; and Downsville, 26 miles, fare $1.50; Lake Delaware, 20 miles, fare $1.50.

The railway here turns sharply north, and ascends the East Branch of the Delaware for a dozen miles to its source on Irish Mountain, passing through a country of dairy farms, long ago settled by Scotch and Scotch-Irish people, where many visitors now find rural entertainment. *Mount Pisgah* * (altitude, 3,425 feet) is conspicuous off at the left; and Vly Mountain and Bloomberg are prominent peaks in the Summit Range at the right, recalling by their names the Dutchmen who first lived at their bases; the latter is visible from Tannersville. In the valley of the Schoharie, beyond those mountains, are Gilboa, Prattsville (both reached by daily stage from Grand Gorge station, fare 50 and 40 cents respectively), Huntersfield, Windham, and various other popular villages and objects of interest already spoken of.

Prattsville has perhaps 1,000 inhabitants, and, in addition to the loveliness of its situation and the miles of maple-shaded roads that diverge from it in all directions, possesses an extraordinary curiosity in what are locally known as the Pratt Rocks, which are daily visited by wondering tourists.

Old Col. Z. Pratt, long since dead, used to own much property in and about Prattsville, including this hillside crested with beetling rocks. "With the view of improving upon nature," Kirk Munro tells us, "the good colonel employed sculptors—of whose skill you can judge when you see their work—to carve from these rocks many quaint devices, for which he furnished the designs. Horses, dogs, and human figures are mingled in the general plan, and as each was finished it was painted white to resemble marble. There they still remain, much to the astonishment of the passing traveler who has not been informed concerning them. Every bowlder on the hillside is also carved into some shape different from that which it originally assumed. The

---

* The same name is also applied to a lofty mountain northwest of Windham, High Peak, at the head of Mitchell Hollow, in Greene County.

whole forms a unique and enduring memorial of the eccentric colonel."

Huntersfield Mountain, six miles northeast, gives one of the most far-reaching views in the Catskills; and other neighboring heights are well worth climbing. Another object of special interest, one mile distant, is Devasago Falls and the narrow cañon into which the current plunges by a leap of fifty feet.

Roxbury, the next station, is an old-time dairy-farming village snugly packed away between hills that are dotted with cattle and pastures and dairy barns. It is of growing importance as a summer resort, and is interesting to the outside world as the boyhood home of Jay Gould, the deceased railway financier, and of John Burroughs, the naturalist-author. It is not generally known, by the way, that Mr. Gould was also author of something besides railway certificates and Wall Street rumors; but it is a fact that when a young man he wrote a history of this region — a book now extremely scarce. A pretty memorial church has been erected and a free library established here, to the memory of her father, by Miss Helen Gould.

At *South Gilboa*, a short distance farther, the "Delaware Divide" is attained, and one has a fine outlook over the valleys and through the mountains, the scene increasing in beauty as the line swings westward around the base of Mount Utsayantha, and runs down to Stamford.

"**Stamford**," to quote the enthusiastic, but not overdrawn, picture in the Ulster & Delaware's little book, "is the prettiest and most charming village in the Catskills. It is seventy-four miles by rail from the river, and 1,767 feet above it. The early settlers were from Stamford, Conn., after which this place was named about a hundred years ago. The situation in the lovely open valley at the headwaters of the Delaware River, on the western border of the Catskills, with lofty mountain-crags rising abruptly and grandly almost from the village streets, is most delightful. Nature has bestowed liberally here, and man may well admire and appreciate. For a summer mountain-home with all the requisites—the best air, the best water, the best scenery, the best drives, and the most wholesome and pleasing moral atmosphere— it will be hard to equal Stamford. Mount Utsayantha towers 3,203 feet in the air, near the village, the sightly crest being reached by a short drive up the slope over a good road. From the tower on this mountain the eye rests upon one of the most magnificent panoramas to be found anywhere, covering an area of 20,000 square miles, and embracing twenty-eight prominent peaks in the Catskill Range. Mount Churchill, a sister peak near by, will also be surmounted by a tower, to which a road is promised. Utsayantha is an Indian name, in connection with which forest tradition contains the details of a sad tragedy in which a beautiful Indian maiden, her babe, and her white husband lost their lives.

"West of Stamford begin the little streams which braid into the great Susquehanna, later. One mile east is Bear Creek, which empties into the Schoharie. Thus within a half-hour's drive one may drink from the headwaters of three great rivers. One hundred years ago a battle between the citizen soldiery and the Indians and Tories was fought on the present village site, which then contained only two houses."

Not until 1872 was Stamford thought of by summer visitors. Then two Brooklyn gentlemen drove over from Prattsville and sauntered into the seminary, then in charge of Dr. S. E. Churchill. Being delighted with the locality, they prevailed upon Doctor Churchill to open his house to summer guests, and from that time to this the business has steadily increased. "Churchill Hall" was erected in 1883, and has since been enlarged. In 1893 he completed a larger and more elegantly appointed hotel, "The Rexmere." Meanwhile other hotels have arisen in the village, which has a population of about 1,500, and does much business, especially in dairy products. Some of these, as the excellent "Delaware House," are open the year round; while others, as the "Grant House," "Greycourt," etc., are large summer hotels only. In addition to all this, many very attractive private cottages are scattered all through the village, which looks as prosperous and well-groomed as if it were all a part of a city park. The village has five thriving churches, a union free school, water-works, electric lights, a National bank, numerous stores, a public library, and two of the best country weekly newspapers in the State. Near the village is "Eagle's Nest," the home of the late "Ned Buntline," the story-writer, and originator of the much-abused "dime novel," though he can not justly be held responsible for the evil imitations which followed and debased his earlier work. The Kortrights, Jefferson, Harpersfield, and other rural communities frequented by city people in summer are within easy driving distance.

Stages from Stamford run daily, except Sunday, throughout the year, to Harpersfield Center, 4½ miles, fare 50 cents; Davenport, 14 miles, fare $1; Oneonta, 27 miles, fare $2; Jefferson, 7 miles, fare 75 cents; Summit, Schoharie County, 14 miles, fare $1.25; Richmondville, 18 miles, fare $1.50.

Hobart, four miles farther down the Delaware, is a pretty little village, with a history antedating the Revolution. It is the western terminus of the Ulster & Delaware track proper; but the new *Delaware & Otsego Railroad* has been completed to *Bloomville*, about nine miles beyond, and trains run to that point. *South Kortright* is an intermediate station, four miles southwest of Hobart. From Bloomville a stage goes daily on to Delhi, eight miles farther (fare, 75 cents), giving a very pleasant ride. A stage also runs to Bovina Center, six miles from Bloomville (fare, 50 cents). The Delhi stage connects with the morning train from Rondout, on Sundays. It is possible to drive across from here to West Davenport, the terminus of the Cooperstown & Charlotte Railroad, and go by rail to *Cooperstown;* but a better road and a more interesting country are seen by driving or taking the stage down the Charlotte River Valley from Stamford, and the distance is little, if any, longer. From Cooperstown it is an easy matter to go down the lake and on to Richfield Springs, or over to the New York Central Railroad and back to Albany, and so make an interesting round-trip.

This rounds out the Catskill tour.

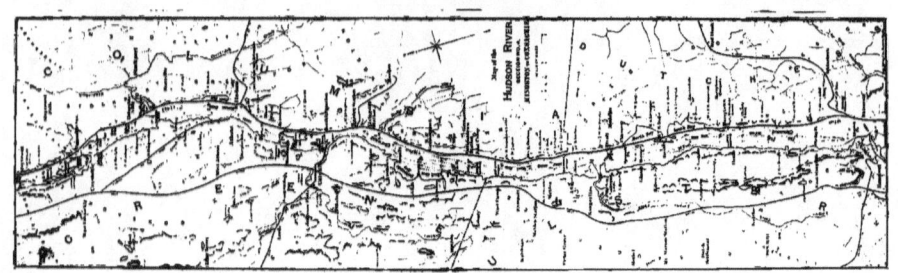

KINGSTON TO CATSKILL AND TO THE MOUNTAIN RESORTS.

Rhinecliff, opposite Rondout, is the landing and railroad station for *Rhinebeck*, 2½ miles inland; stage fare, 25 cents. The day-line boats no longer stop here, but this is the terminus of the *Philadelphia, Reading & New England Railroad.*

Rhinebeck is an ancient, pleasant, and prosperous town on the old post road, now numbering some 2,000 inhabitants, and having two hotels. These, several village boarding-houses, and many of the long-settled surrounding farms, are filled with summer residents from the city. Its first-comer and the Patroon of the region was William Beekman, whose low-eaved stone house is still standing on the high ground near the station, and is now occupied (with additions) by the Hermance family. It was built prior to 1700, and is an excellent example of the Dutch architecture of that period. The round port-holes under the eaves, whence an attack of Indians might be resisted, are still visible; and the fact that here were instituted the first religious services is not only a matter of history, but is attested by the very ancient grave-yard along the brow of the bluff near the house. Some grand views of the river and mountains are given by this road, and a visit to Rhinebeck is well worth the trouble.

A fine villa with a pointed tower, seen a mile above Rhinecliff, is "Ferncliff," the Astor residence, formerly the home of William Astor, and now occupied by John Jacob Astor third. Next comes "Clifton Point," now the home of Louis Ehlers, and especially interesting to members of the Methodist Church in America as having been built by Freeborn Garrettson, the eminent preacher, who married a sister of Chancellor Livingston, and to whose energy is due much of the prosperity of that branch of the Christian Church. Douglass Merrit lives just beyond at "Leacote." Opposite, in succession northward, are the estates of Albert Terry, Charles M. Preston, J. N. Cordts, A. S. Staples, P. S. Gurney, nd Charles A. Shultz, the last just above the little landing called

Flatbush; and still farther along the western bank are passed in succession the cement-works of E. M. Brigham, and the residences of C. O. Livingston, C. Coddington, and Dr. G. F. Shrady. The last is "Pine Ridge," and is a little below the ice-house on Turkey Point. Returning to the **eastern** side of the river: Opposite Doctor Shrady is *Astor's Point*, just below which can be seen the brown house with a square tower owned by F. H. Delano; and just above it is "Rokeby," built by one of the Astors, where J. W. Chanler now lives. The mansion with a Greek-pillared front, next northward, and behind Daisy Islet, is "Edgewater," the home of E. C. Goodwin; and just beyond is the landing and railway station of **Barrytown**, known of old as *Lower Red Hook*, because it served as the landing-place for Red Hook, an old-time posting village two miles inland, and now a station on the Hartford & Connecticut Western Railroad. There is a small hotel on the wharf.

Immediately above the landing is the Aspinwall home, "Massena"; and half-a-mile farther, on a lofty bluff overlooking the cove of South Bay, is *Montgomery Hall*, a magnificent place, the house upon which was built by the widow of that General Montgomery who fell at Quebec, and which is now inhabited by Carleton Hunt. Just north of the Sawkill is St. Stephens (theological) Seminary, near "Annadale," the estate of John Bard; and more inland, behind Cruger's Island, "Devcaux Park," the estate of Col. Charles Livingston, and more lately named "Almonte." This brings the catalogue of things of interest to *Cruger's Island*, a peninsula where Col. J. C. Cruger has spent money freely and well in landscape gardening, and has set up on the southern end of the island a quantity of architectural and statuesque ruins, brought many years ago from the prehistor c cities of Central America. The channel passes close to them on one side and the railroad on the other, but only a mere glimpse of th se interesting objects is attainable. The mansion was recently burned.

The marshy bayou north of Cruger's Island is *North Bay*, and the headland forming its northern shore is **Tivoli**, which takes its name from the "chateau" erected here before the Revolution by one of the Livingstons, but more lately occupied by the family of the late Col. J. L. De Peyster. This old house stands a short distance back of the railway station and landing, where a small village has grown up. Somewhat southward of the chateau stands "Callender House," now occupied by Mrs. Kidd; and at the foot of its lawn, on the shore of North Bay, was built, in 1807, Robert Fulton's first steamboat, the *Clermont*, so named out of compliment to Chancellor Livingston, who was the partner and financial supporter of Fulton in this far-reaching enterprise.

Along the post road here, two miles back from the river, upon the higher ground, live J. N. Lewis, near *Upper Red Hook;* then the Reverend Doctor Platt; and next north, the De Peyster family. Tivoli itself is of importance mainly as the point of steam ferriage to Saugerties; but just above it is seen, among the trees near the shore, an interesting ante-revolutionary residence called "Rose Hill," now the home of Gen. J. Watts De Peyster. It is related that the British, on their way to burn Livingston's manor-house, "Clermont," a little above, in 1777, stopped here under the impression that this was the house to be destroyed; but the owner, with the aid of his well-stocked wine-cellar, convinced them of their mistake, and "Rose Hill" was left unmolested.

The Western Shore, which we have been passing, is less interesting, but worthy of attention. The residences as far as Turkey Point, opposite Barrytown, have already been noted. North of that point the shore is high, diversified in outline, and wooded, and serves as a beautiful foreground to the Catskills, of which we here obtain an uninterrupted view; but it is destitute of buildings deserving mention until the little valley town of *Glasco* is seen, surrounded by brick-yards. Just south of Glasco is the house of Henry Corse, Jr., and north, along the bluff, are the homes of Messrs. Polhemus, O. R. Spaulding, and of Mrs. Vanderpool, a sister of the late President Martin Van Buren. In the rear of these estates runs a highway which is excellent for driving. Upon this road, opposite Barrytown, a notable object is the ancient *Flatbush Church*, near which is Aunt Tren's Lake, now called *Lake Katrine*, and turned into a picnic resort. Still farther inland, in the lowlands along the Esopus, runs the West Shore Railroad, with *Glenerie* and *Mount Marion* as stations, to the station for Saugerties, a mile west of that town.

Saugerties is a brisk and attractive village clustered about the gorge through which the Esopus finds an outlet to the

Hudson. Its beginnings were nearly as long ago as those of Kingston—to whose jurisdiction it was attached when all this region was "Esopus"—and it has grown by slow and substantial degrees. The impression one gets as he strolls about the well-shaded streets, and observes the character of the houses and their surroundings, is that it is a town of a settled and well-to-do population, among which it would be very agreeable to live if you were not tormented by abnormal energy. Grand views of the Catskills are presented, and some of the finest pictures of the river may be had from these high shores, while the rocky cañon of the stream, with its great artificial fall, is an altogether unique feature in the scenery of the Hudson. *Barkley Heights*, south of the creek, is an especially attractive part. The Catskills come nearer to the Hudson at this than at any other point; the Overlook, Kaaterskill, and Mountain houses are in plain sight; and it is only a day's drive to any of them or to Tannersville.

The Platterkill Clove, a great gorge that opens into the very heart of the mountains, directly west of the village, is the special property of Saugerties in the Catskillian collection of glens. The rural district at its entrance is a lovely plain, where nearly every farm-house is filled with city people in summer, and at its head is the *Plaaterkill Hotel*, whose stages meet express trains at Saugerties; but the Clove itself is the wildest of all the great glens that separate the eastern peaks of the range, and the most difficult to travel. "Eighteen water-falls may be counted in a walk up this clove, and the wild grandeur of the scene has defied almost every pen and pencil. The Kaaterskill and Stony cloves are more frequented and less hazardous than the grand old Platterkill, and almost as beautiful; yet with the latter we must feel the sympathy that one gives a defiant conqueror. It rests captive, if you like, by the present day in one sense, but boldly suggestive of the days when its first inhabitants lived in it without touching one stone or curve, one stream or angle, that nature had set there; and the steady stream of progress, or perhaps I should say tourist, may go on another fifty years before the Platterkill will succumb to the imperious claims of man."

Saugerties is an incorporated village, but has no bonded indebtedness, and taxes are low. It has a daily and two weekly newspapers, several public schools, one parochial school, and an academy; seven churches, mountain water introduced by the gravity system, electric and gas lights, telegraph and telephone communication, and several hotels offering good accommodation,

FLEISCHMAN'S SETTLEMENT, DELAWARE COUNTY.

as well as numerous summer boarding-houses in the village and neighborhood. Stage fare to Mt. Airy House, 50 cents.

Saugerties is favorably situated for the location of industrial enterprises. There is a wide-awake board of trade; transportation charges are reasonable; there are two banks of deposit and a savings bank; and abundant water-power and labor. The village is already the seat of several important industries, among which are the Sheffield Company, manufacturing writing-papers, blank-books, and envelopes; the Martin Cantine Company, manufacturing coated papers and card board for lithographing purposes and the factory of the Barkley Fiber Company, devoted to making wood-pulp by the sulphide process. The great white-lead factory at Glenerie belongs here too. Most of these establishments can be seen from the steamer, in the narrow harbor which has been made by the Federal Government, where the wharves measure a mile or more along each side of the creek. Much space there is yet available as sites for manufacturing concerns, and others may be found west of the village, near the railway. One of the chief industries of the place is in the quarrying, dressing, and shipment of bluestone (here of Devonian age), which is largely carried on at the landing called *Malden*, just north of the village. The making of brick is also extensively prosecuted in the neighborhood. The West Shore Railroad, a daily night-line of steamboats, and the ferry to the Hudson River Railroad, at Tivoli, keep Saugerties in close communication with New York, and make it a good place wherein to live or to do business.

Not many special objects remain to be pointed out along the western shore from Saugerties to Catskill, where we leave Ulster and pass into Greene County; the **Eastern Shore**, however, abounds in facts of social and historic interest. Almost opposite Saugerties is "Idele," the old *Chancellor Place*, lately the home of Miss Clarkson, and the first estate in Columbia County, the division-line between it and Dutchess County coming to the river at this point; and half-a-mile above it, opposite the bluestone wharves of Malden, is "**Clermont**," an early manor-house of the Livingstons, whose manorial church still stands about four miles inland. The present owner and occupant is Clermont Livingston, a descendant of that sturdy patriot and statesman of the revolutionary period—one of the Provincial Committee of Safety, and first Chancellor of the State of New York—Robert R. Livingston, from whose time the present structure dates.

THE STORY OF CLERMONT.—The Livingstons of New York have a long and genuine pedigree, descending from long before the days of James I. of Scotland, where an ancestor stood nearest to that king. In 1600 Alexander, the seventh Lord Livingston, was created first Earl of Linlithgow, a title which descended to the fifth earl, who, in 1713, was made a peer of the United Kingdom; and our local name *Linlithgo* is derived from that fact. But this gentleman joined the Pretender, lost his earldom, which has never been restored, and the line is extinct. The fifth Lord Livingston, guardian of Mary, Queen of Scots, whose daughter was one of "the four Marys" who were playmates and maids-of-honor to that unfortunate woman, founded a line of descendants, largely ministers of the Scotch Kirk, whence sprang an adventurous young man named Robert, born in 1654; he, having been exiled with his father to Holland, learned Dutch and Dutch notions of liberty, hastened to America as soon as he came of age, and went to live at Albany, where he became prominent, and remained until 1686. By that time he had purchased from the Indians lands extending for twelve miles along the east bank of the Hudson River north of Roelif Jansen's Kill, extending inland to the Massachusetts boundary, and embracing upward of 160,000 acres, or about 250 square miles. This was created by Governor Dongan into the lordship and manor of Livingston. In 1692 he built a manor-house on the bank of the Hudson at the mouth of Livingston Creek, but did not actually begin to live in it until 1711. One of this Patroon's acts was to procure for Captain Kidd the commission for privateering against pirates, which he turned to thrifty account by becoming head pirate himself; and more than one person has dug in the grounds of the old manor for treasure said to be buried by him. To his eldest son, Phillip, was left all this estate except about 13,000 acres known as the lower manor, which was given to the second son, Robert, who called it "Clermont." Phillip became the patriarch of a family whose members occupied distinguished places in the early history of the United States, and are still prominent; but the lands were divided by his grandson among his heirs, breaking up the old manor, to the ownership of which no special dignity had been attached, of course, since the Declaration of Independence had abolished all American "lordships." The same remark is true of the progeny of the other sons and daughters of this highly endowed family. Meanwhile Robert had built a manor-house at "Clermont"; and here were born another *Robert R.*, his grandson, who became the chancellor, and a group of brothers and sisters who reached almost equal eminence.

Col. Robert R. Livingston was so well known as an influential and ardent republican and soldier that the British were eager to cripple him, so far as was possible, by burning his place. After the demolition of Kingston, therefore, Vaughan, although aware of Burgoyne's surrender and the risk he ran, sailed up the river this far in order to destroy it. A wounded British officer and an attendant surgeon, prisoners on parole, were at the time the guests of the family, who were nursing the sick man. These officers advised Mrs. Livingston to cease her preparations for saving what property she could, offering to protect the place against destruction. She did not consider it safe to rely upon their promises, or at any rate upon their ability. Her negro servants therefore heaped what furniture and valuables they could into two carts, and the family started for a refuge in Massachusetts. The last load was not out of sight when Mrs. Livingston looked back to see the building in flames. The house was speedily rebuilt; and when, in 1824, the Marquis Lafayette made his triumphal visit to the United States, and was proceeding to Albany upon the steamboat *Kent*, which had been chartered for his accommodation by the citizens of New York, a whole festive evening was spent at Clermont, and many a relative of the family was greeted by him as an old comrade in arms.

Having passed the marshy shallow called Livingston Flats, the little landing of *East Camp* appears on the right, with *West Camp* opposite on the western shore. These were early settlements of the German refugees from the Palatinate who were provided with lands here about 1710; and a very interesting old church still stands in the midst of fertile farms back of West Camp, which dates from those early times. The estate near *East Camp* is R. E. Allen's "Riverview"; and just above is seen the rural village *Germantown* (the name recalls the Palatinate refugees, as does also New Hamburgh, etc.), the abode of several families of wealth and social position, and a favorite resort of summer residents.

The view of the Catskills from this part of the river is very fine. One's gaze reaches to the very head of the Kaaterskill Clove, where, with a powerful glass, the cottages and hotels at Twilight Park and Haines' Falls can be discerned; and south of that great glen are seen the graceful summits, beyond Overlook, that smile down upon Phœnicia and the Shandaken Valley. As we pass on up the river, the front range assumes a fanciful resemblance to a colossal human figure lying upon its back—a curiosity of shape which the aborigines taught the first white explorers to recognize. "The peak to the south is the knee; the next to the north is the breast; and two or three above this, the chin, the nose, and the forehead."

Four miles above Germantown the Hudson River Railroad tracks will be seen crossing the mouth of a deep bay. This is the mouth of *Roelif Jansen's Kill*, which played a very important part as a boundary in the early geography, and distribution of lands and jurisdictions; and on the farther side of it is the pretty village *Linlithgo*, just above which are the Burden iron mines and furnaces, and the estate of Hermann Livingston, having the house near the shore at the base of Oak Hill. This is just south of *Catskill* station, on the Hudson River Railroad, where there is a steam ferry (fare, 15 cents) to

Catskill Village.—This old town, which before the completion of the Ulster & Delaware Railroad from Kingston was the only point of entrance to the Catskills for tourists and summer residents, is picturesque and interesting, and has a history that is full of romantic interest. As early as 1678 several square miles of land here was bought from the Indians by Albany men— the first Robert Livingston, Gerritson Van Burgen, Salisbury, and others; and several of the dwellings erected by these first settlers are still in existence and service. Such wars with the Indians and troubles with the British soldiers as Kingston and the lower towns experienced never came to disturb the peace and prosperity of this village growing up along the banks of Wildcat Creek,* and it early became one of the most prosperous communities along the river.

The Catskill of to-day is a large, active place, much resembling Peekskill in the stately appearance of many of its houses, the abundance of mature shade-trees, and the irregular way in which its streets wander up and down the hills over which it has spread. The business part is mainly in one long street, with shops and hotels—a vast amount of bustle in summer and sleepy peace in winter. "Around about, in a sort of stately indifference to the activity of the place as a 'resort,' are the houses of olden time, belonging to families who have authorized Americans in their feeling that pride of race may be consistent with the most simply republican sentiment." And these old places give a dignity to the town. He who runs may read their story, since in few instances have the original forms been altered. They preserve their Dutch symbols, the heavy cross-beams, the generous fire places, or the English architecture of the last century so perfectly that their tale is assuredly written in stone and wood-work."

The village lies in the valley and upon the high banks (chiefly the northern) of this creek. A long pier has been built out from

---

* This is the translation of the Dutch *kat-kil*, which has become "Catskill"; or, in the plural form, *katen-kil*, which has been corrupted into "kaaterskill" or "kanterskill," both of which are ludicrously wrong, but too firmly fixed to be made right. The "cat" may have been the panther (or puma), or nothing worse than the common lynx. The Indians (Iroquois) called the range Onteora—the "land in the sky."

the natural point of land to deep water, and all day-line steamers stop here. There is also a line of night-boats plying between this port and New York. This is the terminus of the *Catskill Mountain Railroad*, which runs to the base of the mountains at two points—*Palenville* and *Cairo*—and whose trains come down to the steamboat landing in summer. The West Shore Railroad has a station on the west side of the town; and a ferry (fare, 15 cents) connects with trains on the Hudson River Railroad; while a neat little steamboat, the *Isabella*, makes four round-trips daily between Catskill and Hudson. Stage fare in Catskill, 10 cents.

Summer hotels abound in the immediate vicinity of Catskill; and the principal business of the whole local district between the Hudson and the mountains is the entertainment of city people during the hot months. It is a fact, indeed, that the area of cultivated land, and the care of farming and dairying, decrease year by year, since all the farmers are becoming boarding-house keepers, though it is hard for an outsider to understand why such a result should follow; why can not an industrious man do both? The largest and oldest of the local hotels is the great white *Prospect Park House*, whose long pillared portico is a conspicuous object on the bluff north of the village. It commands an extensive river landscape, is most attractively situated in every respect, and has long been patronized by a superior class of guests. On Jefferson Heights is the *Grant House*, admirably located upon a breezy, commanding hilltop, not too far from the post office, and in possession of a long list of regular patrons.

Driving and walking routes about Catskill are recommended as follows by Van Loan, a local authority:

"Half-a-mile from the village, along the river-shore, is *Deeper Hook*, near the picnic grounds in the lower grove belonging to the estate of the artist, the late Thomas Cole" [painter of the "Voyage of Life" and other well-known pictures]. "No one should fail to visit *Austin's Glen*, known also as Hope Hollow and Jefferson, about 1½ miles from Catskill. The track follows the course of the stream for some distance, and crosses it at a natural fall. Near a cave in the glen is a spring of ice-cold water. . . . A walk on the '*Snake Road*' and return, by making a circuit of the Grant House, will occupy two hours.

"*For driving:* To *Leeds* (crossing the old stone bridge), and back by the way of Kaaterskill or Belfast Mills, an easy two hours' ride. *To Athens and back;* or turn to the left, one mile out on the Athens road, and passing the *first left* (unless a shorter way back is desired) and then the two *right* hand roads, keep on to

Jefferson, where the turnpike to Catskill can be taken; or by adding ten minutes' time, pass around the Grant House and its grounds, returning by the 'Snake Road.' After passing the toll-gate, two miles from Catskill on the Cairo road, take the first right-hand road at the edge of a piece of woods, and follow it directly north for two miles and a half to *Green's Lake.*"

The Grant House, alluded to above, is situated on the southern edge of Jefferson Heights, 300 feet above tide-water, and commands an almost unobstructed view of not only the Catskills, but also of mountains in Vermont and the Berkshire Hills of Massachusetts, while the valleys of both the Catskill and Kaaterskill creeks are in the foreground of the view, and form delightful walking and riding routes. Every amusement, such as tennis, baseball, croquet, bowling, boating on the creek, and billiards, have been provided for guests; and music is provided morning, afternoon, and evening. Excellent bass and trout fishing is to be had within a short distance from the house. Special attention has been given to the water supply and drainage of this hotel, making it a most desirable place in which to spend the summer months.

"One of the finest rides is to take the direct Catskill Mountain road west to the old King's road, following the latter to a left-hand road that brings you to the brick school-house on the Saugerties road; thence north to its intersection with the mountain road, one mile from the village. Going south of the brick school-house, and taking a road that returns through the woods on the right hand, affords a very fine view of the mountains. A delightful half-day ride is to take the old King's road to High Falls, crossing the bridge at the falls, and take the right-hand road northward to the mountain turnpike near the division of the Palenville and Catskill Mountain House roads, halfway from Catskill to the mountains."

The **Catskill Mountain Railroad** and **Otis Elevating Railway** form one of the principal entrances to the Catskill Mountains, and the direct route to the long-famous *Mountain House.* Its trains also run to Palenville as a southern terminus, and to Cairo northward. The Otis Elevating Ry. connects at Otis Summit with the Kaaterskill Railroad (page 167). The *stages* from Catskill Village pass through Palenville en route to Tannersville; and from Cairo stages run in summer to every point of importance in the northern part of Greene County. This northern "corner" of the mountains is perhaps the most attractive, naturally, of the foot-hill districts, but is less frequented than some others.

The railway journey to the mountains (fare, to Otis Jc., $1) is a foretaste of the enjoyment of your vacation in the highlands.

"The route is well chosen," writes an observant traveler, "and leads you away over a country full of richness and peace; of idly growing things, great fields of corn, stretches of buckwheat with the bloom of August on it; into ravines where the water rushes with an ancient melody in its movement, and out and over a plain beyond which the mountains rise, relegating all smaller things into insignificance. . . . The train takes us up around Catskill proper and into Leeds, and Leeds was really old Catskill—in very truth the place which gave this part of the country a name. Whence comes the name I believe the most faithful chronicler can not say. It is found in various old records. In a letter dated over one hundred years ago, and which the present owner kindly allowed me to read, 'Catskill Village' is mentioned, but the place now known by that name was then referred to as the 'Strand,' or the 'Landing,' for, as I have said, the village of Leeds was then Catskill proper.

"I think it nurtured in men a curious feeling of permanence, proprietorship; of desire to keep nature unchanged, glorious, and true to her first, best impulses; for there at Leeds one finds so few marks of the impress of destroying man; so little which could jar the student of form and color as God has laid it upon his earth. Whether this has come from jealousy, listlessness, or perhaps the appreciation of vastness, one can not say. All that can be reduced to fact is that Leeds village, the old Catskill, lies simply embosomed by the hills and vales which the Indians and Dutch must have known, and it seemed to me a most perfect relic of the past, which is fast becoming too traditional to seem our own."

The Catskill Mountain House is the oldest of the large summer hotels in these mountains, dating back to coaching days.

Originally the access was wholly from Catskill by means of Concord coaches, or by driving in from Hunter or Tannersville. For ten years after the opening of the railroad, in 1882, stages climbed the mountain from Laurenceville. But in 1892 an inclined cable railway, the **Otis Elevating Ry.**, was put into operation from the railroad in the valley to the plateau near the hotel. This hoists passengers in ten minutes (fare, 75 cents) from *Otis Junction* to *Otis Summit;* and it has become not only the direct route to the hotels, but one of the regular routes to the Kaaterskill and Laurel houses, Haines' Falls, Twilight Park, Santa Cruz Park, Tannersville, etc.

The Otis Elevating Ry. is 7,000 feet long, and in that distance it ascends 1,600 feet and attains an elevation of 2,200 feet above the Hudson River. In length, elevation overcome, and carrying capacity, it exceeds any other incline railway in the world. It was built and first opened for travel in 1892. It is operated by stationary engines and steel-wire cables. A passenger and baggage car are attached to each end of double cables, which pass around immense drums located at the summit of the incline. Thus, when one train ascends the other descends, the trains passing each other midway. By this arrangement trains carrying 75 to 100 passengers can be run in both directions every fifteen minutes, when necessary, the time required for a trip being only ten minutes. The ascent of the mountains by the incline railway is a novel and delightful experience, and alone worth a visit to the Catskills. As the train ascends, the magnificent panorama of the Valley of the Hudson is gradually unfolded, and the Hudson River and the Berkshire Hills in the distance seem to rise up to the view of the passenger. The time required for the trip from Catskill Landing to the summit of the mountains is ordinarily fifty minutes.

The completion of this quick and easy means of access has resulted in increasing the travel to the many resorts on this route. A limited train operated during the summer season makes the trip from New York to Otis Summit in three and one-half hours.

The Mountain House stands upon the verge of one of the eastern ledges of South, or Pine Orchard, Mountain, 2,250 feet above tide-water, and by reason of its peculiarly advantageous location on the front of the range commands a view of the Hudson Valley which is more extensive than that embraced by the outlook of any other hotel.

The park surrounding the hotel has a valley frontage of over three miles in extent, and consists of about five square miles of forests and farming-lands, traversed in all directions by many miles of carriage roads and paths, and including within its boundaries North and South lakes, both plentifully stocked with various kinds of fish, and well supplied with boats. Signs and guide-marks indicate the paths to various places or objects of interest. The *top of South Mountain* is easily reached; a path makes the circuit of its summit lower down; plain paths lead to *Kaaterskill Falls*, along each side of the lake, and steps descend to the bottom of the cataract. The *Palenville Overlook*, or *High Rock*, 1,728 feet above the bed of the creek, and *Moses Rock* on the *Long Level*, may be taken in another circuitous walk. These are south of the hotel. Good roads and paths lead to similar grand outlooks northward—*Artist's Rock*, *Prospect Rock*, the *Sunset Rock*, *Bear's Den*, *Newman's Ledge*, and the *crest of North*

OTIS ELEVATING RAILROAD, CATSKILL MOUNTAINS.

Copyright, 1892, by Loeffler, Tompkinsville, S.I.

Mountain, the summit next north of South Mountain, whence magnificent views north, east, and south are obtained. Many longer excursions by driving are possible — going one way and returning by another.

The Hotel Kaaterskill is an immense and splendidly-furnished hotel, 2,495 feet above the level of the Hudson River. The view from the hotel piazza is awe-inspiring when first seen, and of never-ceasing interest when grown more familiar. The extension of the railroads almost to the doors of the hotel, within the past few years, has been of great convenience to guests, who can now approach either by the way of Phœnicia and Stony Clove, or by way of Catskill and the Otis Elevating Railway. This ease and rapidity of access is highly appreciated by busy New Yorkers, who can run up to the Kaaterskill on Saturday afternoon and back to the city on Monday morning without the least delay en route. The hotel has been lately improved and made more than ever attractive to its patrons. The precautions against fire have been a matter of especial care. The tanks on the roof are said to hold 200,000 gallons, and the watchmen and male employes are organized into a well-drilled brigade of firemen, acquainted with the apparatus and instructed as to proper action in an emergency. The neighborhood of the Hotel Kaaterskill is intersected in all directions by carriage roads and paths, which connect with those of the old Mountain House; and a carriage road from Palenville winds up the acclivities of the Kaaterskill Clove, despite the assertion of engineers that it was impracticable to build such a road.

"So numerous and varied," says an appreciative writer, "are the attractions and points of interest to be visited near and from the Hotel Kaaterskill, that an energetic guest could be kept constantly on the go for twenty consecutive days, visiting a new scene of wonderful beauty each day, and being amply repaid for each separate effort. Of the many fascinating points within easy walking distance of the hotel, none is more worthy a visit than *Sunset Rock*, half a-mile distant. It is a bare table-rock, overhanging Kaaterskill Clove, with an almost sheer descent of 1,500 feet. Directly opposite rises, grand and dark, 4,000 feet in the air, the *Kaaterskill High Peak*, offering to view its entire face from base to summit. Its sides are closed with a royal evergreen mantle, streaked here and there with the ermine of falling water, and woven of whispering pines, dark-hued firs, sturdy spruces, and the stately, sweet-scented balsams, with tops as straight and sharp as lance-tips. . . . Looking down the Clove, its embracing mountains form a wondrous frame for the fair picture of the valley of the Hudson widespread beyond, with gleams of water in the distance. Turning toward the setting sun, the glisten of *Haines' Falls* is seen at the head of the Clove, and grand and somber Hunter Mountain rises far inland. While the western sun still bathes the rock in its light, the deep valley below is dark and tremulous with the shadows of evening. The true lover of nature has no need of artist tongues to tell him that he sees a *perfect* picture from Sunset Rock; he knows as he gazes, that were aught added, or one feature taken from it, its completeness would be marred; and that though other views may be more extended or more grand, none can be more truly beautiful.

"One of the most charming drives from the hotel is down the *mountain road*, with its 'swan's neck' and 'horseshoe' curves, to Palenville, and then up the romantic Clove, in which there are many tempting bits of tumbling waters, dark pools, sequestered nooks, and grassy glades, to the Kaaterskill and Haines' Falls, the two principal cascades in the Catskills. The last grade, near the upper end of the Clove, is the steepest on the whole road, and on surmounting it the head of the Great Land Slide is crossed. Here, each winter, the road is torn from the hillside and hurled into the abyss 600 feet below.

And oft both path and hill were torn
Where wintry torrents down had borne,
And heaped upon the 'cumbered land
Its wreck of gravel, rock, and sand.

"From the summit of the Clove the return to the hotel can be made by way of the back road over the mountain.

"The finest all-day drive from the Old Mountain House or the Hotel Kaaterskill is to the Overlook Mountain House, over the new *Plaaterkill Mountain road*. The distance is about fifteen miles, and the route back from the mountains is to Tannersville around Clum Hill, and over the Plaaterkill turnpike to the very headwaters of the Schoharie and the upper end of Plaaterkill Clove. From here the new road, four miles in length, opened in 1880, winds at a dizzy height along the side of Plaaterkill Mountain, above the clove of the same name."

The **Laurel House** is a long-established and somewhat less expensive hotel than the others, situated about a mile west of the Hotel Kaaterskill, at Laurel House station on the Stony Clove line, and near Kaaterskill Falls. It is only a short distance farther to Haines' Falls and Tannersville.

KAATERSKILL CLOVE AND RIP VAN WINKLE.

This great ravine, long ago named Kaaterskill Clove by the Dutch settlers, separates High Peak from South Mountain, and is the channel of the Kaaterskill, which empties into the Catskill just above Catskill Village. West of High Peak (which is the loftiest point of the front range as seen from the Hudson, and nowadays sometimes called Lincoln Peak) is Roundtop, from the farther slopes of which springs the Schoharie, a tributary of the Mohawk. Fortunately, the natural beauties of this gorge sustain the legendary interest with which Indian tradition and the imagination of Irving have endowed it. A fine road ascends the Clove from Palenville, at its entrance, to Haines' Corners, at its head; and the best way to see it is to drive through, at leisure, in your own conveyance, or to walk; but two lines of stages make trips daily in summer between Catskill and Tannersville via Palenville and the Clove. They are very comfortable covered wagons (fare, $1); about four hours are consumed in the trip, and as the passenger is expected to walk up the last mile and a half or so of steepest road, he has plenty of time and chance to see afoot the best part of the ravine.

The old stage-road to the mountains, however, did not go up this Clove, but wound its way up the Sleepy Hollow Ravine, north of the Mountain House. This road is still kept in good repair and is available for cyclers coming down, but hardly in going up.

The most sympathetic description of this once delightful stage journey is contained in an article by Mrs. Lucy C. Lillie in *Harper's Magazine* for September, 1893, from which the following extracts are made:

"It seems to me that the early spring and late autumn are the seasons when this mythically historic spot should be seen to its best advantage, for the shifting elements of the summer-time force upon it too business-like an aspect. In the very mildest part of one October I remember driving up the hilly curve that brings on to the brief sweep of land which is a sort of halt before the mountain's final ascent. There to the right stands the dilapidated old house, bearing a historic picture of Rip and his flagon, and to the left is a terrific gorge, crowded by trees and ferns, and which in its lavish break westward shows one of those rich and smiling valleys which meet one at every opening in this luxurious country.

"The Rip Van Winkle House, it seems to me, is only a shell to bear on its outer side the cracked and worn picture of the dear old sleeper of these hills. Turning away from the gorge, we asked a man, lounging about, where the picture came from, and he informed us it had been there over forty years, and no one seemed to know its origin. It is not altogether bad in color, and the drawing is not worse than the best sort of a sign-board, while it has a certain charm of antiquity which gives it character. It hangs just above the tumble-down little doorway of the house, and to the left, high up among the rocks and their underbrush, is the spot where Rip was supposed to take his sleep of twenty years.*

"From the moment the real heights are entered upon there comes a new feeling in the air—a consciousness, dim at first, but fast growing into exhilaration, that we are reaching the final uplands of the world. The roads are now almost perfect, and the tales of overturned stages and runaway horses are fast growing mythical. These last miles up the mountain are at twilight full of melancholy charm, and I think that as we go on and upward the sense of isolation even from humanity so grows that the darkness falls as though a shrouding of nature were only what one might expect. Sounds are few; movement is, as it were, only part of the still-life about one, and the green to right and left darkens into impenetrable night. Then suddenly comes a revelation. Here on the very summit of the highest mountain-peak we come upon a great lawn and terrace illumined by electric light, a hotel all doors and windows and vivid animation. A band is playing; there is a vista of a long room with whirling figures, while everything round and about is suggestive of youth and brilliancy, fashion and luxury. . . .

"Once up on the mountain-top, the traveler feels impelled or urged on into the ordinary stream of summer action at a summer resort. Before one stretches a view of hill and dale, of valley land, which is beautiful enough to bear every analysis. . . . The variety seems almost endless, and new pathways are opening on every side. For a time we hesitated about revisiting the Kaaterskill Falls, dear to our childhood, since they are so completely under business management; but, after all, we were entirely repaid even for the laborious climbing up and down the cleft, at the foot of which one can see the falls in all their glory leaping and tumbling over the finely irregular rock; and in spite of the business-like manner in which the visit must be made, there is some interest and amusement to be derived even from the spirit of speculation and 'sight-seeing' of the native and the visitor. There is a little summer-house at the entrance to the falls, where you pay your 25 cents, and may invest still further, if you like, in candy—the real old-fashioned sticks

---

* While Irving, perhaps purposely, left indefinite the precise spot, if any he had in view as the locality of the imaginary adventures of Rip Van Winkle, common consent for many years has made this Clove and "Rip's Rock" the place. No intelligent person, probably, believes that such a character ever really existed or had any such an experience; but it is not surprising that many believe the story to have been derived from a tradition in circulation among the Dutch pioneers, and handed down to Irving's time. But this is not true. Irving did nothing more, as indeed he hints in a foot-note, than rewrite, with his humorous grace, and apply to the Catskills and the Dutch character, a superstition which has reappeared in every European land and nation since earliest times, that certain notable persons were not really dead but only sleeping or imprisoned in the earth, awaiting the termination of a period, or the breaking of a spell, or some other event which should set them free. The Rip Van Winkle house still stands as a part of another.

of candy—or such beverages as root beer, lemonade, or soda-water, and there are always interesting and entertaining fragments of conversation floating about. . . . It certainly is not inspiring to have the falls 'turned on' to order, but those in authority declare that this is done by no means simply from speculation, for there has been long felt a danger of the water giving out if not held in check. Soon, however, the scene itself dispels the commonplace feeling which came first. Surely this might well be the scene of that old tradition of the hunter and his gourd. And upon the rocks, even in the noisy waters high up on either side, seems the spell of the mountain's magic—the peculiar loneliness and sense of each rock, each stream, each tall fir, communing with itself, repeating over and again the strange stories of the past."

Catskill to Hudson.—Resuming the voyage up the great river, the steamer passes close under the beautiful Catskill shore, to avoid the grassy flats called Roger's Island, near the eastern bank. In revolutionary times this island was densely wooded; and it is related that in the narrow channel behind its curtain a great number of river-craft were safely hidden, in 1777, when the English fleet came up the river; but the marauders turned back before reaching this point. On the hill behind it are the country seats of F. E. Church, the artist, and Doctor Sabine. The shores above the island grow hilly, and the eye is attracted to a long and lofty ridge upon the right, which is beautifully cultivated, and suggests a reminiscence.

The ancient name, it is said, was Rorabuch, but this hill has been known as Mount Merino ever since the first decade of this century, when a *furore* over the rearing of merino sheep was introduced among farmers of the Eastern States, and the whole of this hill was then devoted to flocks of that breed. Although a few merinos had been introduced previously, it was not until Robert R. Livingston turned his attention to the subject, wrote a widespread pamphlet about it, and sent home a large importation of blooded stock from Spain and France, where he was then United States Minister, that public interest was aroused. Enormous sums were paid for the animals at first, but their price soon fell to figures little in advance of those for native stock, and the vast sheep-pastures were again plowed for grain. The extensive wool industry of Vermont, however, dates from this period; and unquestionably the grade of American sheep was elevated, so that the general result of the speculation was beneficial.

Mount Merino gives the rambler one of the most enchanting landscapes in the whole Hudson Valley. On the opposite bluffy shore are the estates of George Griffin, W. O. Morrison, and Mr. Guntley. As soon as Mount Merino is passed, the grass-grown shallows of Hudson Flats divide the channel, and the steamer swerves to the right and slows up at the wharf of

The City of Hudson.—Hudson is a town of 10,000 people crowning a bold bluff on the eastern shore. It has a curious history, quite different from that of most of the valley towns.

Dutch and English farmers and fishermen were settled all along these hill-slopes, from the earliest times, as tenants of the lower manor of the patroonery of the Van Rensselaers, but nothing in the shape of a village arose until 1783, when a purchase of lands was made by a company of merchants from Massachusetts and Rhode Island for the purpose of pursuing the whaling business, since during the Revolution the whale fisheries of Nantucket were broken up by the English. Settlers arrived at once, and were so numerous and influential that in April, 1785, the town was incorporated as a city called *Hudson*, the third city in the State, and having much wider limits than at present. This name was peculiarly apt, because here, or very near here, Henry Hudson ended the voyage of the *Half Moon*, and upon his return from his farther boat voyage halted for two days while he stored his vessel with wood and water and bade a ceremonious farewell to the natives, who had treated him with the greatest cordiality. This locality* was therefore peculiarly identified with the navigator. The city stands at the head of ship navigation—a fact which had recommended it to the choice of its commercial promoters; and preparations were at once made for sending out whaling-ships. Their early voyages were very successful, and reminders of this adventurous and almost forgotten commerce may be seen in the city to-day, as when, for example, the stranger comes upon a whale's jaw standing as a tall sign-post in the main street. A large trade was done with New York, Boston, and Providence, and Southern ports, principally with Charleston, S. C., in provisions and general produce, bringing in return cargoes of rice and cotton, sugar, rum, and molasses. In 1790 the city was made a port of entry, and with the growth of its commerce it bade fair to become the second city in the State. Another natural and important factor of growth was its ship-yards. Ship-building was carried on so extensively that at one time more vessels were owned in the city

---

* It should be mentioned, however, that the best historians do not now accept this claim, but assert that the real place was higher up; some say in the mouth of Kinderhook, or Stockport, Creek, and others near Schodack. *N'importe!*

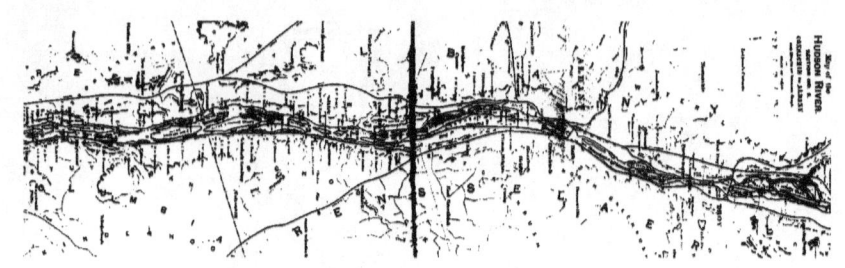

cl
to

al /B. T.E. Bronk
th
bu
pi
M
thr
fis
ar
A
th
pr   NEW
ne
an
da
ce
th   N. DAM
id
sh
of   SARATOGA
fo
su
fo
ex
tal
No
pr
pro
ru
an
se
of
ex   R.

acc
the
N

of Hudson than in the city of New York. During the Revolution in France, and the War of 1812 at home, many of the vessels owned in Hudson were employed in the carrying trade, and several of these were captured or destroyed by the French and English, several were lost by shipwreck, and when steam navigation became a certainty the decline of the commercial prosperity of the city was complete. "In 1815," says an authority, "the city was closed as a port of entry; an effort to revive the whaling interests was made, but with indifferent success, and in 1845 the last ship engaged in the business was sold." The high hopes of Hudson were then quenched; but this was due not to the fact that the expectations were replaced—for under the conditions of transportation which obtained at the time when the town was founded the town at the head of navigation was in the best commercial position—but because, with the rise of steamboats and railroads—new conditions—the city at the mouth of the river had so much advantage.

Hudson stands upon a slate bluff which rises abruptly from the river, and from whose brow, now a public promenade, a very wide and pleasurable view of the river is presented. It is sixty feet above the beach, and across the wide moat of the Hudson the long front of the Catskills rises like some Titanic fortification.

This bluff is the end of a narrow ridge which slopes gradually upward for a mile and a-half to *Prospect Hill*, the high, rounded eminence behind the town. Warren Street, the main thoroughfare, extends along the crest of this ridge, with the neighboring streets sloping downward on each side. The town is very compactly built, its streets are deeply shaded, and many of its houses are old and excellent; the best of them cluster about the pretty square, with its noble trees, in front of the portico of the court house. The city has electric cars, steam ferries to Athens and Catskill (see p. 185), and a small steamboat now plies between Hudson and Albany The State Reformatory for Women is conspicuous upon a green knoll south of the city.

Columbia County and its little capital boast of many citizens of consequence in the past as well as the present. President Martin Van Buren lived here as a young man, and passed his declining years near by. Samuel J. Tilden spent his boyhood in this vicinity, and is buried at New Lebanon, not far away. Here, in the early decades of this century, were living such prominent men as the once famous orator Elisha Williams, and the lawyers Ambrose Spencer, William Van Ness, Thomas P. Grosvenor, Jacob R. Van Rensselaer, Col. Elisha Jenkins, and others.

In the days when these men were young and fashionable, they would go in midsummer to the *Columbia White Sulphur Springs*, four miles east of the city, where all the world made merry, as now they do at Saratoga. A hotel still opens its doors, and a few lovers of the old resort annually assemble there to preserve the traditions; but these springs are rarely set down in the lists of fashion's watering-places.

Not far distant, and a station on the Boston & Albany branch road, is the quaint and historic village of *Claverack*, now known principally as the seat of "Claverack College," a prosperous school of wide repute for both sexes.

"The handsome and substantial college buildings, surrounded by beautiful and well-shaded lawns, and commanding most charming views of the romantic scenery in which the neighborhood abounds, are the features of the village. The old Dutch church, with its staring date of 1767 on its western side, shines out in old-fashioned red among the towering oaks that keep ward over it and its adjoining cemetery. On the opposite crest is 'Fairview,' the stately mansion built by the late Doctor Flack, who was the founder of the college, and its president for more than thirty years. Down the village street are the residences of the descendants of the Muhlers, the Ostranders, and the Van Rensselaers, and in a quaint old yellow brick, dormer-windowed house are to be seen the *lares* and *penates* of Gen. James Watson and other distinguished Webbs. The 'Spook Rock,' in a shady swirl of the Claverack Creek, is visited on moonlight nights by the neighboring swains and their sweethearts, who linger to see it turn in its shiny bed when it hears the institute bell."

The distance from Hudson to the *Berkshire Hills* is only thirty miles, and this way comes a large part of the travel between that favorite part of Massachusetts and the metropolis. Many New Yorkers, sending their horses and carriages up by boat, drive over from here. Perhaps more would do so if the excellence of the roads and the varied and unsuspected beauty of the scenery in this neighborhood were more widely understood. From some of the higher points on the country roads, the hills of Berkshire, the Taghkanick, and even the Green Mountains, are visible, as well as the ever-present Catskills. Beautiful glens and quaint hamlets abound, reminding one of the better-known but no worthier region about Tarrytown.

Athens is the classical name of a little ship-building and brick-making town opposite Hudson, and connected with it by steam-ferry. It missed the goal half a century ago, when it failed to carry out its contemplated design of bringing the Erie Canal to the Hudson at this point. Four miles above Athens the promontory long known to old pilots as "Chaney Tinker" now bears a light-house, and the prosaic name *Four-mile Point;* John ?. Burchell has a house just below it and George Houghtaling another immediately above it.

Nearly opposite is the broad mouth of **Kinderhook Creek**, with the railway station *Stockport* and the rural hamlet *Columbiaville* on its banks. This district was settled very early in the history of the State, and queer old "cross-roads" may be searched out up the valley of this stream and that of its large southern tributary, Claverack Creek. In Kinderhook Village, a few miles northwest, was born and reared *Martin Van Buren*, Governor of New York, Jackson's Secretary of State, Vice-President, and finally President of the United States from 1837 to 1841. About 1848 he retired to an estate there, where he resided until his death in 1862.

Half-a-dozen miles farther north the river is narrowed by a hilly headland called *Nutten Hook* (sometimes corrupted into "Newtown Hook"), on the eastern shore, where there is a railway station called *Coxsackie*, and a small hamlet, whence a steam-ferry crosses to *Coxsackie Landing* on the western bank.

Coxsackie is said to be from an Indian word meaning "cut-banks," and is locally pronounced "Cook-sackie." It is chiefly a trading-town, having a station a mile inland on the West Shore Railroad, and surrounded by a large area of fine farms, where hundreds of town-people find summer board.

Stuyvesant, the landing and railway station on the east side of the river, just above Coxsackie station, was formerly the "port" of Kinderhook, and noted for its shipments of grain; but now it is of little importance.

The head of natural ship-navigation in the Hudson has now been reached; and the steamboat channel henceforth winds between low islands and marshy flats, which by and by nearly fill the river, while the shores exhibit fertility and the scenes of peaceful cultivation, in respect to which there is little that is adventurous or picturesque in story to relate.

The elevated sites of the substantial farm-houses and occasional country-seats along these shores command an inspiring view of the northern Catskills, of which *Black Head* (3,965 feet) is most conspicuous. Northwest of and beyond that massive summit are the serrations of the range that stretches northwestward into Schoharie County, with *Windham High Peak* (3,500 feet), Mount Zoar, Mount Hayden, *Mount Pisgah*, and Sutton Hill as successive peaks of prominence. Along their base flows the Catskill Creek, and nearer us is the course of Potuck Creek, its principal northern tributary. The valleys of all these streams are highly cultivated, largely by the descendants of the original Dutch settlers, and it is said that that language is still frequently heard in the more remote hamlets.

New Baltimore, the next landing above Stuyvesant, is a little town on the western shore, noted for its industry in building small river-craft, such as sloops and barges. Just above it is the mouth of *Haanakrois Creek*, which marks the end of Greene County (entered just north of Saugerties) and the beginning of Albany County. Immediately opposite is the boundary-line between Columbia County and its neighbor northward on that side of the river—Rensselaer County; so that in the rocky islet on the left of the channel four counties corner. This prominent little **Barren Island** was once far more prominent, actually *compelling* attention. Its true name is *Beeren* (or "Bears"), and on its summit once stood the "castle" of Rensselaerstein, from whose wall Nicholas Kroon, the agent of Killian Van Rensselaer, the Patroon, compelled passing vessels to dip their colors and pay tribute, or take the chances of being sunk by the ordnance of the fort. It has now become a favorite picnic resort for excursionists from Albany and Troy; and a small steamer plies daily between the island and Coeyman's Landing.

In the earliest times the Dutch gave the name *Claverach*, or "Clover Reach," to this whole district—a breadth of term which has caused much indefiniteness in some historical narratives. It was all embraced in a vast grant of land to the first Van Rensselaer, of whom we shall hear more when we come to the story of Albany. Disputes as to ownership under this grant arose; and in 1704 it was conveyed by Killian Van Rensselaer, the head of the family at that time, to his brother Hendrick. He in turn devised it to his son Johannes, who erected it, under English royal sanction, into the Lower Manor of Rensselaerwyck.

Immediately above Beeren Island, on the western bank, is **Coeyman's** (pronounced "Queeman's"), a small landing and village, a mile or more west of which is the junction where the main line of the West Shore Railroad begins to bend westward toward Buffalo, while its Albany branch keeps on northward. Opposite it another small and pretty village, called **Schodack**, is seen; and five miles farther brings the traveler to the flourishing town of **Castleton**, built upon the front of a steep hill from which the spires of Albany and its towering capitol are distinctly visible.

Castleton Bar, formerly known as the "Overslaugh," has always been a serious impediment to navigation at this point. As early as 1790 State appropriations were made for the purpose of improving the channel, but all efforts were unavailing until the present system of dykes was begun by the State in 1863. In 1868 the United States Government assumed the work of completing the dykes, and they may now be seen stretching for several miles along the river, effectually accomplishing the purpose for which they were intended.

The Boston & Albany Railroad passes through the northeastern edge of Castleton, and has a station called *Schodack Depot*, recalling the fact that near there (some five miles north) was the place which the Indians called Schoti-ack, where was kept ever burning the central council fire of the Mohegan Indians, who deemed that spot their capital, so far as such a term could be applied to their confederacy.

THE CAPITAL CITY.

Albany stands upon the west bank of the Hudson, 145 miles above New York and about ten miles south of the mouth of the Mohawk River. Opposite, on the east bank, is the old town of Greenbush, or East Albany, and the population of both shores is dense for a dozen miles above, where the cities of Troy, West Troy, Cohoes, Lansingburgh, Waterford, etc., succeed one another with little that is "truly rural" between them.

The steamboat wharves at Albany are close to the business center of the city and to the two railway stations, which are themselves close together at the river-side. The New York Central & Hudson River Railroad and the Boston & Albany Railroad unite in East Albany, and cross the river into the Union Station, where, also, certain through northern trains of the Delaware & Hudson system enter, so that passengers between New York and the north (Montreal) do not need to change stations. The West Shore Railroad and the Delaware & Hudson Canal Company's Railroad use jointly a station between the Union Station and the river, just around the corner of a single block. Both of these stations are only about five minutes' walk from the landing of all the Hudson River steamboat lines. All of the hotels of the city, also, are within walking distance, Stanwix Hall, Delavan, and minor hotels being just across the street from the exit of both stations; the "Kenmore," the largest hotel, one block farther away.

The Union Station contains a large dining-room, but fruit and edibles may be bought far more cheaply just in rear of the station.

Historical Sketch of Albany.—It will be remembered that Hudson's men ascended the river in their small boat as far as the mouth of the Mohawk. Whether it was by their recommendation or not, the adventurers who followed them chose this point as the site of one of the first Indian trading-posts. It was well chosen, for here naturally came to the river the great trail that crossed over to the Mohawk at Schenectady, and then followed that valley westward to the lake country and to Ontario; and also trails southwestward to the Susquehanna, and trails and canoe roads north and east. It was a central point on the Indian highways, as it has become upon the transportation routes of civilization; and moreover it was the head of natural sloop navigation.

Albany, according to Lewis Morgan, author of *The League of the Iroquois*, owes its Iroquois name to the openings there between the Hudson and the Mohawk. Long anterior to the foundation of the city this site was well known under the Seneca name *Ska-neh'-ta-de*, whence followed the name of the Hudson, *Skä-neh'-ta-de Ga-hun'-da*, "the river beyond the openings." It would thus appear that Schenectady has appropriated the name which rightfully belongs to the city upon the Hudson.

In 1614, as we read in H. P. Phelps' admirable *Albany Handbook and Guide to the Capitol* (Albany: Brandow & Barton, 1884), Henry Corstænsen, under a grant of the United New Netherlands Company, erected a stockaded trading-house on the island just below the present city. It was garrisoned by ten or twelve men, who had a cannon and twelve stone-guns with which to defend themselves. Here they carried on an extensive fur trade with the Indians, until the spring freshet of 1617 nearly destroyed their domicile, when they moved "up town" and erected a new fort on the hill near the Normanskill. The West India Company erected a fort in 1623 on a spot near what is now the steamboat landing, and called it *Fort Orange*, in honor of the prince who presided over the Netherlands; but only eight families were resident here. In 1629 the feudal system of *patroonship* was instituted in America by act of the Dutch States General. Any member of the West India Company who should plant a colony of fifty or more adults in Dutch America was to be acknowledged a "Patroon of New Netherlands," and was given permission to acquire lands extending sixteen miles along any navigable river, and inland indefinitely. "The Patroons possessed," as Phelps points out, "absolute title to the soil; had a monopoly of fishing, hunting, and grinding; of all mines and minerals, and a preëmption right of buying the colonists' surplus grain or cattle; their courts had jurisdiction in civil and criminal cases, in the latter even punishment by death; colonists could not leave the colony without written permission, and after their terms of service were fulfilled they were compelled to return to Holland. The tenants were in fact little better than serfs, and modifications of the enactment soon followed; not out of regard for the people, but because the Patroons waxed arrogant and came into conflict with the West India Company. None was more conspicuous in this respect than the Patroon of this region, Killian Van Rensselaer. He was a pearl merchant of Amsterdam and one of the West India Company's directors, and acquired lands which soon included a tract called Rensselaerwyck, forty-eight by twenty-four miles in extent, reaching from Beeren Island to the Mohawk. His colonists began to arrive in 1630, at once built a brewery, and soon constituted a village separate from Fort Orange, named Beaverswyck. The lordly pretensions of this Patroon, who arrogated to himself baronial powers and privileges that interfered with the company's fur trade, led to quarrels in which he was compelled to let go of the land about Fort Orange, although he kept possession of all the remainder; and the results of that feudal tenure led to the 'anti-rent war' of forty years ago, and to long litigations that are scarcely ended yet, for the estate still exists as a land word in this and in Rensselaer counties. The fifth Patroon, Stephen, was the last to receive the title and entire estate, and the entail ceased at his death in 1839."

When in 1664 the province fell into the hands of the English, the name of the settlement was changed to **Albany,** in honor of the Duke of York and Albany, who had modestly attached his first title to the seaport at the mouth of the river; and in 1686 the town was incorporated a city.

Albany, as the center of the trails and fur trade south of the St. Lawrence, was much resorted to by Indians and by the scarcely less savage French *coureurs du bois,* who ended each transaction by a grand spree. But the town was always well fortified with palisades, and during the terrible closing years of that century, when the Indian massacre at Schenectady (1690) was only one of many such outrages, Albany was safe within its stockades, which reached from the river back to Lodge Street, and from Steuben Street on the north to Hudson on the south side. Here, in the Indian and Canadian wars half a century later, rendezvoused the armies of Amherst and Abercrombie, and then proceeded against the Champlain forts; and here were lighted early the fires of patriotism which burned steadily during all the period of the Revolution, when the place was constantly a depot of supplies, and an outpost always threatened, but never reached, by British expeditions from Canada or from the Indian country

This was the meeting-place of the Continental Congress of 1754, in which all the Colonies north of Virginia convened by delegates to discuss the proposal of a federal union. The plan proposed by Benjamin Franklin was agreed to, but none of the Colonies would ratify it because it delegated too much power to the general government; while the king refused to approve of it, on the other hand, because it did not go far enough in that direction. But the Constitution of the United States, adopted only a dozen years later, was so closely similar that the idea of the Union may be said to have been first formulated here in Albany in 1754. Washington visited the town in 1783, and dined in the Schuyler mansion; and Lafayette, who had commanded the post for a time during the war, revisited the city in 1784. In 1790 the census showed that Albany County had a population of 75,150 (almost twice as much as New York County), and the city, 3,506. It was on the emigrant road to the Genesee country, "the West" of that day, and grew rapidly. In 1797 it was made the capital of the State, and by 1800 numbered 5,349 citizens, and in 1810, 10,762. The first steamboat began running here in 1811, and the next year Greenbush was chosen as the headquarters and rendezvous for General Dearborn, the commander-in chief of the armies in the second war with Great Britain, and thousands of troops were gathered in and about the city. This stimulated the growth of the town to 12,541 in 1820, and the opening of the Erie Canal to this point in 1825 (the occasion of great local rejoicing) doubled these figures, which had increased to 33,000 in 1830. Two years later (1832) saw the first railroad train running between Albany and Schenectady; but it was not until 1851 that the Hudson River road gave a through rail connection to New York, the first train making the run in three hours and fifty-five minutes, including stops; nor until 1853 that the consolidated railroads were opened westward to Niagara Falls and Buffalo, and north to Montreal; and it was six years later (1859) before the opening of the Delaware & Hudson's route to Binghamton and the Pennsylvania coal region. Within late years the city's advancement has been steady, and the population now exceeds 100,000.

Besides its political and social prominence the city is largely engaged in lumber, grain, and shipping interests, and in manufacturing, particularly stoves and other ironware.

The **tour of Albany** and its sights is easily accomplished. The capitol, State museum, and most notable buildings are all within walking distance of the boat landing, railway stations, and hotels; and for farther explorations electric street-cars and public carriages are available in all directions, the cars running north as far as Troy, west to the stock-yards and shops of West Albany, and south to "The Island."

The *steamboat landing* is an open space at the foot of Broadway, whence a walk of five minutes to the right (northward) leads you to the foot of State Street, the business center, where all street-cars converge.

The covered way from the exit of the Union Station, or Maiden Lane from the Delaware & Hudson Station, takes you in two minutes to the same central point. *Broadway* is the oldest, most varied, and important of the north and south streets. Its great width opposite the Union Depot is due to the fact that the middle was formerly occupied by a market; and its extensions southward and northward were, respectively, the Albany Turnpike and the Troy Road. Its junction with State Street forms a proper starting-point for any tour of the city.

State Street is the wide avenue which, starting at Broadway, slopes straight up the hill to the capitol, and then, with a slight southern displacement by this obstruction, stretches west to and beyond Washington Park, as the "high street" of the city. Its great width is due to the fact that originally it was a double street, in the center of which stood the public buildings of the early history of the town. A picture of it at the opening of this century is preserved in Mrs. Grant's *Memoirs of an American Lady:*

"The city of Albany was stretched along the banks of the Hudson; one very wide and long street lay parallel to the river, the intermediate space between it and the shore being occupied by gardens. A small but steep hill rose above the center of the town, on which stood a fort intended (but very ill adapted) for the defense of the place and of the neighboring country. From

THE CHASM, CATSKILL CREEK.

the foot of this hill another street was built, sloping pretty rapidly down till it joined the one before mentioned that ran along the river. This street was still wider than the other; it was only paved on each side, the middle being occupied by public edifices. These consisted of a market-place, or guard-house, a town hall, and the English and Dutch churches. The English church, belonging to the Episcopal persuasion and in the diocese of the Bishop of London, stood at the foot of the hill at the upper end of the street. The Dutch church was situated at the bottom of the descent where the street terminated; two irregular streets, not so broad but equally long, ran parallel to those, and a few even ones opened between them. The town in proportion to its population occupied a great space of ground. This city, in short, was a kind of semi-rural establishment; every house had its garden, well, and a little green behind; before every door a tree was planted, rendered interesting by being coeval with some beloved member of the family; many of their trees were of a prodigious size and extraordinary beauty, but without regularity, each one planting the kind that best pleased him, or which he thought would afford the most agreeable shade to the open portico at his door, which was surrounded by seats, and ascended by a few steps. It was in these that each domestic group was seated in summer evenings to enjoy the balmy twilight or serenely clear moonlight. Each family had a cow, fed in common pasture at the end of the town. In the evening they returned all together, of their own accord—with their tinkling bells hung at their necks —along the wide and grassy street to their wonted sheltering trees, to be milked at their masters' doors."

THE STATE CAPITOL.

Although the Legislature convened first in Albany in 1797, a special building was not completed until 1808. Then the "old capitol" was built on the hill, just in front of the present structure, the site of which was then occupied by the old English fortification, Fort Frederic. In the course of half a century this building was outgrown, and as early as 1863 a proposal looking toward a new one was introduced into the Legislature. Various cities made strenuous efforts to have the capital changed to their towns; but the general sentiment of the State, outside of New York City, was in favor of its remaining at Albany; and this city was munificent in its grant of land adequate for the purpose. Two appropriations, aggregating $500,000, were made, and in 1869 foundations were begun for a building expected to cost $4,000,000, after plans by Thomas Fuller. The foundations are of course of the most substantial character, resting upon a bed of concrete four feet in thickness, fifteen feet below the surface, and inclosing a sub-basement containing 114 different apartments. The corner-stone was laid with masonic ceremonies on June 24, 1871, and since then the work has progressed, now rapidly, now slowly, to the present time, under changing commissions, superintendents, and architectural advisers. By the end of 1878 it was completed so far as to be partly occupied, and on the evening of January 7, 1879, the new capitol was first occupied, the Senate meeting in the chamber intended for the Court of Appeals and the Assembly in its own chamber. This event was signalized by a large and brilliant reception, in which the city of Albany entertained 8,000 people, including many highly eminent men and women. A more formal public occupation occurred on the evening of February 11th; but the Senate Chamber was not occupied until March 10, 1881.

The site of this great building, which is so conspicuous from every approach to Albany, is the central hilltop of the city, which had been crowned with the "castle," or "fort," of the colonial town from the earliest times. The surface of the park is 155 feet above the Hudson, and embraces $7\frac{3}{4}$ acres.

"The size of the structure," says Phelps, "impresses the beholder at once. It is 300 feet north and south by 400 feet east and west, and with the porticos will cover three acres and seven square feet. The walls are 108 feet high from the water-table, and all this is worked out of solid granite brought, most of it, from Hallowell, Me. . . .
"The impression produced varies with various persons. One accomplished writer finds it 'not unlike that made by the photographs of those gigantic structures in the northern and eastern parts of India, which are seen in full series on the walls of the South Kensington, and by their barbaric profusion of ornamentation and true magnificence of design give the stay-at-home Briton some faint inkling of the empire which has invested his queen with another and more high-sounding title. Yet when close at hand the building does not bear out this connection with Indian architecture of the grand style; it might be mere chance that at a distance there is a similarity; or it may be that the smallness of size in the decorations as compared to the structure itself explains fully why there is a tendency to confuse the eye by the number of projections, arches, pillars, shallow recesses, and what not, which variegate the different façades. The confusion is not entirely displeasing; it gives a sense of unstinted riches, and so far represents exactly the spirit that has reared the pile.'

"On the other hand, Mr. Edward A. Freeman, the English historian, was, by the general look of the city, carried so completely into another part of the world 'that if any one had come up and told me in French, old or new, that the new capitol was "le chateau de Monseigneur le Duc d'Albanie," I could almost have believed him.'"

The building is constructed around a central square court, and is in architectural plan a modified style of Italian Renaissance. The roof, at least so far as the east front (looking down State Street) is concerned, is to be further modified by the extension there of a great gable, which will lend mass and dignity to that, its principal aspect. The center of the structure is to be surmounted by a lofty tower, capped with dome and pinnacles.

The grand marble approach to the east front was finally completed during 1898. It consists of an immense and magnificent flight of stone steps, 100 feet in width, broken by landings and terraces, leading up to the level of the second story. Beneath this, supported by ornamental pillars and arches, is a passage-way for carriages; while the heavy balustrades of the sloping approach, and its wing-like terraces, are elaborately and variously carved. It is not possible to judge fairly of the architectural effect of the great structure until the tower is erected, and the whole is brought into a structural harmony now lacking. The total cost of the finished capitol will be not less than $20,000,000.

The entrances, pending the completion of the east front, are in the north front, on Washington Avenue, and in the south front, on State Street. These admit to the second floor.

The first, or ground, floor has little of interest to the sightseer. Its rooms are devoted to committees and to various departmental offices.

The second, or entrance, floor, however, contains not only many offices, including that of the Secretary of State, but one object of special interest, the Governor's Room. The "Golden Corridor" has been cut up into offices.

The Governor's Room is situated in the southeast corner of the second, or entrance, story, and is reached by the *South-side Corridor*. This corridor is lighted by elevated windows, and is wainscoted with colored marbles, lending a richness and variety of color to the hall which are exceedingly pleasing. The Executive Chamber itself is a room 60 x 40 feet in dimensions, wainscoted to a height of fifteen or sixteen feet with mahogany set in square panels. Above the line of carved molding that surmounts it are hangings of Spanish leather, and the ceiling is paneled in dark wood.

The Halls of the Courts and Legislature and the Library give to the *third floor* a higher interest than belongs to any other. Elevators on both sides of the buildings will carry one to these upper stories, or the ascent may be made by one or other of the three noble staircases, of which the Western is the newest and most remarkable.

The Western Staircase occupies a great square opening or well in the western part of the capitol, and undoubtedly is the most ornate thing of its kind in the country. It is wholly of stone and double, the flights meeting in central platforms borne upon pillars, and diverging picturesquely to the floor-landings; while the whole ends at the top in decorated finials to the balustrades, leaving a large open space, replete with intricate carving, beneath the low glass dome that illuminates the whole with a flood of light. The material of the staircase, its surrounding balustrades, supports, etc., is pale-red Corschill freestone; while the steps are of a paler tint of Medina sandstone. Everywhere the chisel of the carver has been employed in decorations which are harmonious in general style yet differ in detail, so that one's eye never rests twice upon the same ornament. Peering forth from the profuse and intricate designs of leaves, flowers, fruits, and ribbons peer the faces of many well-known men, mainly heroes of the early history of the State, but including also statesmen of national renown. These portrait-heads, which are often excellent in drawing, are labeled, and in some cases are accompanied by symbols; and they are not, perhaps, out of place in such a building as a part of such an unconventional performance as this is. Especial attention has been given to the balustrade in the six openings of the third story, and to the surrounding walls.

The Senate Staircase ascends from the ground floor, east of the entrance on the south side, to the highest gallery, and is of massive brown sandstone, supported by, and supporting, arches whose pillars and edges are ornamented with elaborate carvings, lighted by openings, and overlooked by balconies. The greatness and strength of the structure, the elaborateness of the decoration, and the harmony and softness of the coloring combine to give an effect of dignity and richness perhaps unequaled in the world. It takes its name from the fact that it leads to the room in which the Senate sits, to which the visitor is conducted by an ornate passage way called the Corridor of Columns.

The Senate Chamber is at the east end of the south side, and was decorated by the late H. H. Richardson, who is regarded as America's greatest architect. Passing through lobbies wainscoted with marble, a room is entered whose sumptuous adornment is beyond realization until one has studied it long and closely. The light comes through great windows of stained glass, "iridescent and opalescent," set in frames of stone most intricately carved. Between the windows the wall is of Tennessee marble; but above them is a broad space paneled with Mexican onyx. Above this paneling is a string-course of simply carved marble, and above this an upper tier of windows, six in number. Surmounting all is set a broad golden frieze, consisting of a surface of gilded lead, beaten by hammers and stamps into an arabesque ornament in low relief that is exceedingly effective. From this frieze, and supported upon carved corbels of stone, spring the great beams of the oak ceiling, elaborately paneled and decorated. The series of arches underneath which the balcony-like galleries are placed, the grand fire-places on each side of the entrance door, and the heavy, ornate chandeliers are other very notable features in the magnificent design of this palatial hall.

"The doorway and fire-places are constructed of marble, as is the space between them. The openings of the fire-places are about six feet in height and something more in breadth. The cheerful effect of these when filled with blazing logs, the flames of which are reflected on the polished onyx and marble from all sides of the room, may well be imagined. . . . The chimney-pieces are finished with and surmounted by hoods slanting back to the wall at a steep angle, and ornamented with crockets and carved bands. The whole chimney-pieces are about half as high as the room, reaching to the string-course below the gold frieze. Above the doorway and wall space of Knoxville marble we see the wall-space up to the frieze covered with the Mexican onyx panel, and like the frieze in greater extent of surface than elsewhere. So placed, these two great fields of onyx and gold catch the broad southern light and afford a great diversity in the play of color; and offer the necessary repose to the eye after looking at surfaces broken by the arches of the windows on the south, east, and west walls."

The Assembly Chamber, at the other end of the building, on the same floor, is perhaps equally magnificent in a different way. It is larger and less jeweled, so to speak; but the sense of grandeur is very striking. It measures 84 x 140 feet, but the galleries restrict the floor-space of the chamber proper to eighty-four by fifty-five feet.

The elevated Speaker's desk faces the entrance; behind it is the press gallery, and before and beneath it the long desk of the Assembly clerks. The seats of the members are at small, red topped desks, arranged in six concentric rows. These desks, and the long desks of the Speaker and clerks, are all of dark and richly polished mahogany. At the rear is a lobby, shut off from the floor by a broad rail. The limits of the "floor" are defined by four enormous pillars of rose granite, which spring from white marble bases to white marble capitals. These originally supported a massive grained arch of stone, the largest in the world, whose peak was fifty-six feet above the floor. This was flanked and interwoven with other noble arches of creamy sandstone, "divided by the sweeping lines of deeper toned ribs, . . . and fretted with wide belts of ornament climbing their climbing courses, touched with the gleam of gold, and standing out from hollows filled with deep ultramarine and burning vermilion, to the 'dark backward and abysm' of the remotest vault." At that time the north and south walls were covered by great allegorical paintings from the brush of Richard M. Hunt—the only work of the sort he ever did. They represented the Flight of Night and The Discoverer. Unfortunately, however, the mechanical workmanship of this splendid stone canopy was found to be defective, and it became necessary to take it down. The arches overhead have, therefore, disappeared.

In their place is a ceiling which is itself sufficiently beautiful. It is of carved and polished oak. Massive beams stretch from pillar to pillar in four directions, dividing the ceiling into great sections. These beams and brackets are elaborately carved, and the spaces between them are divided into many small square panels, each deeply recessed and carved profusely, but in excellent taste, so that the effect is exceedingly fine, whether seen by daylight or lamplight.

The walls are finely in keeping. On each side of the room are three great windows, each capped by an arched space filled with stained glass; and the wall about these rounded heads, and the spandrels between them, are filled with a broad design, colored and cut in low relief, as if largely tiled. Above this is a horizontal band of graystone panels, and above that again a row of many windows, just under the ceiling, which are filled with stained glass, rich and thick, flooding the auditorium and the rose-red pillars and the carved oak and mahogany of ceiling and furniture with a vari-colored radiance.

The Court-Room of the Court of Appeals, in the southeast corner of this same (the third) floor, over the Executive Chamber, is another apartment worthy of examination. It is 53 x 35 feet in dimensions, and lofty in proportion, and is finished in oak, with carved stone about the windows, and much carving upon the rails that divide the panels, over the great fire-place of Sienna marble and onyx, and about the august seat of the justices of this highest of State Courts. Adjoining are a suite of other rooms devoted to the purposes of the court, all appropriately arranged and decorated, and like this court-room adorned with valuable portraits of distinguished men.

The State Library occupies extensive quarters on this same floor at the west end of the capitol, and should not be overlooked by the visitor interested in books. Its history begins in 1818, and it has grown to something like 150,000 volumes. It is sustained by a moderate annual appropriation, and is open to consultation by any person. While every sort of book is to be found upon its shelves, its specialties are the Law Library—in which it is excelled only by the Library of Congress—and its books relating to American history and development. Among these are many nearly unique, and of great value in the market as well as to students. Many manuscripts of this nature are included. "In 1853 the Legislature authorized the purchase of the correspondence and other papers of George Clinton, the first Governor of the State. These manuscripts have been bound in twenty-three folio volumes, and a calendar since added. A copious index to all names mentioned in these papers is now in preparation. Enough of other Clinton manuscripts have since been procured to fill ten similar volumes. The papers found on the person of Major André by his captors at Tarrytown were among the Clinton manuscripts, and have been framed and put under glass. The papers of Sir William Johnson, covering a period of the history of Central New York from 1738 to 1774, were also purchased and arranged and bound in twenty-two folio volumes." These papers have been thoroughly indexed, and the catalogue of the whole library, including its 65,000 or more pamphlets, is very complete.

"In addition to the books, other articles of value and interest have drifted in as to a safe place of deposit for the inspection of visitors. Among these are a sword and pistol and the surveying instruments of Washington; the swords presented to General Worth by the United States, by New York State, and by the city of Hudson for brilliant services in the Mexican War; busts of some of the eminent statesmen of New York; portraits in oil of many of the governors and regents of the university, and a numismatic collection of considerable value. It is a reference library, and only members of the Legislature, heads of departments of the State government, and the trustees of the library have the privilege of taking books to their residences. The library is open daily from 9 A. M. to 5 P. M., except Sundays, and holidays, and from the 5th to the 20th of August; during sessions of the Legislature till 6 P. M., except Saturdays, when it closes at 5 P. M."

The fourth, or gallery, floor is so called because it gives access to the public galleries of the Senate, Assembly, and Court chambers. It contains, besides these entrances, the rooms of a number of government departments, and one of its corridors, that at the west end on the south side, is devoted to a **museum of military records and relics**, which to the right-thinking patriot is perhaps the most impressive sight in Albany.

"This collection," Mr. Phelps tells us in his *Handbook*, which should be in the hands of every intelligent visitor at the capitol, "grew out of a desire to perpetuate in some way the patriotic memories of the War of the Rebellion. It was at first proposed to erect a suitable building for the purpose, and over $30,000 was subscribed by towns and by individuals. This money is now on deposit, and the interest helps to support the bureau, which is under the charge of the Adjutant-General. The objects of greatest interest are the *battle-flags* of the various State regiments, 804 in number, some of them torn in shreds, others still bearing plainly the names of the battles in which the regiments participated. These are in cases in the Senate gallery corridor. There are twenty-eight rebel ensigns captured from the enemy, and many other trophies to interest the curious. Over 3,000 photographs have been collected, and many are framed and on exhibition. There is also a large collection of newspapers in which the history of the war was written in the time of it; many specimens of ordnance; some relics of the Revolutionary War and of the War of 1812; an interesting collection of Lincoln memorials, including a piece of the bloody shirt taken from his person on the night of the assassination. Another interesting group is the clothes worn by Colonel Ellsworth when he was shot down in Alexandria, and the rebel flag which he took from the Marshall House, an act which led to his untimely death."

When on this floor the curious visitor will take occasion to look out upon the great interior court, and examine the coats-of-arms carved over the six dormer windows that open upon it from the attic. These coats-of-arms are those of the six colonial families deemed most prominent in the history of the State, which are as follows: On the north side, east, *Livingston;* middle, *Schuyler;* west, *Stuyvesant*—on the south side, east, *Tompkins;* middle, *Clinton;* west, *Jay.*

But there is much else to see in Albany besides this magnificent capitol. Many notable buildings surround, or are within easy distance of, this elm-shaded Capitol Square at the head of the broad and historic State Street. The old-fashioned brownstone building at the northwestern corner is the *Boys' Academy,* which has been a famous school ever since 1815; and the bit of green in front of it is called *Academy Park.*

"It was in the upper room of this building that Joseph Henry, who from 1826 to 1832 was one of the professors, first demonstrated the theory of the magnetic telegraph in transmitting intelligence, by ringing a bell through a mile of wire strung around the room. It only remained for Professor Morse to invent the code of signals and the machine for making them, and the thing was done. As has been well said, 'The click heard from every joint of those mystic wires, which now link together every city and village all over this continent, is but the echo of that little bell which first sounded in the upper room of the Albany Academy.' It was in this building that the well-known Bullions grammars were written, and first used as text-books by their author, professor of Latin and Greek in the institution. For many years T. Romeyn Beck, who created the science of medical jurisprudence, was the principal, and at all times the institution has maintained an enviable reputation. On the 26th of June, 1863, a semi-centennial celebration was held, when it was found that more than 5,000 students had been educated here."—*Phelps.*

The slope of Academy and Capitol parks, separated by Washington Avenue, extends down to Eagle Street, upon which, facing Academy Park, are two remarkable buildings—the State Hall and the City Hall.

The *State Hall* is the large red-domed structure of Sing Sing marble, on the corner of Steuben Street, which has been occupied by various commissions and other State departments since 1842.

The High School stands upon the next corner north; and a short distance away, on Elk Street, is the great St. Agnes Seminary. Next to it, on the corner of Maiden Lane, is the

City Hall.—This conspicuous and beautiful building is the masterpiece of the artist-architect H. H. Richardson. It is built of reddish granite in a freely modified Gothic style, and is surmounted by a square tower 202 feet high. This building was erected in 1883 at a total cost of about $325,000. The handsome granite edifice on Maiden Lane, behind it, is Masonic Hall.

A few doors down State Street, on the south side, near Lodge Street, is the large plain brick building called *Geological Hall*, dark and unsuitable, in which is now housed the

State Museum of Natural History.—It is well worth a visit, and should be regarded with more interest and pride than has hitherto been accorded to it by the people of the State generally. The *Entrance Hall* is devoted to an exhibit of building-stones dressed in various ways so as to display their good qualities. At the right is the large and handsome cabinet of minerals. The other rooms upon this (the ground) floor are devoted mainly to offices, store-rooms, and the quarters of the State Agricultural Society. The *second floor* is devoted to geology and paleontology primarily of this State; and the range of rocks found in New York is so extensive that the formations here represented constitute the most complete series of paleozoic rocks known in the world. This series will be found in a continuous line of table-cases around the room, which, examined from left to right, show the regular superposition of geological formations. The student is assisted by a long colored "section" of the geology of the State, up to the base of the coal measures. A full illustrative series of the ores of the State, especially of iron, is also found here.

The *third floor* is given up to collections of rock specimens and fossils exhibiting the geological formations of New York since the carboniferous period, and including the very complete and remarkable skeleton of the mastodon discovered many years ago at Cohoes.

The *zoological* and *ethnological collections* on the fourth floor, however, are those of most popular interest. The former are especially strong in ornithology and conchology, but contain many American mammals, some of them rare, as the white goat of the northern Rocky Mountains. The birds are largely of the De Rham collection; while the shells are of the private collections of two famous conchologists, Gould and P. P. Carpenter.

"All the collections are arranged for study and comparison, and the museum is strictly an educational institution, which is made available by thousands of students and by the public, and its influence is gradually pervading the entire community. Being a State institution the museum should be considered as cosmopolitan. Its intentions are to cover the whole field of natural research, and to be a center for the dissemination of a technical and popular knowledge of the products, fauna, and flora of the entire State. With this view it should be an object of interest for the remote portions of the State as well as the immediate locality."

The beautiful Norman-Gothic tower of **St. Peter's Episcopal Church**, Opposite Geological Hall, will attract admiring attention. This building is the third which has stood upon this site; but the original house of worship was the "English church" mentioned by Mrs. Grant in the citation heretofore quoted, and stood in the middle of State Street opposite its present position. It is built of Schenectady bluestone with New Jersey brownstone trimmings, and will seat about 1,000 persons. The tower, one of the richest specimens of French Gothic in this country, contains a chime of eleven bells, and another bell marked 1751, which is used only to ring in the new year. "A communion service, the gift of Queen Anne to a projected chapel among the Onondagas which was never built, was given to this church at the frontier post in 1716, and has been in use ever since. It consists of seven pieces of solid silver, each of them bearing the royal arms and a curious inscription. The vault in the vestry-room of the church also contains the parchment conveying the original grant of land by George I. and the charter of the parish given by George III. The memorial windows of the church, of which there are a great number, are very fine specimens of English decorated glass."

State Street is devoted to business houses for the most part— banks, newspapers, and office buildings. It is crossed in the middle by *Pearl Street*, running north and south, and containing the best stores and the most prominent office buildings, of which the new Albany Savings Bank, a Corinthian marble building erected in 1898, the "D. & H." Building, and the Kenmore Hotel are the most conspicuous and handsome. At the foot of State Street stands the

Federal Building, in "free Renaissance" style, which has cost about $600,000, exclusive of the ground, and is occupied by the *Post Office*, United States Courts, and Custom House.

The best **residence part of** Albany is upon the high ground near and west of the capitol, and especially along Washington Avenue—a broad, beautifully shaded thoroughfare, lined with stately homes. Half-a-mile above the capitol is *Washington Park*, a beautiful pleasure-ground of over eighty acres, containing miles of walks and driveways, and a lake 1,600 feet long.

"The park is reached by the State Street line of trolley-cars, which go within a short distance of it (at Knox Street); but more directly by the Hamilton Street line, which runs along Madison Avenue directly on the border. In the season for flowers no one should miss seeing the beautiful display of 40,000 bedded plants, most of which are placed near Willett Street, between Hudson and Lancaster. A band plays in the cupola of the lake-house nearly every week in the summer, and is listened to by thousands who walk or drive about the beautiful grounds. In the skating season the lake is of course the great place of resort; but at all seasons of the year, when the weather will permit, the park is frequented by hundreds daily.

"The special features of the park, aside from the artistic manner in which it is laid out and the careful manner in which it is tended, are its noble trees, which were there when the land was taken for park purposes; and the scenery afforded by the distant Catskill Mountains and the Helderbergs."

One who wishes to see the quaint older part of the city, which will remind him much more of a southern than a northern town, should go southward along the narrow street (Lodge) beside Geological Hall, cross the market (whence an extremely picturesque presentation of the towering capitol is obtained), and then wander beyond until he is tired of the hilly narrow streets. Half-a-mile or so south of the capitol he will come upon the old *Schuyler Mansion*, now a Roman Catholic asylum, which was the home in revolutionary days of the aristocratic, but patriotic and kindly, Schuylers. It is a historic and interesting old house, but it does not give the impression of the elegance and wealth that belonged to the rich colonial families as did the old home of Patroon Van Rensselaer, out at the head of North Broadway; but that grand mansion was moved, stone by stone and timber by timber, and re-erected in Williamstown, Mass., in 1897. Electric cars run to Greenbush, Kenwood, Watervliet, and Troy.

THE UPPER HUDSON COUNTRY.

The Upper Hudson is a very different river from that which has been followed so closely between Albany and New York Bay. The Boreas, North, Rocky, and Cedar rivers gather from the innermost glens of the Adirondacks to form its rollicking youth, and escape from the mountains down a course that is only a long tumbling through rocky rifts. The wilderness beauty of this uppermost torrent is profaned by many dams, and it is only below Eldridge's that even the hardiest canoeists dare put in their boats; and few of these are willing to follow the bold example set by Mr. Charles Farnham, the pioneer canoeist of that region, the story of whose running these rapids is briskly told in Vol. XXI of *Scribner's Monthly*, p. 857. Read this account if you want to know how it seems to run Spruce Mountain Rift and the Horse Race—the two worst rapids of the mountain-gorge. Down to the Glen the river is so furious that in a freshet only the most reckless lumbermen venture on its rapids. The ten miles from the Glen to Thurman is not much better. Says Mr. Farnham:

"The Hudson about Thurman changes from a wild mountain torrent to a stream of charming pastoral character. The valley here and there expands a little, and gives room for bits of cultivation among varied hills and dales. The gloom of the forest is broken by a few fields and a farm-house, that are very welcome to the eye. The hills often shut the course of the river from view with bold points and narrow passes, quite like a miniature of the grander Highlands. The islands in the broad stream are picturesque with arching elms. The shores are varied with mossy rocks under golden beeches; with fields where brown shocks of buckwheat peep over the bank; or with green pastures and orchards near a home. The placid river was a long gallery of autumnal pictures. I floated a day through its gorgeous halls of crimson, gold, and green, flooded with sunlight; I drifted as idly and as quietly as the fleets of leaves that came and went with the zephyr. After the rush and nervous combat on the rapids, these tranquil beauties and these dreamy hours were inexpressibly delightful.

"The roar of Hadley's Falls broke the spell, and announced one of the most interesting episodes in the cruise. . . . The gorge of the river here" [below the falls] "is very narrow, crooked, and walled in with precipitous rocks. The current is swift, tortuous, and turbulent. Just below the foot of the fall is a steep plunge, or shoot, where the water almost falls over some rocks, and rolls up crested waves of quite formidable appearance. A few yards below this is a second plunge, rather rougher than the first. Elsewhere the current is deep, and safe enough if it does not dash you against the cavernous walls of rock. The best channel is in the center of each shoot. . . . The passage was short, but swift and exciting; and its successful termination was not the worst of it.

"The Hudson returns at Jessup's Landing to the ways of its youth by plunging down a great fall and then running seven miles as a wild rapid between high mountains. I unwisely followed the counsel of the most prudent villagers instead of the most enterprising, and had my canoe carted four miles down the river to New Bridge. This mistake lost me over three miles of strong, swift water, deeper and safer than the rifts about Riverside and the Glen. But I made up the loss by camping here several days and hunting gray squirrels. The mountains about are delightful hunting-grounds. Every peak commands an extensive view—of the deep gorge where the river foams and roars, of the wide valley of the Hudson rolling through the plain from Glen's Falls to Troy, and of the Green Mountains along the eastern horizon. Every evening the neighbors collected about my camp-fire for stories. They brought me combs of wild honey and sweet apples to roast. These bright fall days in the woods, and the jovial hours of the evening, were some of the pleasantest of the trip. But finally I launched on the last rapids, and soon left the mountains and the rifts for the plain and the still waters of every-day life.

"The quiet Hudson below Glen's Falls offered no exciting passages, but this part of my trip was quite as delightful as any other, for the peaceful scenery, the rest on smooth waters, and the presence of civilization were all exceedingly welcome after the rough wilderness. At Northumberland I left the Hudson and followed the canal on its west bank, to avoid some dams in the river; and at the same time to follow a more elevated route for better views. The canal offered also a new phase of life, and many pleasant civilities. Toward sundown I paddled up to a canalboat loaded with lumber, and rested from a long day's pull by towing alongside. The captain chatted to me while he manned the long tiller, his wife came up from the cabin to look at the canoe, and their two children leaned over the rail as near as possible to the *Allegro*, and almost devoured her with curiosity. . . . The boat and its people seemed so attractive that I chartered them all to take the *Allegro* on board for the the night. She was soon placed in a hollow between the piles of lumber, covered with the tent, and opened to receive calls from all hands. Then the family took me still more into their circle. As we went into their cabin, and I inspected their diminutive but neat quarters, I thought it compared favorably with the cabin of the *Allegro;* for the beds, stove, stores, and furniture were all within reach of a central seat. After a chat I bade them good-night, and went on deck to turn in. The silence of a misty night was scarcely broken by the tread of the horses on the tow-path. Now and then the man at the helm called out to the driver in a slow, sleepy voice. The boat, as well as everything else, seemed in perfect rest; but when the headlight glared on a bridge or a tree it seemed as if Nature were on a silent march to the rear. I soon fell asleep, after a long day of labor at the paddle; but the night seemed almost a dream, for I knew that we traveled, yet felt not the slightest motion; that some one watched over our progress, although he rarely spoke; and more than all I enjoyed again the delightful feeling of home.

"I turned out just before sunrise to enjoy every minute of the last day of my cruise; . . . and thus we floated slowly and idly through a charming country, while watching the various operations of locking and weighing the boat, and other peculiar scenes of canal life. As we advanced, the country became still fuller of human interests. The sound of flails floated over the banks, the hum of villages grew louder and more frequent. Then the smoky breath of Troy rang with shrill whistles and the heavy toils of commerce!"

Albany is the central point of departure for this upper valley of the Hudson. Nearer to it are other attractive places of summer travel and residence. Eastward are the Berkshire Hills and Lebanon Springs, reached by the Boston & Albany Railroad. Southward, along the line of the Delaware & Hudson Railroad, is Howe's Cave—a vast cavern almost as great as the Mammoth Cave—opening near the station, where a hotel-village has grown up as the foremost of the summer resorts along the base of the Helderberg Mountains. This is forty miles from Albany. Farther is the branch line to *Sharon Springs* and Cherry Valley, while still farther south the western Catskills and Cooperstown are reached by this line, which passes through a beautiful and storied farming country all the way to Binghampton and the Wyoming Valley of Pennsylvania.

West of Albany goes the great four-track system of the New York Central Railroad, up the valley of the Mohawk, following the great prehistoric Indian highway to the west. The Central Railroad also runs a line to Troy, with trains every half-hour all day; this passes along the eastern bank of the river through East Albany, Greenbush, and the iron-works district of Troy.

Troy is the head of steamboat navigation upon the river, and one of the foremost manufacturing cities in the country, especially in shirts, collars, and cuffs, in laundrying and laundry machinery, and in iron-work, locomotives, and railway-cars. Its streets present great animation, and some imposing business blocks. The principal public buildings are the fine new Court House, a handsome marble Federal Building, accommodating the Post Office and Federal Courts, and the lofty Soldiers' Monument. Troy has famous schools, of which the Rensselaer Polytechnic, for boys, and the Willard Seminary, for girls, are best known. The latter has the beautiful Sage Memorial Building. In its Union Depot center the New York Central, Delaware & Hudson, Fitchburgh, and Central Vermont railroads, and electric cars run to Albany, Cohoes, and Lansingburgh.

The most interesting tours north of Albany, however, are those over the admirable lines of the **Delaware & Hudson Canal Co.'s railroads,** which run to Saratoga, Lake George, Rutland, Vt., and along Lake Champlain to various entrances to the Adirondacks, and to Montreal.

Leaving Albany, the traveler passes through the great *lumber district* of that city— which is the largest lumber market in the eastern United States—out into charming suburbs and past the *Rural Cemetery,* where many people of note have been buried amid the most charming surroundings; and so on past the United States arsenal and gun-foundry at *Watervliet,* and *West Troy,* to the the manufacturing city of *Cohoes.* Here the Mohawk River is crossed on a magnificent double-truss iron bridge 960 feet long, from which a good view of the falls may be had. The river at this point joins the Hudson through a series of branch streams, or "sprouts," forming many islands of much beauty. *Waterford* and *Mechanicville* are large manufacturing towns passed in succession, the latter the home and resting-place of Ellsworth—the first victim of the Civil War—and the junction-point of branch lines to Schenectady and Troy.

The main line now leaves the Hudson and strikes northwestward through the camp-meeting grounds of *Round Lake* and the pretty village of *Ballston Spa* to Saratoga, the queen of American summer resorts. The railroad runs through the heart of the village, and from the car-windows one can get a good view of the principal hotels and the main street.

Saratoga Springs is the most prominent inland summer resort in the United States, and in some respects is as remarkable as any in the world, resembling the famous Bath Wells of England in the last century with all the brilliant additions of modern luxury and convenience. The permanent population of the town is about 12,000, but at the height of the summer season this population is often doubled in number, and the whole of it seems to be given over to gayety.

The principal reason for the growth and prosperity of this resort is found in the presence of the mineral springs which have made it famous for more than a century. Some of them yield chalybeate waters, others contain iodine or sulphur, and all are strongly impregnated with carbonic acid gas. Their temperature is usually from 46° to 50° F., and most of them furnish water pleasant to drink, though this can hardly be said of those most in repute medicinally; possibly the nauseous taste has done something toward the faith in their efficacy. The waters principally used are both tonic and cathartic in their action upon the human system, and are considered especially beneficial to the stomach and liver, and in cases of rheumatism, calculus, and similar disorders. About thirty of these springs exist, all told, of which the principal ones are:

Congress Spring, Columbian Spring, Hamilton Spring, Putnam Spring, Washington Spring, Geyser Spring, Saratoga Vichy Spring, Saratoga Kissingen, Champion Spouting Spring, Carlsbad Spring, Lafayette Spring, High Rock Spring, Star Spring, Seltzer Spring, Magnetic Spring, Flat Rock Spring, Pavillion Spring, Royal Spring, Empire Spring, Red Spring, Excelsior Spring, Union Spring, White Sulphur Springs, Eureka Spring.

Saratoga Springs was one of the earliest settlements in that part of the state, its beneficent fountains, its agreeable climate, and lovely situation, its agricultural surroundings, and convenient position on the highway to the north, uniting to give it stability and making it the summer resort of fashionable folk. In antebellum days this was the favorite resort of rich Southerners, and to this fact it owes some of its peculiar customs and attractions. These people and their wealthy successors, who flock thither from all parts of the country, are the support of the great hotels, whose vastness and splendor are still something to wonder at, and make the spectacle of the gay town in midsummer, but scores of smaller hotels and boarding houses hold a quieter life and the beautiful shady streets are lined with thousands of delightful homes.

The height of the season is in July and August, when the greatest crowd is present, conventions are meeting daily, and the races offer a supreme attraction. The admirable service of the excellent Delaware & Hudson Railroad is taxed to its utmost, and several special trains are run daily. The Saratoga Races are among the leading American events of their kind, and attract the best horses in the land. The track is on Union Avenue, and its equipments in every particular are of the finest description.

The country surrounding Saratoga Springs is hilly and beautiful, and the roads are excellent, so that driving is one of the foremost pleasures. One of the special objects of a driving excursion is to Saratoga Lake, about four miles southeast of the village. The lake is a charming place for boating, and has many houses and gardens of entertainment upon its shores, and it is reached by an electric railway, and also by a public tally-ho coach, which runs once a day, starting from the United States Hotel and stopping at Thomas' Hotel, a favorite place for eating game and fish dinners, served with the celebrated "Saratoga chips." Woodlawn Park, a fine expanse of 1,200 acres, a short distance from the town, is also open to the public, although owned by Judge Hilton, who has his private residence there.

Broadway, the principal street of Saratoga and one of the most beautiful in the United States, is shaded by fine elm trees for a distance of three miles, and is kept in perfect order. The chief hotels, the best shops, and most of the principal residences are situated on this street, and it is thronged with prettily dressed loungers in the morning and gay carriages as evening draws on, while in the evening it sparkles with light and is ringing with music and laughter.

A long account might justly be written about the hotels of Saratoga, which maintain to this day their early reputation. Some of them are among the largest and best appointed in the world, and probably more distinguished names are written upon their registers each year than anywhere else in the country. It is said that 20,000 guests can be accommodated by them at once, and this capacity is sometimes taxed to the utmost. A directory of these hotels will be found in the alphabetical list on page 229.

From Saratoga the *Adirondack Railroad* reaches northward into the Southern Adirondacks. It reaches the Upper Hudson at Hadley, and then follows the valley as far as North Creek; and much of the way the brawling stream can be seen, though not at its worst. Thurman, the Glen, and other places mentioned in the canoe trip related a few paragraphs back, are stations on this line; but the rural wildness of the valley has been little disturbed by its presence. From the terminus at *North Creek* stages run in summer into the mountains in several directions, and especially to Blue Mountain Lake and the lakes beyond there—Raquette, the Fulton Chain, Long Lake, and numberless others.

Saratoga is in the midst of a country deeply overlaid with memories of the utmost interest to Americans, and full of incidents picturesque to foreigners. Here Arnold and Schuyler and Gates won renown, and Burgoyne obtained a greater fame by defeat, perhaps, than ever he would have secured by success. But the memories go back to far older and fiercer stories than that; and this is especially true a little farther north, in the region of Lake George and the southern end of Lake Champlain, where French and English and Iroquois, noble and simple, troop past in a long procession of soldiers and priests and explorers as we summon the characters of local history during three centuries past. At *Fort Edward*, which was a camp-ground in 1690, and in 1759 was the site of a strong fort, where was gathered Amherst's great expedition, which resulted in the conquest of Canada, one changes cars for *Caldwell*, at the foot of **Lake George;** and in summer one may make the circuit of that lake and return the next day, or at the upper end may pursue his journey northward by rail or boat, as pleases him.

Fort Ann is a historic village beyond Fort Edward; and next comes Whitehall, where a branch line will carry the traveler to *Rutland*, Vt., and so into the Green Mountains or on to the White Hills. Then comes **Fort Ticonderoga**, whose grim ruins crown the headland where Dieskau, and Montcalm, and Abercrombie, and Amherst, and Ethan Allan, and Burgoyne commanded in turn armies and an armament that were long ago turned to dust. What memories of ambition and political intrigue and war these names Ticonderoga and Crown Point and Champlain arouse! And how thrilling is it to wander about these crumbling walls and **retrace the old redoubts where such men struggled!**

The shining expanse of beautiful Champlain is plowed by the keels of swift steamers, and at all these ports the excursionists may embark for the northerly landings—Burlington, Plattsburgh, etc.—or he may continue in the railway-cars, along the cliff-bordered western verge of the lake, and enjoy some of the most striking scenery in the country.

From Crown Point a railway extends westward to Paradox Lake, whence stages run to Schroon Lake, and on across to Tahawas and the headwaters of the Hudson. *Westport* gives another popular entrance (by stage) to the Adirondacks.

"Tally-ho stages meet trains at Westport to convey passengers to Elizabethtown, an enjoyable ride of eight miles through Raven Pass, whence stage lines run daily to Keene Valley. It is probable that unless the traveler's time is limited he will yield to the temptation to tarry a few days at Elizabethtown before exploring the wonders beyond, and he will be wise to do so. Here are the most comfortable of hotels, filled in summer with hundreds of guests representing the best elements of American social life. Good drives radiate in all directions. Easy trails lead to the summits of Mount Hurricane and the Giant of the Valley. The village itself is one of unusual beauty and salubrity. The lovely Pleasant Valley in which it lies is comparable only with the famed Keene Valley, a few miles beyond. The streams and lakes in the vicinity will furnish good sport to the angler, and the forests unfailing attractions to the sportsman. The drive over Symonds Hill and back, via the Pleasant Valley road along the windings of the Bouquet River, and to Split Rock Falls, where the river descends a hundred feet through a wild chasm in a series of picturesque cataracts, should be taken. Wood Hill, but a few minutes' easy walk from the hotels, should be visited for the prospect of mountains and the view up Pleasant Valley to be had from its summit. Cobble Hill, a short distance southwest of the village, presents a formidable climb; but those who are willing to perform the little hard work necessary to reach its top will be amply repaid by the outlook. The view from the sharp peak of Hurricane Mountain, which is easily ascended from the Elizabethtown side, is one of the best high views to be had in the Adirondack Mountains; second only, perhaps, to that from White Face. Nowhere else can the full glory of an American autumn be seen in greater brilliancy than on the hillsides and in the valley around Elizabethtown. The road to Lake Placid follows a westerly course, running alongside the bed of a rushing mountain stream, and passing many lovely cascades and pools. Ascending gradually the narrowing valley, we arrive in about an hour at the top of Pitch-off Pass, under a noble cliff, and are at an altitude of 1,710 feet. To the right, but a short distance away, the bare and shining peak of Hurricane is seen. At our feet, a thousand feet below, Keene Valley lies spread out before us in almost its entire extent, a vision of loveliness with its soft green meadows and graceful elms; beyond it, range upon range of grand mountain forms; and still farther, the pyramidal peak of White Face, rising high above all, presents itself for the first time to the observer—an exalted type of mountain sublimity which is quickly lost to the eye as we descend into the valley. Looking to the south, a new surprise opens before us in the first view of the Gothics, whose graceful outlines present a strangeness of effect not to be found elsewhere, so far as the writer knows, throughout the entire domain of mountain scenery. A few minutes later the dark cone of Mount Marcy is seen a few miles southwest; but the glimpse of the monarch is as fleeting as that of White Face. We have now descended to the valley, and if the tourist has a day or two to spare he will do well to stop here before pursuing his journey, for he is in one of the loveliest vales that the sun shines upon. For six miles up the valley lovers of nature have dotted it with summer homes, and good hotels and boarding-houses are located in the most picturesque situations. The Au Sable Ponds are most conveniently visited from Beede's, at the head of Keene Valley.

"The large hotels of Lake Placid are now in sight. We descend a short hill, cross a branch of the Au Sable, and when within half-a-mile of Lake Placid experience a momentary feeling of disappointment because our surroundings have suddenly grown uninteresting. A few rods beyond, however, a turn in the woods reveals that we have before us and around us one of the most entrancing scenes in all nature; a picture so glorious that the imagination can scarcely compass it, or conceive of a single element wanting to make it perfect."

From Port Kent, farther on, one can easily visit the *Au Sable Chasm* by rail; or pass on to the great **Hotel Champlain**, at Bluff Point, near Plattsburgh.

This new and elegant hotel stands in the midst of spacious, cultivated grounds, upon a bold promontory overlooking the water, and commanding a very wide view of the lake and the green, and Adirondack Mountains. No less than 363 acres in the hotel grounds, mostly wooded, have been laid out in walks and drives. The hotel is 400 feet long, having an average width of about fifty feet and a central width of ninety feet. This immense and costly structure is surmounted by three towers—one at each end, and a central tower 125 feet high. It is intended that the "Champlain" shall be the model summer hotel of its kind. "The house and its furnishings are of the highest class, and every convenience that can conduce to the pleasure and comfort of its guests has been provided. Such has been the rapid growth in popularity of Lake Champlain that the opening of this fine home for summer pleasure seekers signalizes an era of interest in this incomparable region that has placed its shores in the first rank of summer resorts."

A short distance beyond, 168 miles from Albany, is the old and interesting town of *Plattsburgh*, much resorted to in summer, and the terminus of the Chateaugay Railroad, which runs up the Saranac Valley to Saranac Lake. Twenty-four miles farther brings the traveler to *Rouse's Point*, on the Canadian boundary-line, and only fifty miles from **Montreal**—a fit ending to the "Tour of the Hudson."

ALPHABETICAL LIST OF HOTELS IN THE HUDSON VALLEY AND CATSKILLS.

Those Hotels bearing the star (*) are open only in summer.

Albany, Albany Co. Pop. 100,000. Hotels: *The Kenmore,* $4; *Stanwix Hall,* $3 to $4; *Globe,* $2; *Hotel Vendome,* $2; *Keeler's* (Eur.), 75 cents upward; *Mansion House,* $2.

Arkville, Delaware Co. Pop. 113. Hotels: *Commercial House,* $1.50; *Arkville Hotel,* $1.50; *Hoffman House,** special rates; *Locust Grove House.*

Athens, Greene Co. Pop. 2,500. Hotels: *Stewart House,* $2; *The Arlington,* $2.

Big Indian, Ulster Co. Hotels: *Joslyn House,** $2; *Big Indian,* $2; *Slide Mountain House,** $1.50; *Forest Home.*

Bloomville, Delaware Co. Pop. 236. Hotel: *Bloomville,* $1.50.

Cairo, Greene Co. Pop. 859. Hotels: *Columbian,** $3; *Winter Clove,** $2; *Glenbrook House,** $2; *Walter's,* $2; *The Rockwood,* $1.50; *Chichester Hotel,* $1.50; *Glen Falls House,* $1.50; *Maple Lawn,* $1.50; *Maple Grove House,* $1.50; *Malacska House,* $1.50; *Hine House,* $2; *Jenning's,* $2.

Castleton, Rensselaer Co. Pop. 1,300. Hotels: *Rensselaerwyck,* $2; *Signer House,* $2.

Catskill, Greene Co. Pop. 5,000. Hotels: *Airy Grove House,* $2; *Irving House,* $2 to $3; *Summit Hill House,* $2; *Embogcht,* $2; *Hart House* (Landing), $2; *Union* (Landing), $2 to $3; *Mountain House,** $4 to $5; *Prospect Park Hotel,** $3 to $4; *Grant House,** $3; *Glenwood,** $2.50; *The Saulpaugh,* $2 to $3; *Smith's,* $1.50; *Gay's,* $2.

Coeyman's, Albany Co. Pop. 963. Hotel: *Gedney House,* $1.50.

Cold Spring, Putnam Co. Pop. 2,500. Hotel: *Burnett House,* $2 to $2 50.

Cornwall, Orange Co. Pop. 2,356. Hotels: *Grand Central,* $2 to $2.50; *Cornwall,* $2; *Elm Park,* $2; *Mountain House,** $3; *Elmer House,** $2.50 to $3; *Glen Ridge,** $3; *Grand View,** $2.50; *Linden Park,** $2; *The Cornell,** $2; *Smith House,** $2.50; *Bay View House,** $2; *Taylor House,** $2; *Ward House,** $2; *Storm King House,** $1.50; *Palmer House,** $1.50.

Coxsackie, Greene Co. Pop. 2,200. Hotels: *Cummings,* $2; *New Eagle Hotel,* $2; *Larrabee House,* $1.50.

Dobb's Ferry, Westchester Co. Pop. 2,083. Hotels: *Hotel Riverview,* special rates; *Hotel Bellevue;** *Livingston House,* special rates; *Emmet House,* $2; *Union Hotel,* $1.50.

East Windham, Greene Co. Pop. 110. Hotels: *Butts House,** $2; *Summit House,** $2; *Grand View Mountain House,* special rates.

Esopus, Ulster Co. Pop. 340. Hotels: *Esopus Hotel,* $1.50; *Valley House,* $1.50.

Fishkill-on-Hudson, Dutchess Co. Pop. 3,617. Hotels: *Colonial Inn,* $2 to $2.50; *Holland House,* $2; *Flannery's,* $2; *Standard Hotel,* $2.

Fleischmann's, see GRIFFIN'S CORNERS.

Garrison's, Putnam Co. Pop. 160. Hotels: *Highland House,** $2.50 to $3; *Garrison's,* special rates.

Germantown, Columbia Co. Pop. 460. Hotels: *Central,* $2; *Mountain View Hotel,* $2.

Griffin's Corners, Ulster Co. Pop. 365. Hotels: *Lasher House,* $2; *Switzerland,** $2; *Maple Grove,* $2.

Haines' Falls, Greene Co. Hotels: *Glen Park House,* $2; *Haines' Falls House,** $2; *Shady Grove House,** $2; *Sunset View House,** $2; *The Antlers; Vista,** special rates; *Vendome,** $1.50 to $2; *The Loxhurst,* special rates; *Laurel House.*

Hastings, Westchester Co. Pop. 1,466. Hotels: *International,* $2; *Warburton House,* $3.

Haverstraw, Rockland Co. Pop. 5,170. Hotels: *United States,* $2; *Rockland House,* $1.

ALPHABETICAL LIST OF HOTELS.

Hensonville, Greene Co. Pop. 288. Hotels: *Orchard Grove House*,* $2; *Bloodgood House*,* $1.50.

Highland (village), Ulster Co. Pop. 1,570. Hotels: *Bellevue Villa*,* $2; *Highland House*,* $2; *Dobbs' House*, $1.50.

Highland Falls, Orange Co. Pop. 2,237. Hotels: *Cranston** (see West Point); *Highland Villa*,* $2.50; *Highland Falls*,* $2; *Brookside Cottage*,* $1.50; *Howard's*; *The Villa*, $2.

Highmount, see SUMMIT MOUNTAIN.

Hobart, Delaware Co. Pop. 850. Hotels: *Barrett House*, $1.50; *Liberty Hall*, $1.50.

Hudson, Columbia Co. Pop. 10,027. Hotels: *Worth House*, $2.50; *Waldron House*, $2; *Hotel Lincoln*, $2; *Central*, $2; *City*, $2; *St. Charles*, $2; *Curtiss House*, $2.

Hunter, Greene Co. Pop. 500. Hotels: *Hotel St. Charles*,* $2.50 to $4; *The Arlington*, $2; *Hunter*, $2.50; *West End*, $2; *Central*, $2; *Hunter Mountain Prospect House*,* $2; *The Kaatsberg*,* $2.

Hyde Park, Dutchess Co. Pop. 738. Hotels: *Horning House*, $2; *Park Hotel*, $2.

Jewett's, Greene Co. Hotels: *Jewett's Heights House*,* $2; *Tower Mountain House*,* special rates.

Kaaterskill, Greene Co. Hotels: *Hotel Kaaterskill*,* $5.

Kingston, Ulster Co. Pop. 21,261. Hotels (in Kingston proper): *Eagle*, $2 to $2.50; *Clinton*, $1.50. In old Rondout: *New Mansion House*, $2 to $2.50; *Oriental House*, special rates.

Lexington, Greene Co. Pop. 448. Hotels: *Monroe House*,* $2.50; *O'Hara House*,* $2.25; *Lexington House*,* $2.

Longyear (Cockburn House), see MOUNT PLEASANT.

Margaretville, Delaware Co. Pop. 700. Hotels: *Ackerly*,* $2.50; *Dimmick House*,* $1.50; *Maple Grove*, $1.50; *Riverside*, $1.50.

Marlboro, Ulster Co. Pop. 870. Hotels: *Exchange*, $2; *Pleasant View House*, $2; *Atkins*, $1.50.

Matteawan, Dutchess Co. Pop. 4,278. Hotel: *Dibble House*, $2.

Milton, Ulster Co. Pop. 531. Hotel: *Milton House*, $1.50.

Montgomery, Orange Co. Pop. 1,024. Hotels: *National*, $2; *Palace*, $2; *Empire House*, $1.50; *Wallkill House*, $2.

Mount Pleasant, Ulster Co. Hotels: *Cockburn House*,* $2.50; *The Maples*,* $1.50; *Winne House*,* $2.

New Baltimore, Greene Co. Pop. 810. Hotels: *Riverside House*,* $2; *Windsor Hotel*, $1.50.

Newburgh, Orange Co. Pop. 23,087. Hotels: *Palatine*, $3 to $4; *United States*, $2.50 to $3; *Holland's*, $2.

New Hamburgh, Dutchess Co. Pop. 573. Hotels: *Central*, special rates; *Traver House*, special rates.

Nyack, Rockland Co. Pop. 4,111. Hotels: *Palmer House*, $2; *Tappan Zee House*,* $4; *St. George*, $2 to $3; *The Avallon;* *Ivanhoe House*, $1.50 to $2.

Palenville, Greene Co. Pop. 362. Hotels: *Palenville*,* special rates; *Stony Brook House*,* $2 to $3; *Pine Grove*,* $2; *Maple Grove*,* $2; *Winchelsea*,* $2; *Echo House*,* $2; *Drummond Falls*,* $1.50 to $2; *Airy Hill House*,* special rates; *Central House*, $1.50.

Peekskill, Westchester Co. Pop. 9,676. Hotels: *Eagle*, $2 to $3; *Hudson Avenue Hotel*, $2; *Exchange*, $1.50; *Allen House*, $2.

Phœnicia, Ulster Co. Pop. 354. Hotels: *Tremper House*,* $3 to $4; *The Martin*,* $2; *The Europea*, special rates.

Piermont, Rockland Co. Pop. 1,400. Hotels: *The Windsor; Haring House; Hotel Riverview*, $2 to $2.50.

Pine Hill, Ulster Co. Pop. 400. Hotels: *Winterton*, $2.50; *Rip Van Winkle*,* $3; *Alpine*,* $2.50; *Bonnie View House*,* $2; *Cornish House*,* $2; *Hotel Ulster*,* $2; *Brewerton*,* $2.

Platte Clove, Greene Co. Hotel: *Plaaterkill Falls Mountain House*,* $2. Stage from Saugerties, 75 cents.

Poughkeepsie, Dutchess Co. Pop. 22,206. Hotels: *Nelson House*, $2.50 to $3.50; *Morgan House*, $2.50 to $3.

Prattsville,• Greene Co. Pop. 384. Hotels: *Central*, $2; *Devasego*, $1.50; *Fowler House*,* $1.50; *Stanley Hall; The Graham*, special rates.

Rhinebeck, Dutchess Co. Pop. 1,654. Hotel: *Rhinebeck Hotel*, $2.

Rhinecliff, Dutchess Co. Pop. 600. Hotel: *Rhinecliff*,* $2.

Rockland Lake, Rockland Co. Pop. 470. Hotels: *Grand Rockland Hotel,* * $2.50 to $4; *Overlook Mountain House,* $2.50.

Rondout, *Mansion House,* $2 to $2.50.

Roxbury, Delaware Co. Pop. 744. Hotels: *Delaware Valley,* $2; *Lauren Villa,* * $2; *Falls House,* special rates.

Saratoga Springs, Saratoga Co. Pop. 12,000. *United States Hotel,* $5.

Saugerties, Ulster Co. Pop. 4,188. Hotels: *Palmer,* $2; *Phœnix Hotel,* $2; *Mt. Airy House,* * $2; *Maple Grove.* *

Shandaken, Ulster Co. Hotels: *Palace,* * $3; *The Clarendon,* special rates.

Shokan, Ulster Co. Hotels: *Hamilton House,* $2; *High Point,* * $1.50; *Cool Breeze House,* $2.

Sing Sing, Westchester Co. Pop. 9,352. Hotels: *American,* $2.50; *Hotel Keenan,* $2; *Phenix House,* $2; *Crosier,* $2; *St. Cloud,* $1.50.

Slide Mountain, see BIG INDIAN.

Staatsburg, Dutchess Co. Pop. 220. Hotel: *Nackle,* $1.50.

Stamford, Delaware Co. Pop. 1,000. Hotels: *Churchill Hall,* * $3 to $4; *Greycourt Inn,* * $2.50; *Simpson Terrace,* * $2; *The Westholm; Grant House.* * $2; *Delaware House,* $2; *Hamilton House,* $2; *Cold Spring,* * $2.

Stuyvesant Falls, Columbia Co. Pop. 930. Hotels: *Stuyvesant Falls House,* $2; *Milner,* $2; *Hotel Star,* $2.

Summit Mountain, Ulster Co. Hotels: *New Grand Hotel,* $4 to $4.50; *Grampian,* $3; *Rossmore**; *Summit Ridge,* $2.

Tannersville, Greene Co. Pop. 271. Hotels: *Blythewood,* $2.50; *Pleasant View,* * special rates; *Fabian House,* * $2.50; *Campbell House,* * $2.50; *Cascade House,* $2; *Mansion House,* * $2.50; *Waverly House,* * special rates; *Belvedere,* $2.50; *Mountain Summit House,* $2 to $3; *American,* $1.50 to $2.

Tarrytown, Westchester Co. Pop. 3,562. Hotels: *Florence House,* $2; *Mott House,* $2.50; *Park House,* $2.

Troy, Rensselaer Co. Pop. 60,700. Hotels: *Troy House,* $3; *Fifth Avenue,* $2.50 to $3; *Mansion House,* $2 to $2.50; *Revere House,* $1.50 to $2.

West Point, Orange Co. Pop. 1,164. *West Point Hotel,* $3.50; *Cranston's,** $4 to $5. *Fort Putnam Hotel.** $2.

Windham, Greene Co. Pop. 700. Hotels: *Osborn House,* $1.50; *Munson House,** $2; *Soper Place House,** $1.50; *Centre House,* $2; *Munger House,* $1.50; *Coe's Hotel,* $2.

Woodstock, Ulster Co. Pop. 267. Hotels: *Woodstock,* $2; *Mountain Home,* $2; *Overlook Mountain House,* $3 to $3.50.

Yonkers, Westchester Co. Pop. 32,038. Hotels: *Getty House,* $2.50 to $3; *Barden's Hotel,* special rates; *Hollywood Inn,* special rates; *Hotel Wynnstay,* special rates.

INDEX.

A.

	PAGE.
Abbey, Henry	154
Abbottsford	48
ALBANY	200–226
Historical Sketch of	200–203
Railway Stations	200
State Capitol	205–213
" Library	211
" Museum of Natural History	214
Alpine Gorge	46
André's Capture and Execution	66
" " Monument to	56
Anthony's Nose	16, 79, 80, 125
Aqueducts, Croton, New and Old	47, 48
Arkville	172
Arnold's Treason, Story of	65–68
Astor's Point	178
Athens	196
Audubon Park	30
Au Sable Chasm	225
Austin's Glen	185

B.

Ball Mountain	60
Ballston Spa	220
Balmville	119
Barkley Heights	180
Barr, Amelia E., Home at Cornwall	114
Barren Island	198
Barrytown (Lower Red Hook)	178
Beacon Hills	106, 124, 126
Bear Mount	79, 82
Beecher, Henry Ward, at Peekskill	74
Belle Ayr	172
Bergen Hill and Neck	26, 28, 33, 34
Berkshire Hills	47, 196, 219
Beverly Dock	86
Big Indian	168, 169

	PAGE.
Bishop's Falls	159
Black Creek	140
Black Dome	165
Blackhead	165, 198
Black Rock	79, 111
Bloomville	157, 176
Boiceville	158, 162
Breakneck Mountain (The Turk's Face)	85, 111, 124
Broadway along the Hudson	43
Bull Hill (Mt. Taurus)	85, 106, 108
Bull's Ferry	34
Burgoyne, General	81, 85
Burr, Aaron	27
Burroughs, John	130, 139

C.

Cairo	185, 186
Caldwell	223
Canoeing on the Upper Hudson	217
"Castle Phillipse"	40, 56
Castleton	199
Catskill	184
" Creek	164, 186, 198
" Driving and Walking Routes	185
" Mountain House	187
CATSKILLS, THE	
First view of	188
Gateway of	158
Railway Fare in	164
Routes to	156
Washington Irving and the	155
Catskill Station	184
Chain Point	81
Church, F. E., County Seat of	193
Claremont Heights	29
Claverack	196
Clinton, Sir Henry	69, 81
Closter	46, 60
Clum Hill	165, 190
Coeyman's	199
Cohoes	200, 220
Cold Spring	107
Columbiaville	197
Constitution Island	95, 106
Continental Village	73
Cooper's *The Spy*	42
Cooperstown	176, 219
Cooper, Susan Fenimore	18

	PAGE.
Cornwall	112–115, 124
Country Seats	See Maps.
Coxsackie	197
Cranston's	85, 86
Cro' Nest	85, 106, 108, 124
Croton Bay	64
" Point	46, 61, 63
" River	48
" Station	64
Crown Point	224
Cruger's	64
" Island	178
Crum Elbow	138

D.

Danskammer	128
Deeper Hook	185
Deep Notch	168, 171
Delaware and Hudson Canal	22, 143
Denning's Point	126
Depew, Chauncy M., and Peekskill	74
Devasago Falls	174
Diedrich Hook	60
Dinsmore's Point	141
Dobb's Ferry	30, 44–46
Drake, Joseph Rodman	109
Dunderberg, The	73, 78, 82
Durham	186
Dutchess Junction	125, 127
Dutch Traders	16

E.

Eagle Valley	109
East Albany	200, 220
East Camp	183
Edgewater	32
Eldorado	27, 28
Elizabethtown	224
Elka Park	167
Ellison House, The	121
Elysian Fields	26
Englewood	34, 35, 60
Erie Canal	22, 203
Esopus	140, 141, 152
" Creek	141, 158, 159, 179
" Valley, Ernest Ingersoll on, in Harper's	159, 161
" Wars	148

F.

FERRIES: PAGE.
    Catskill Station to Catskill 185
    Fishkill to Newburgh 119, 125
    Fort Lee to New York 28, 33
    Garrison's to West Point 37
    Hudson to Athens 197
    Peekskill to Jones' Point 75
    Poughkeepsie to Highland 135
    Rhinebeck to Rondout 157
    Rhinecliff to Kingston 143
    Storm King Station to Cornwall 108
    Tarrytown to Nyack 59
    Tivoli to Saugerties 181
    Weehawken to New York 28
Fishkill 125–127, 151
    "   Mountains 126, 139
Fleischmann's 172
Foote, Mary Hallock 129
Forrest's (Edwin) Font Hill 38
Fort Ann 223
  " Clinton 80–85
  " Constitution 31, 33
  " Edward 11, 223
  " George 31
  " Independence 73, 81
  " Lafayette 69
  " Lee 31, 33
  " Montgomery 70, 80–85
  " Orange 201
  " Putnam 85
  " Ticonderoga 223
  " Tryon 31
  " Washington 31, 32
Four-Mile Point 197
Fulton's (Robert) First Steamboat 179

G.

Garrison's 87
Germantown 183
Glasco 179
Glenerie 179
Glen's Falls 218
Glenwood 39
Gomez Explores the Hudson 16
Gould, George, Summer Residence of 172
    "   Jay, Country Seat of 51
Grand Hotel 171
Grant's Tomb 29

Grassy Point ... 68
Great Chip Rock Reach ... 46
Greenbush ... 200, 220
Green Mountains ... 196, 223
"Greystone," Samuel J. Tilden's Home ... 43
Guttenberg ... 28

H.

Haanakrois Creek ... 198
Hadley ... 223
Haines' Corners ... 167, 190
" Falls ... 167, 188, 189
Half Moon, The ... 17, 18, 194
Hamilton, Alexander ... 27
Hampton Point ... 128
Harlem Ship Canal ... 30
Hastings ... 43
Haverstraw ... 64
Haverstraw Bay ... 64, 65
High Bridge ... 48
Highland ... 135, 137
Highland Falls ... 86
Highland Forts, Fall of the ... 81
Highlands, The ... 76, 77, 85
Highland Village ... 137
High Peak ... 142, 162, 165
High Point Mountain ... 158, 159
High Tor ... 65
Hobart ... 157, 176
Hoboken ... 26
Hook Mountain, (Point-No-Point) ... 47, 60
Horse Race, The ... 79, 217
Hotel Champlain ... 225
" Kaaterskill ... 164, 167, 188
Hudson, (City of) ... 17, 21, 194
Hudson-Delaware Divide ... 157
Hudson, Henry ... 16-18, 194

HUDSON RIVER:
    After the Revolution ... 21, 22
    Breaking up of ... 14
    Broadest Part ... 64
    Channel ... 13
    Discovery of ... 16
    Dumping into ... 13
    During the Revolution ... 19, 21
    First Steamboats ... 21, 203
    John Burroughs on ... 11, 14, 130
    Life on ... 142

HUDSON RIVER—Continued   PAGE.
    Local Historians of 44, 81, 83, 94, 118, 121, 150, 152, 169, 185
    Most Beautiful Part 139
    Names 16, 18, 19, 201
    Navigability of 12
    New York City Shore.. 25
    Professor Newberry's Theory about.................................. 12
    Sources of 11, 217, 224
    Washington Irving on 22
    Winter Navigation of 13
Hunter 164
   " Mountain 164, 165, 189
Huntersfield Mountain 174
Hussey's Mountain 141, 142
Hyde Park 138

I.

Ice and Ice Harvest 13, 129-132
 " Boating 135
"Idlewild," Home of N. P. Willis 120
Indian Head 46
Inwood 30
Iona Island 79
Irvington 49
Irving, Washington 37, 49-55, 78

J.

Jeffrey's Hook 30, 31
Jersey City 25, 72
Jessup's Landing 218
Jones' Point, (Caldwell Landing) 75, 77

K.

Kaal Rock 132
Kaaterskill Clove 162, 167, 190, 191
   " Falls 188, 189, 192
   " High Peak 189
   " Station 164
Keen Valley 224
Kellogg, Clara Louise, Former Home of 107
Kidd's Plug Cliff 109
   " Point 77
Kinderhook Creek 197
   " Village 197
King Estate and Mansion 27
King's Bridge 30, 31, 37
   " Ferry 68, 82
Kingland's Point 54, 58

KINGSTON: PAGE.
  Cement..143-145
  Historical Sketch of..................................147, 153
  New York's First Court and Legislature at................151
  Old Houses...149
Kosciusko, Thaddeus...95, 97

L.

Lafayette's Headquarters....................................27, 121
Lake Champlain...220, 224
  " George..220, 223
  " Katrine..179
  " Placid..225
Lansingburgh..200
Laurel House Station......................................167, 190
Lebanon Springs...219
Leeds..185, 187
Leonia...59
Linlithgo...184
Little Tor..65
Livingston Family, The..182
  " Manor-House at Tarrytown..................................45
  " " " ("Clermont")..............................153, 181-183
Lost Clove, The...169
Low Point (Carthage Landing)..............................124, 128
Ludlow...39

M.

Malden..181
Manhattanville...29
Manhattes, The..18, 38
Manito Mount..75, 79
Marlborough...128
Matteawan...125
McEntee, Jarvis...154
Mechanicville...220
Millbrook...135
Milton..129
Monka Hill (Summit Mountain)..................................171
Montgomery Creek...80
  " Hall...178
Montreal...220, 226
Montrose..64, 68
Moodna, The (Murderer's Creek)....................112, 114, 115, 120
Morse, Prof. S. F. B., Home of................................132
Morton, Levi P., Summer Home of...............................141
Mountain House.....................................141, 167, 186, 188

	PAGE.
Mount Cornell	146, 162
" Garfield	163
" Hymettus	138
" Lincoln, (High Peak)	165
" Marcy	225
" Merino	193
" Pisgah	164, 173, 198
" Pleasant	162
" Rascal	79
" Sheridan	163, 168
" St. Vincent	38
" Tyceteneyck	158, 159
" Utsayantha	174, 175

N.

Ned Buntline's "Eagle's Nest"	175
Nepperhan, The	40, 42
Neutral Ground, The	43
New Baltimore	198
NEWBURGH	116-125
Driving Routes	119
Historical Sketch of	117
Tower of Victory	123, 124
Washington's Headquarters	121
Newburgh Bay	112, 116
New Hamburgh	124, 128
New Paltz Landing	137
New Windsor	69, 115, 120, 124
New York City, Limits of	38
North Bay	178, 179
" Beacon	127
" Creek	223
" Mountain	165, 188
" River	19, 26
Nutten Hook	197
Nyack	59

O.

Olive	158
Oneonta	176
Onteora Park	165, 166
Oscawanna Island	68
Otis Elevator, The	167, 168, 186, 187
Overlook Mountain	141, 157

P.

Palatinate Settlements, The	117, 128, 183
Palisades, The	35, 46
Palenville	185, 190

Panther Mountain.. 163
Patroons, The.. 201
Paulding, James K.. 140
Peakamoose.. 162
PEEKSKILL...73-76
    Drum Hill... 75
    Paulding's Tomb... 74
    State Camp of the National Guard.............................. 75
Peekskill Bay... 75
Pelham Wharf.. 140
Phillipse Family, The..40-42
Phœnicia..162, 168
Piermont...46, 47
Pine Hill.. 171
Plaaterkill Clove... 180
    "   Mountain Road... 190
Pleasant Valley..32, 224
Plum Point..15, 120
Pocantico Creek.. 54
Pollopel's Island...112, 124
Port Ewen... 142
    " Kent... 225
Ponhockie... 152
POUGHKEEPSIE..133-137
    Cantilever Bridge... 132
    Hudson River State Hospital................................... 137
    Vassar College.. 133
Putnam, Gen. Israel...73, 81-83

R.

Railway Fare in the Catskills..................................... 164
RAILWAYS:
    Adirondack.. 223
    Boston & Albany.................................199, 200, 219
    Catskill Mountain.............................168, 185, 186
    Chateaugay... 226
    Cooperstown & Charlotte...................................157, 176
    Delaware & Hudson....................... 200, 203, 219, 220
    "   " Otsego... 176
    Erie..23, 118
    Kaaterskill... 164
    Newburgh, Dutchess & Connecticut.............................. 125
    New York & Northern... 24
    "   " Central & Hudson River 23, 27, 37, 200, 219
    "   " Ontario & Western....................................... 24
    Otis Elevator.................................168, 186, 187
    Philadelphia & New England.................................... 143
    "   Reading & New England.................................... 177

RAILWAYS—Continued.   PAGE.
    Stony Clove & Catskill Mountain. 162, 164, 168
    Ulster & Delaware................................142, 162, 163, 167, 168
    West Shore 23, 28, 69, 199, 200
Red Hook.. 178
Redoubt Mountain... 87
Refugees, The..34, 35
Rensselaerwyck..119, 202
Rhinebeck. 138, 177
Rhinecliff.. 177
Richards, T. Addison.. 44
Ridgefield..59, 60
Rip Van Winkle..190, 191
Riverdale... 38
Riverside Park and Drive... 28
Roa Hook.. 75
Rockland and Rockland Lake... 63
"Rockwood," Home of William Rockefeller...................... 58
Roger's Island..186, 193
Roe, E. P., Cornwall, Home of.. 113
Roelof Jansen's Kill..182, 183
Rondout..142, 143, 146
   "   Creek..141, 158, 163
Roseton.. 128
Roundtop...162, 165, 167, 190
Rouse's Point... 226
Roxbury... 174

S.

Saranac Lake... 226
Saratoga...220, 223
Saugerties...179-181
Scarborough.. 58
Schodack... 199
Schoharie, The..164, 173, 190
Schroon Lake... 224
Schuyler Mansion, The 216
Shad-Fishing..15, 38, 64
Shadyside... 32
Shandaken... 168
Sharon Springs... 219
Shaupeneak... 141
Shawangunk Range..129, 146
Shokan...158, 159
Sing Sing..60-63
   "   " State Prison.. 62
Sinnipink, (The Hessians' Lake)................................79, 83
Skinners and Cow Boys.. 42
Sleepy Hollow..53-56

Slide Mountain	162, 169, 170
Sneden's Landing, (Paramus)	45, 46
ρitzenberg, The	73
Spruce Mountain Rift	217
Spuyten Duyvil	37
Staatsburgh	141

STAGE LINES:
- Arkville to Downsville ... 173
- Big Indian to Claryville ... 170
- Cairo to Windham ... 186
- Catskill to Tannersville, (via Palenville and The Clove) ... 186
- Grand Gorge Station to Prattsville ... 173
- Hunter to Windham ... 164
- North Creek to Adironack Lakes ... 223
- Paradox Lake to Schroon Lake ... 224
- Raven Pass to Keene Valley ... 224
- Shandaken to Lexington ... 168
- Stamford to Richmondville ... 176
- West Point to Highland Falls ... 86
- Westport to the Adirondacks ... 224

Stamford	174
State Capitol	205-213
State Deer Park	169

STEAMBOAT LINES:
- Albany ... 23, 200
- Catskill ... 23, 185
- Haverstraw and Newburgh ... 75
- Kingston ... 23, 139, 143
- Newburgh ... 23
- Peekskill ... 75
- Pleasant Valley ... 33
- Poughkeepsie ... 135
- Saugerties ... 181
- Sing Sing ... 62
- Troy ... 23

Stevens' Point	26
Stony Clove	163
Stony Point, Battle of	68-72
Storm King (Butter Hill)	106, 108, 111, 124
Stuyvesant	197
Sugar Loaf	85, 86, 162, 165
"Sunnyside," Home of Washington Irving	49, 50

T.

Table Mountain	162
Tannersville	165
Tappan	47, 60, 67
" Reach	60

	PAGE.
Tappan Sea	46, 51, 53, 58
Tarrytown	53-57
Teller's Point	63
Temple Hill	121
Thurman	217
Tippet's Hill (Constable's Point)	30, 31, 38
Tivoli	178
Tomkins Cove	73
Treason Hill	65
Trinity Cemetery	29
Troy	11, 21, 220
Tubby Hook	30
Twilight Park	167, 188

U.

"Undercliffe," Home of Col. George P. Morris	108
Union Hill	26, 28

V.

Van Buren, Martin	197
Van Cortlandt Manor	63
Vanderberg Cove	111
Van der Lyn, John	153, 154
Van Rensselaer, Patroon	202, 216
Vaughan's Expedition	152
Vaux, Calvert	113
Verdrietig Hook	60
Verplank's Point	68, 69, 82
Verrazano Enters the Hudson	16

VIEWS MENTIONED IN THE GUIDE:

Catskills, of	138, 141, 183, 198
Crescent Reach, from	85
Croton, from	64
Haverstraw Bay, of	65
Highlands, of	76
" " from Montrose	64
Huntersfield Mountain, from	174
Hurricane " "	224
Kuyckuyêt, from the	146
Mount Pisgah, from	164
" Utsayantha, from	174
Overlook House Observatory, from	157
Sing Sing, from	61
Slide Mountain, from	170
South Beacon, "	127
" Gilboa, "	174
Tower Hill, from	47
" of Victory, from	123
Vly Mountain	173

W.

	PAGE
Wappinger's Creek and Falls	128, 136
Warner, Susan B.	101, 107
Washington, George	41, 67, 96
Washington Heights	30, 33
Washington's Headquarters	30, 34, 45, 69, 72, 115, 121
Waterford	220
Watervliet	220
Wayne, Gen. Anthony	34, 70, 119
Weehawken	26
"Week in New York, A," by Ernest Ingersoll	28
West Camp	183
" Davenport	176
" Haverstraw	65
" Hoboken	26
" Hurley	157
" Nyack	60
West Park	139
WEST POINT	88–105
Battle Monument	98
Camptown	100
Corps of Cadets	102
Historical Sketch of	95–97
Parade, The	93
United States Military Academy	89–94
West Point Foundry	107
Westport	224
West Troy	220
Wildcat Creek	184
Willis, N. P.	17, 77, 120
Windham	164, 173, 186
" High Peak	198
Wittemberg Mountain	146, 162
Woodland Valley	163

Y.

YONKERS	39–43
Manor Hall	40
Revolutionary History	42
St. John's Church	40, 42

ADVERTISEMENTS.

Broadway Central Hotel, New York City, . Page vii
Catskill & New York Steamboat Co., . . " xvi
Central Hudson Steamboat Co., The . " xv
Citizen Steamboat Co., ... " vi
Delaware & Hudson R. R., . . . " xi
Green's Hotel, Philadelphia, Pa., . . " iii
Hotel Empire, New York City, Opposite page 7
Hotel Lafayette, Philadelphia, Pa., . " " 3
Hotel Kenmore, Albany, N. Y., Opposite page 9, and page xiv
Hudson River Day Line, ... Back cover.
Mansion House, Troy, N. Y., . . Page ix
Nelson House, Poughkeepsie, N. Y., . Opposite page 133
New York Central & Hudson River Railroad, . Page i
Palatine, The, Newburgh, N. Y., Opposite page 133
People's Line, ... Page viii
Stanwix Hall, Albany, N. Y., Opposite page 5
Seaboard Air Line, ... Page ii
Ten Eyck, The, Albany, N. Y., . . Opposite page 9
Thousand Island House, Alexandria Bay, N. Y., . Page xii
United States Hotel, Saratoga Springs, N. Y., Pages iv and v
Wabash Railroad, The, ... Page xiii
West Shore Railroad, ... " x

TRAVEL NOTES.

THE CLYDE LINE.

No steamers sailing out of New York are more deservedly popular than those of the Clyde Line to Charleston and Jacksonville, Florida. One of these admirable steamships may be taken every other day at 3 P. M., from the pier beneath the New York approach to the Brooklyn Bridge, and Charleston is reached about noon of the second day, and Jacksonville some twenty-four hours later, giving several hours for rambling about Charleston, while the steamer is disposing of its business at that always interesting port.

The oceanic fleet of the Clyde Line now consists of half a dozen steamships, built of steel after the most approved methods, and officered, manned, and equipped in the most effective and comfortable manner. The three largest of these steamers, the *Iroquois*, *Comanche*, and *Algonquin*, measure about 4,000 tons each, and are new in construction and equipped and furnished in the most modern manner. The other three, *Cherokee*, *Seminole*, and *Carib*, are a little smaller, but otherwise just as good and comfortable, and the large number of habitual travelers upon this line confess that there is little choice among the whole fleet. Each steamer, besides all the known improvements in machinery, life-protecting appliances, etc., is luxuriously furnished, provided with electric lights, bells, fans, etc., and has most of its staterooms opening upon the upper deck, while all are well ventilated. The fare served on this line has long had a high reputation for abundance and excellent cooking — none better is served in any ocean service — due not only to good stewardship, but the variety of marketing afforded by the weekly visits of each boat to both southern and northern points of supply.

While the Clyde Line lays especial stress upon the carriage of travelers to and from the southern winter resorts (and it must not be forgotten that the line of splendid St. Johns River boats, between Jacksonville and Palatka, is managed by this company), it also has a large amount of general passenger business, as it sells tickets and checks baggage between New York and all interior points in the South and Southwest, by way either of Charleston or of Jacksonville. There are a large number of travelers who much prefer to make a part of their journey by water, and to these the Clyde Line offers a delightful sea voyage, rates cheaper than the railroad charges overland, and greater rest and comfort on the way.

GREEN'S HOTEL, PHILADELPHIA.

No hotel in Philadelphia is more widely or better known among business men and good livers generally, than Green's. It has outlived most of the competitors of its early days, and has survived them by intelligently keeping abreast of the demand of the times. It has stood so long in the now enlarged and commodious building at the corner of Chestnut and Eighth streets, that the locality hardly needs mention. It is an advantageous situation, being just midway between the wholesale commercial districts, nearer the river, and the retail shopping streets somewhat above that point. It is convenient also to the postoffice, Independence Hall, and several other historical points, many of the principal theaters, and to all the railway stations and points of departure for the seaside.

This hotel now contains no less than 250 rooms, offering homelike quarters to ladies and families as well as to business men traveling alone. It is fully supplied with elevators, fire-escapes, electric lights and bells, baths, and all other requirements of a modern hostelry. The management is entirely in accordance with the European plan, rooms renting at $1 and $1.50 a day, and meals offered in what the proprietor asserts to be the "finest restaurant in Philadelphia." This restaurant is one of the institutions of the Quaker City, long renowned, especially for its methods of serving oysters and game. It is of large size, handsomely adorned, able to give a simple, well-cooked lunch, or serve an elaborate dinner, and gives, by its host of well-trained colored waiters, an air of the old-time hospitality which has so long attracted patrons who enjoy the best.

HOTEL EMPIRE, NEW YORK.

One of the newest and greatest of the modern and imposing hotels that have been erected in the upper part of the city of New York, of late, is the Hotel Empire. It occupies an admirable central position on the Boulevard at 63d Street, near Central Park, and one accessible by a great number of lines of transportation. Stations of the Sixth and Ninth Avenue Elevated railways are only a couple of blocks away, and electric cars pass the door, reaching all parts of the great town. At the same time the hotel is sufficiently removed from the roar and dust of Broadway or the business avenues to insure that quiet and good air which is so desirable in one's abiding place.

This hotel is of great size, imposing appearance, and fire-proof construction. Its arrangements and conveniences include the most recent improvements in hotel structure and equipment, and the art of the decorator has been lavishly employed. In this manner safety, sanitation, comfort, and beauty have combined to render the hotel so luxurious that to call it "homelike" would be to compare it only with the palaces of the wealthiest. Guests are entertained at the Hotel Empire according to the American plan (which is preferred by the many families which make it an almost permanent home), or upon the European plan. For the accommodation of the latter class an elegant restaurant is maintained, which is regarded as among those of the highest class in the city in all respects. Nowhere can better cooking be found, or more skillful service. The experience of many fastidious travelers sustains the truth of these assertions.

HOTEL LAFAYETTE, PHILADELPHIA.

The Hotel Lafayette is one of the handsomest hotels, not only in Philadelphia, but in the whole country, and forms one of a group of the finest buildings in the metropolis of Pennsylvania. It is on the fashionable side of Broad Street and in the midst of that part of Philadelphia of greatest interest to tourists. The City Hall is only a block distant, both of the great railway terminals are near at hand, several of the best theaters are in the immediate neighborhood, and many of the leading churches of the city are within easy walking distance, while the Academy of Art, the great libraries, and the Museum of Natural Science are convenient of access. Probably no other hotel in Philadelphia is so admirably situated for pleasure and shopping visits to the city, while the best cars to Fairmount Park and other places of suburban interest pass the building. This fine hotel has no less than 350 rooms, which are rented on the European plan, at rates from $1.00 a day upward. All are neatly and comfortably furnished, and many exhibit the elaborateness and beauty usually associated with our notions of a palace. Of course, all the conveniences and appointments required of modern hotels are present, and the service is excellent. The ladies' parlors and gentlemen's writing-rooms on the southern side of the house are models of luxury and convenience. The restaurants attached to this great hotel are famous among travelers for their good cooking and elegant service. One lovely room looks out upon the gay promenade of Broad Street, and another is more retired. One of the features so popular as to draw a large amount of daily patronage from the professional and business men of taste whose offices abound in this neighborhood, is the regular luncheon served at noon in the restaurant-room at the corner of Broad and Sansom streets. This luncheon is equally popular with guests. It would be hard to find anywhere in American cities a more satisfactory home for the traveler and his wife than the Hotel Lafayette affords.

UNITED STATES HOTEL, SARATOGA, N. Y.

The United States Hotel at Saratoga Springs is so far-famed and so thoroughly popular that it hardly seems possible to say anything new regarding it. It is one of the institutions of America. Within its walls gather each year thousands of the representatives of the world of fashion, wealth, and refinement. It is in itself a great social capital, and is on a scale so grand that its very magnitude is impressive. Within a court formed by three sides of the hotel is one of the loveliest private gardens in America, filled with beautiful fountains, the rarest of shrubs, and no more brilliant scene is to be found anywhere than is here presented each evening, when the park and the surrounding piazzas are thronged with the gay concourse of guests. The finest music is rendered morning, afternoon, and evening on the broad porches, and even a glimpse of the brilliant scenes for which the United States Hotel is famous will long linger in the mind.

Its very immensity is a charm in itself, for there is in the great corridors, parlors, and dining rooms a sense of freedom from all restraint. It is like roaming about a great baronial palace, yourself a prince, with vistas, through the hallways and from the windows on the one side, of fairy-like gardens, with glistening fountains, and the air fragrant with the verdure, and on the other, the gay boulevards of the city of Saratoga, alive with the handsome equipages and trappings of fashion and wealth. The cuisine of the United States is to the uninitiated a marvel, and to those accustomed to all the good things of life a joy and satisfaction.

The markets of New York are drawn upon heavily each day for all the luxuries and delicacies of the season, and the fertile country about Saratoga for vegetables and the dairy products for which the region is famous.

This hotel is one of the most perfectly appointed and beautiful in the world, and the visitor who spends a day, a month, or a season within its hospitable portals will ever recur with pleasure to the experience.

THE YARMOUTH LINE.

Steamers of the Yarmouth Steamship Co. sail from Lewis Wharf, Boston, for Yarmouth, N. S., at noon every Tuesday and Friday throughout the year. From July until October additional sailings are made from Boston at same hour on Monday and Thursday. Connections are made next morning at Yarmouth by train and boat for all points in the Maritime Provinces. The boats of the Yarmouth Steamship Line go direct from Boston to Yarmouth, the nearest point in Nova Scotia. It is much the quickest and most convenient route. In fact, the people of this country owe a great debt of gratitude to the Yarmouth Steamship Line; for had it not been for this enterprising company, the beauties of Nova Scotia would have been known to comparatively few. For when it was necessary, in order to reach the land of Evangeline, to make a long, tedious, and expensive railroad tour through Maine and New Brunswick, it was far too inaccessible for the majority of people. But when, some few years ago, the Yarmouth Company built the beautiful steel steamer *Yarmouth*, which made the distance from Boston to Yarmouth in fourteen or fifteen hours, they brought this delightful land within reach of all; and when the further fact is taken into consideration that this trip, this ocean voyage to a foreign land and back, can be made for the trifling sum of $9, there is really no reason why every American should not be able to go abroad every summer. So popular did this steamship line become after the *Yarmouth* was placed in service, that two years ago another boat, larger, still swifter, and handsomer, was added to the line — the *Boston*. The *Boston* is a steel boat, built on the Clyde, measuring some 255 feet, of 1,700 tons burden, and having over 4,500 horse power. She is beautifully furnished in saloon, in cabin, and stateroom. She has some eighty staterooms, and can accommodate 350 passengers. In fact, the *Boston* and the *Yarmouth* are by far the two handsomest coasters that leave Boston. Both are stanch, speedy, and strong, and admirably officered and manned.

"TRAVEL IS THE ROYAL ROAD TO LEARNING."

Only night-line having Dining Rooms on Main Deck

Powerful Search-Lights on Each Steamer

PEOPLES LINE

NEW YORK TO ALBANY

Steamer **ADIRONDACK,**   Steamer **DEAN RICHMOND,**
Capt. S. J. ROE.   Capt. J. H. MANVILLE.

Leave NEW YORK from Pier 41, North River, foot of Canal Street, at 6.00 P. M., daily, Sundays excepted.

We Ticket and Check Baggage to Albany, Troy, Saratoga, Bluff Point, and all points on Lake George and Lake Champlain, and the Adirondack Regions. Also via N. Y. C. & H. R. R. R. for all connecting points West.

Saturday Night Steamer Connects at Albany Sunday morning

FOR SARATOGA AND NORTHERN POINTS

ALBANY TO NEW YORK

Leave ALBANY at 8.00 P. M. (Sundays excepted), or on arrival of Evening Trains from the North, West and East.

W. W. EVERETT,   J. H. ALLAIRE,   E. C. EARLE,
President,   Gen'l Ticket Agt.,   Gen'l Freight Agt.
NEW YORK.   NEW YORK.

M. B. WATERS, Gen'l Pass'r Agent, Albany, N. Y.

The Largest and Best Located Hotel in the City

Mansion House

M. CROWLEY, PROPRIETOR
AMERICAN PLAN

The Picturesque and ONLY All-Rail Route running Through Drawing-Room Cars between

New York, Philadelphia and Bloomville,

AND BETWEEN

Washington, Baltimore, Philadelphia, Long Branch, New York, and Kingston, to Saratoga and Lake George,

DURING THE SUMMER SEASON

THE FAVORITE ROUTE OF BUSINESS AND PLEASURE TRAVEL BETWEEN

EAST, WEST, NORTHWEST, AND SOUTHWEST.

THE FAST EXPRESS TRAINS over this line have elegant Palace and Sleeping Cars between New York, Boston, Kingston, Albany, Utica, Syracuse, Rochester, Buffalo, and Niagara Falls, to Hamilton, Toronto, Detroit, Cleveland, Chicago, and St. Louis, without change.

For tickets, time tables, and full information apply to any Ticket Agent, **WEST SHORE RAILROAD,** or address

C. E. LAMBERT, General Passenger Agent,

Room 440 Grand Central Station.   **New York.**

Delaware & Hudson R. R.

THE SHORTEST, QUICKEST and BEST LINE

BETWEEN

NEW YORK and MONTREAL.

The Best Line to the Principal Resorts in the Adirondack Mountains.

THE ROUTE VIA

MONTREAL, LAKE CHAMPLAIN, LAKE GEORGE, SARATOGA AND THE HUDSON RIVER,

Is the greatest highway of summer pleasure travel in America. Send four cents postage, for fine descriptive guide, to

J. W. BURDICK,
GENERAL PASSENGER AGENT,
ALBANY, N. Y.

THE WABASH RAILROAD

Forms an important link with all lines

From the EAST, via
BUFFALO and SUSPENSION BRIDGE
To the WEST,
NORTHWEST and SOUTHWEST

FOUR SOLID-VESTIBULED TRAINS, DAILY,
FROM BUFFALO AND SUSPENSION BRIDGE TO

Detroit, Chicago, St. Louis, Hannibal, Quincy, Keokuk, Kansas City, and Omaha

The Famous "**Continental Limited**," leaves **New York**, daily at 1 p. m.; **Boston**, daily, 9.30 a. m.; arrives **Detroit** 7.00 a. m.; **Chicago** 3 p. m.; **St. Louis** 6.52 p. m the following day, and **Kansas City** the second morning at 7.15.

Palace Sleeping Cars, Reclining Chair Cars (SEATS FREE),
Dining Cars (Table d' Hote and a la Carte).

THE POPULAR ROUTE VIA NIAGARA FALLS
at which point a stopover from one to ten days allowed.

Connections in UNION STATIONS
at ALL JUNCTION POINTS.

Through Sleeping Car Service in connection with lines from NEW YORK and BOSTON to DETROIT, CHICAGO, and ST. LOUIS.

For information in regard to rates, time tables, or reservation of sleeping car space, apply to your nearest ticket agent or to

H. B. McCLELLAN, GEN'L EASTERN AGENT,
387 BROADWAY, NEW YORK.

J. D. McBEATH, NEW ENGLAND PASS'R AGENT
5 STATE STREET, BOSTON, MASS.

J. RAMSEY, JR., VICE-PRES. AND GEN'L MANAGER,　} ST. LOUIS.
C. S. CRANE, GEN'L PASS'R AND TICKET AGENT,

Hotel Kenmore

Leading Hotel of
ALBANY, N. Y.

STRICTLY FIRST CLASS.

Rates......$3.00 and upwards per day.

CUISINE NOTED FOR ITS EXCELLENCE.

Centrally Located
on principal shopping thoroughfare. Convenient to STATE CAPITOL, other public buildings, and places of interest. FREE OMNIBUSES at all trains and boats.

H. J. ROCKWELL & SON.

CENTRAL-HUDSON STEAMBOAT COMPANY'S DAILY LINE FOR NEWBURGH

Landing at Cranston's, West Point, Cold Spring, and Cornwall — Fishkill (by Ferry),

Also places on the NEWBURGH, ORANGE LAKE & WALDEN ELECTRIC R. R.

For Passengers and Freight.

The New and Elegant Iron Screw Steamers

"Homer Ramsdell" and "Newburgh,"

The Fastest Propellers On the Hudson River,

Leave New York from New Pier 24, foot of Franklin Street, daily, except Sunday, at 5.00 p. m. (Sundays at 9.00 a. m., foot West 132d Street, 9.25 a. m., from June 1st to October 1st.) Leave Newburgh, daily, except Sunday, 7.00 p. m., Sunday 6.30 p. m., and from May 21st to Sept. 10th Saturday Steamer will leave New York at 3.00 p. m. instead of five o'clock.

The up trip Sunday morning affords one of the pleasantest and most select Excursions of any line running from New York. **Fare 50 cents.** And in connection with the Newburgh & Walden Electric Railway, gives to the New York public something novel in the way of an Excursion through the most charming parts of Orange County, to Orange Lake and Walden, making a most delightful trip.

And an unusually pleasant trip is offered by the Mary Powell, leaving New York every afternoon except Sunday, and returning by this line from West Point or Cornwall, tickets for which are for sale on the Powell.

This line offers unsurpassed service in every particular. Large and luxuriously furnished saloons and staterooms, heated by steam and lighted by electricity. The trip by the up-steamer affords a most enjoyable sail up the Hudson in the early evening, past the wonderful Palisades and through the far-famed Highlands, the most beautiful part of the river.

S.A.L.

SEABOARD AIR LINE
THE POPULAR LINE
NORTH AND SOUTH
Double Daily Service.

The Famous Atlanta Special Solid Vestibule Limited

"THE CYCLONE"

SOLID TRAINS FROM PORTSMOUTH TO ATLANTA.

Make Travel a Pleasure and Use the Seaboard Air Line.

SOUTHERN PINES, ATHENS, RALEIGH, ATLANTA, MACON, MOBILE, NEW ORLEANS, AND PACIFIC COAST POINTS.

TICKETS ON SALE AT ALL PRINCIPAL TICKET OFFICES IN UNITED STATES AND CANADA.

Ask Ticket Agent for Ticket via
SEABOARD AIR LINE.
$3 — SAVE — $3.

For Time Tables, Information, Reservation, call on or address
A. B. FARNSWORTH, GEN'L EASTERN PASS'R AGENT,
371 BROADWAY, NEW YORK.

E. ST. JOHN,	H. W. B. GLOVER,	L. S. ALLEN,
Vice-Pres't and Gen'l Mgr..	Traffic Manager,	Gen'l Pass'r Agent.

PORTSMOUTH, VA.

GREEN'S HOTEL

Corner Eighth and Chestnut Sts., PHILADELPHIA.
MAHLON W. NEWTON, PROPRIETOR.

FOR LADIES AND GENTLEMEN.   EUROPEAN PLAN.

250 Rooms at $1.00 and $1.50 per day. This hotel is centrally located, and in the very heart of the city, being but one square from the Post Office, and easy of access to all Theaters, Railway Stations, Public Buildings, and Points of Interest Finest Restaurant in Philadelphia. Headquarters for Commercial Travelers

Maps and Guides

TO

All of the Principal Cities

AND

EVERY COUNTRY IN THE WORLD.

Road Maps

FOR

Driving, Wheeling, or Walking.

Globes, Map Racks, Spring Map Rollers, Wall and Pocket Maps, Historical Maps, Classical, Biblical, Historical, Anatomical, Astronomical, Physical, and General Atlases of all kinds kept in stock.

Address

RAND, MCNALLY & CO.,

Map Publishers and Engravers,

160 to 174 Adams Street, CHICAGO.

142 Fifth Avenue, NEW YORK.

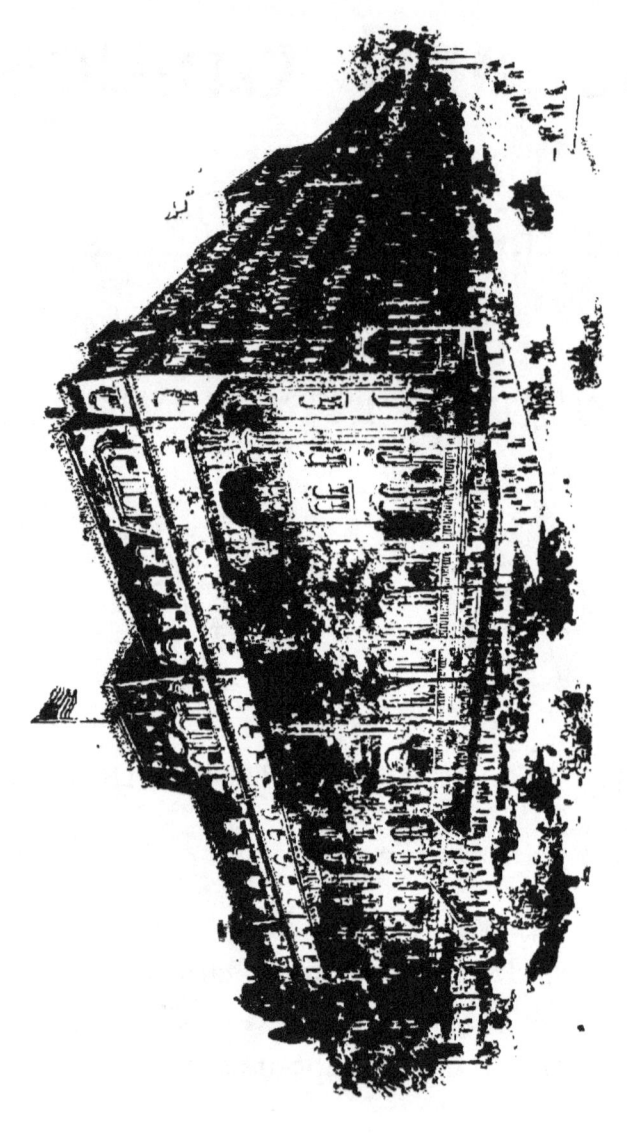

United States Hotel

Saratoga Springs, N. Y.

 ONE OF THE LARGEST HOTELS IN THE WORLD...

17 Rooms

Line of buildings over 1,500 feet long, 6 stories high, covering and enclosing 7 acres of ground, 238 feet front on Broadway, 675 feet frontage on Division Street.

e Summer Residence of the Most Refined Circles
American Fashion and Society.

Orchestra, Hops, Germans, Balls, Concerts, Entertainments, etc. Most elegantly furnished Parlors, Ball Room, Public and Private Dining Rooms, Reading Rooms, etc. Private Suites of any size in COTTAGE WING.

RATOGA HAS
One of the Finest and Most Picturesque Golf Links in the United States, and miles of First-class Cycle Paths.

GAGE & PERRY,
EN JUNE 15TH TO OCTOBER.   **PROPRIETORS.**

Summer Tours

Via

Hudson River

...TROY LINE...

At reduced rates to Adirondack Mountains Saratoga, Lake George, Lake Champlain, Green Mountains, Montreal, and all resorts reached by Delaware & Hudson or Fitchburg railroads and connections.

RATES TO ABOVE RESORTS ALWAYS LOWER THAN BY ANY OTHER ROUTE.

SPECIAL NOTICE.—Dining Room on Steamer Saratoga is entirely new, and is located on main deck, aft. Many other improvements in decorations and fittings have been made to this steamer as well as the "City of Troy," affording unexcelled accommodations for passenger service.

Powerful search-lights on each steamer.

Steamers Saratoga or City of Troy leave West 10th Street Pier, daily, 6.00 p. m., except Saturday.

Sunday Steamers touch at Albany.

Leave Troy week days, except Saturday, about 7.40 p. m., on arrival of D. & H. train. Sunday boat leaves Troy at 6.00 p. m., Albany 7.00 p. m.

Send for list of routes and rates for Excursion tours.

R. L. HORNBY,
General Ticket Agent,
West 10th Street Pier, New York.

Catskill Mountains..

Shortest, Cheapest, and Best Route from New York

To Hotel Kaaterskill, Catskill Mountain House, Laurel House, Kaaterskill Falls, Haines Falls, Twilight Park, Santa Cruz Park, Sunset Park, Onteora Park, Palenville, Tannersville, Prospect Park Hotel, Grant House, Summit Hill House, Cairo, Durham, Windham, and all points of interest in the Mountain Region.

CATSKILL EVENING LINE STEAMERS
"KAATERSKILL" and "ONTEORA"

Leave New York from Pier 43, N. R., foot of Christopher Street, every week day at 6.00 p. m., Saturdays at 1.30 and 6.00 p. m. (1.30 boat from July 1 to Sept. 2, both inclusive). Leave Catskill daily, except Saturday, at 7.00 p. m., Sundays at 7.00 and 10.00 p. m. (the 10.00 o'clock boat from July 9 to Sept. 3, both inclusive)   FARE, ONE DOLLAR.

Special trains connect at Catskill via Catskill Mountain Ry., Cairo R. R., Otis Elevating Ry., and Catskill and Tannersville R. R.

Tickets sold and baggage checked through. Bicycles carried free.

Special attention paid to the transportation of horses and carriages.

Folder containing list of hotels and boarding houses, with locations, rates, and other information, sent free to any address.

G. M. SNYDER, PRESIDENT,   **W. J. HUGHES, TREASURER,**
Foot of Christopher St., New York.   Catskill, N. Y.

Hudson River by Daylight

The Most Charming Inland Water Trip on the American Continent.

THE PALACE IRON STEAMERS

"NEW YORK" AND "ALBANY"

OF THE

HUDSON RIVER DAY LINE,

Leave New York Daily, Except Sunday, from Desbrosses Street Pier, 8.40 a. m.; Twenty-second Street Pier, N. R., 9.00 a. m. From Albany 8.30 a. m.

THE FAVORITE ROUTE TO AND FROM THE

CATSKILL MOUNTAINS, SARATOGA AND THE ADIRONDACKS, HOTEL CHAMPLAIN AND THE NORTH, NIAGARA FALLS AND THE WEST, THE THOUSAND ISLANDS AND THE ST. LAWRENCE RIVER.

Appreciating the demand of the better class of tourists for comfort and luxury, the management of the Day Line have perfected their service in every manner possible, keeping it fully abreast of the times. The elegant steamers are as famous as is the majestic river on which they run. Built of iron, of great speed and superb appointments, they are the finest of their class afloat. No freight of any description is carried, the steamers being designed exclusively for the passenger service. Richly furnished private parlors, giving absolute seclusion and privacy to small parties or families, are provided, and handsomely appointed dining rooms, with superior service, are on the main deck, affording an uninterrupted view of the magnificent scenery for which the Hudson is renowned.

ATTRACTIVE DAILY EXCURSIONS TO
WEST POINT, NEWBURGH, AND POUGHKEEPSIE.

Send six cents for copy of "Summer Excursion Book."

E. E. OLCOTT, General Manager.   F. B. HIBBARD, General Passenger Agent.

DESBROSSES STREET PIER, NEW YORK.

www.ingramcontent.com/pod-product-compliance
Lightning Source LLC
Chambersburg PA
CBHW021202230426